WHERE ARE THE MEN?

THE JOURNEY TO DISCIPLESHIP IN JESUS

PHILIP MONNIN

This book is also available in eBook format.

Cover design by Caleb Porter
www.portergraphicdesign.com

ISBN-13: 978-0-9969639-0-9

TABLE OF CONTENTS

AUTHOR'S NOTE

I am a fellow disciple-in-training. I am not a perfect man. I don't live a flawless life. I am still working to become a better husband and father. My marriage is not the model of everything Jesus intended marriage to be. Each day I must deal with the twists and turns of life and contend with the enemy of my soul.

Following Jesus is not about having it all together. It does not require a theological degree or particular level of education. It pays no attention to social standing, positions, or possessions. It is not concerned with the length of church membership or the absence of it. It is not contingent upon what has or has not been done with a life.

Discipleship is an open invitation to all who belong to Jesus. All that is required is a willing heart eager for the walk and then taking the next step with Him.

This book is the result of my learning to walk with Jesus. Its purpose is to shine some light on the path forward, providing a *means* for you to learn to walk with Jesus on your own unique journey, while leaving the *method* up to Him.

The *Notes* at the end of each chapter contain very important information that further explains the main points of the chapter, along with Scripture references that provide insight into God's perspective on the subject matter. These *Notes* are the 'book within the book' and will greatly enhance your understanding.

There is a *Study Guide* section included at the end of each chapter and a list of related word definitions in the *Appendix*. These will help you plumb the depths of what you have just read. It is suitable for use as an individual or in a group setting.

Are you ready? Let's go for a walk with Jesus!

Philip Monnin   April 2020

INTRODUCTION

Most men have decided that following Jesus consists of merely holding the fort until Jesus returns. It has become all about having an adequate defense instead of a powerful offense. Of playing *to not lose* instead of playing *to win*. Of taking the safe way of the *inconsequential* instead of risking all for the *substantial*. It is trying to win the game by running out the clock of life—as dutiful husbands and fathers, by reading the Bible and going to church, by participating part-time in Christianized activities. It is about *occupying* instead of *subduing*.

And in that void between our occupying and the call to subdue stands Jesus. He looks to see who is with Him and asks, 'Where are the men?'

જ્જ

Walking with Jesus is not as simple as we thought it would be. For many, it is a daily struggle for consistency, meaning, and joy. We look in the mirror and do not like what stares back at us. *Who is that man with the hollow, weary eyes? Where is the joy of his salvation? Why does he feel less than real, a mere shadow of what he knows he should be? Is there any authenticity beyond the façade of his public persona? Why does defeat haunt him each step along the way?*

We grasp for answers, but the solution eludes us. We try new things, but we find them to be temporary and ineffective. We stumble and fall, wondering how many more times we will be able to get back up. We settle for less than we should, moving quietly in the shadows just beyond the glorious.

We don't know what to do.

୨◦ఌ

There is a solution, a unique pathway forward for each of us.

It begins with the realization that our struggling is in vain...that the forces arrayed against us are too strong to overcome on a human level...that every man-made solution—the seminars, the groups, the retreats, the programs—are insufficient for what lies ahead...that we need supernatural help to climb out of the quicksand-filled ditch that threatens to suffocate us.

Next, we must reach out and grasp tightly to Jesus' hand. He alone can lead us out of our individual darkness and into His glorious light. He alone can make our steps sure along the path He has chosen for us. He alone can breathe life into what is dead in our lives.

And finally, we must willingly walk the difficult path before us—the way of discipleship. This path begins at our present state, winds its way through our many challenges, and ends at our appointed place of destiny. It is traversed one step at a time, day by day.

Each man has his own path of discipleship to walk, but he never walks alone. Jesus is there every step of the way—leading, helping, teaching, and encouraging him to become all He intends him to be.

୨◦ఌ

It is possible to walk triumphantly with Jesus. He is calling out to each of us today.

Come, let us walk with Him. Step by step.

ಐ PART 1 ೞ
THE PRELUDE

Most of us have lived some portion of our lives as believers in Jesus. It could have been for a few days or for many years. We might consider our relationship with Him as being deep or admit it is superficial. Maybe we have fully experienced His reality in our lives or are looking around and wondering what it is we are missing. Our life might demonstrate the level of purity we believe Christianity demands of a man or it may not. We could have a clear idea of why we are here on earth or may be wondering what this is all about. Perhaps we are walking on the straight and narrow path or traveling down the broad boulevard toward sure destruction—not damnation, but destruction just the same.

Regardless of how we see ourselves in the statements above, two basic truths remain—we are *who* we are, and we are *where* we are. Good, bad, or ugly, we can't change those facts. Each of us owns the reality of the quality of our walk and the distance we have traveled with Jesus since that day He miraculously entered into our lives and began to transform us into His likeness.

The chapters in this section provide a baseline and take us back to the beginning so we can examine the basics of our life as a Christian. If we are truly willing to look at who we have become and where we have gone with our lives since that day we first pledged our allegiance to Jesus, He can begin the process of teaching us to walk closely with Him.

OUT FROM OUR PAST

When we read about the Roman soldiers mocking Jesus and spitting on Him, it is easy to marvel at their cruelty and total disregard toward the God of all creation. To mock someone is to defy that person by treating them as less than who they are, as less than their worth as a person. It is an uncaring act of ridicule. Spitting on a person is one of the most base forms of contempt that can be demonstrated. It is the low evilness of a man expressed perfectly.

At some level, we discount these acts of contempt by the Roman soldiers because of the time and the setting. After all, maybe these soldiers did not know who Jesus was. Perhaps they were just pawns in a larger game that was being played out.

But what about each of us? Those who know who Jesus truly is? Those who clearly understand what He did for us? Those who have pledged to follow Him no matter what? Are we not likewise guilty of the same sins as those soldiers from so long ago?[1] Have we not done exactly the same things to Jesus for years with how we have lived our lives before Him, even though we knew He was the God of creation and the Author of our salvation? Have we not spit on Jesus in our blatant rejection of His rightful claim as the Lord and Owner of our lives? Are we mocking Him now with our divided hearts as we declare our devotion to Him while we live as we please?

The truth in our answers to these questions should shock us. And sicken us.

But this can be a thing of our past. Jesus can intervene

in our shameful behaviors and put them behind us. This is the Jesus who awaits each of us—the One who calls us to walk with Him as His disciples on a journey of true significance.

OUR JOURNEY

Our stories may be different. We may be struggling with immaturity or irresponsibility, drugs or alcohol, gambling or gaming addiction, pornography or illicit affairs, homosexual desires/activity or gender identity issues, materialism or food, or some other sinful life choice. The messes made of our lives and relationships might be greater or lesser than those of other men we know.

It does not matter. The journey from wherever we are today to becoming a disciple of Jesus is the same. The steps are the same. The forsaking of our sin and turning away is the same. The need to realign our concept of God to His reality is the same. The need to understand who Jesus is for our lives is the same. The need to understand what has driven us all these years is the same. The need to be healed fully is the same.

Jesus is ready. Let's take a walk. With Jesus.

♦♦♦ CHAPTER NOTES ♦♦♦

1. The Cruelty Of Man

Man's cruelty knows no bounds. Man's contempt knows no limits. All of us have been guilty of cruelty and contempt toward Jesus. In doing so, we have become partakers with all who mistreat Him.

(Mark 15:16-19) And the soldiers led Him away inside the palace (that is, the governor's headquarters), and they called together the whole battalion. And they clothed Him in a purple cloak, and twisting together a crown of thorns, they put it on Him. And they began to salute Him, "Hail, King of the Jews!" And they were striking His head with a reed and spitting on Him and kneeling down in homage to Him.

All of us have a past *since* our beginning – not our physical beginning, but our spiritual beginning as a Christ follower. Below are questions that will help you unlock the truth of this past.

1) Describe your salvation experience.

2) Think back. What were your expectations of this new life as a Christian?

3) How has this life lived up to or not lived up to those expectations?

4) Has your walk with Jesus moved forward since your early days with Him, or has it remained the same, or even gone backwards? Has it become closer and more intimate, stagnated, or faded slowly away? How?

5) When you look back, are you pleased or disappointed? How so?

6) Think of what Jesus went through to purchase your salvation. In light of this, how would you rate your walk with Him? *(Resist the temptation to compare yourself to others or to shift blame to someone, something, or some circumstance.)*

7) Think of a time when someone else mocked you. How did it make you feel?

8) Think of a time when you mocked someone else. As you replay the incident in your mind, what do you feel inside?

9) Is your life as a Christian mocking Jesus? Are you professing to be His follower while living like you please? *(Again, do not compare yourself to others.)*

10) When you think of your Christian experience this way, describe how it makes you feel.

11) If you had a chance to put your past life as a Christian behind you and begin again with a fresh walk and a new relationship with Jesus, would you take it?

12) What constraints would you put on this new walk and relationship?

WDJW?

Years ago, a fad swept through the Christian community. As fads go, it was deeper than most. For as long as it lasted, much good came out of it. Remember *WWJD?—What Would Jesus Do?* People from all walks of life wore bracelets asking WWJD? Cars sported bumper stickers asking WWJD? People of every age, gender, and race wore shirts asking WWJD?

What would Jesus do in the everyday moments of life? How would He act? What would He think? What would He say? Where would He go? Where would He not go? How would He handle the issues of life as they presented themselves? Yes, this was a very valid question. The *WWJD?* paraphernalia was a reminder to put on Jesus' mind, and see things through His eyes as we went about our daily business.

But there is another question that is more important, more urgent. WDJW?—What Does Jesus Want?

Let us first start with what He *doesn't* want. Jesus isn't looking for more converts just for the sake of having them. This may be a surprising statement for many of us, perhaps even shocking. It is one we will rarely, if ever, hear spoken in our modern-day Christian experience, for the Church today has made its evangelical business primarily one of attracting people and gathering them as converts.

When Jesus gave us the Great Commission, He did not command us to make converts. He commanded us to make disciples.[1] With this command, Jesus made a huge statement on what He considered important.

Jesus does not call us to a cheap version of salvation where one merely avoids hell and attains heaven. It was never His intent for people to think they have arrived on the day of their salvation and no further action or commitment is needed. No. Salvation is the beginning point in the life-long pursuit of a relationship with Jesus and our becoming more like Him. Salvation is our call to action. From there we can follow where He leads us and accomplish all He has for us to do.

Jesus doesn't want more converts. He wants what He has always wanted. He is searching the world over for men whose hearts are truly His.[2] He is looking for men who pant after Him, who thirst for all of Him.[3] He desires men who will forsake all to follow His call.

Jesus wants disciples.

CHRIST FOLLOWERS

Following Jesus. It sounds so simple. So basic. So peaceful.

After all, is He not the Good Shepherd? Are we not His sheep? Won't a shepherd watch the sheep and keep them from the wolves? Won't the sheep cruise around from lush pasture to lush pasture, eating their fill each day, doing what sheep do without a care in the world? Won't He gently prod them to move on to the next field, the next place of His choosing? Won't they willingly go?

Is this what following Jesus is all about?

For many of us, this is our idea of following Jesus. We know we are in the flock through our salvation experience. We know that we are one of the sheep instead of one of the goats. We know that God is love, so everything will be fine...kind of. We want to believe that our troubles are now behind us. We have learned, or are learning, the rules of being an acceptable sheep—going to church, being better than we were before, giving our money, getting our families into church programs, volunteering to serve. We move from one thing to the next, from pasture to pasture. We go about our business, but we do it in sheep's clothing...more or less. We have a routine. We are at peace with our Shepherd...at least we think we are.

But in the quiet moments of our lives, deep down in our souls, is this what we believe it means to truly follow Jesus?[4]

If we are honest with ourselves, most of us will admit that following Jesus is much more than just doing these things. We know from experience it is not simple or basic. Even though we know it should bring peace to our souls, we have found no guarantee of peace in our lives beyond that.

Even the Scriptures we read paint a different picture for us. In them, Jesus tells us His followers would not be above Him in anything, and that we should expect the same trials and treatment He experienced—if He was mistreated, we should expect the same; if He was ostracized by those in power, we would be as well; if He was seen as a threat to the religious equilibrium, we would likewise be seen as a threat; if He was ridiculed for being a radical, we would suffer the same fate.[5]

So, what does it mean to follow Jesus, to become His disciple?

The answer to this question has eluded most men for two thousand years. Sure, there were times when men moved closer to the answer than today and the implications seemed clearer. There have been pockets of revival at various times that fostered a truer sense of what this meant. And, as always, there have been the few—a remnant—who have understood and embraced the reality of what it meant to truly be a disciple.

But for most of us, we are clueless. We have never come to the place of understanding. The truth be told, we never really gave it much thought. We were in. That is what really mattered! The eternal question was answered. We had no worries about it. We just dove right into the Christian experience and went with the flow of the general church population, doing what was expected. Perhaps some of us challenged the popular conventions in a few areas, but mostly our view of following Jesus was the same as the one we just read. Predictable. Lackadaisical. Subdued. Safe. Running with the herd.

As a consequence, our lives are a reflection of that view. Dutiful. Fleshly. Following with one leg on each side of the fence. Minimal commitment with even less connectedness. Making few waves. Easily tripped by the cords of our sin.

And our lives lack significance and are more or less a waste for Jesus.

WHO ARE WE FOLLOWING?

A disciple is a pupil or an apprentice. A disciple is one who follows and learns how to become like the one he follows. The purpose of becoming a disciple of Jesus is to become like Him. Step by step. Day by day. Week by week. Month by month. Year by year. For a lifetime.

Being a disciple of Jesus is not a part-time activity. It does not get a time slot in our daily calendar. It is not something that we 'work into our schedule'. It is not relegated to the time crumbs between our work and our next activity. It is not for Sunday only. No. Discipleship is a full-time occupation. In fact, it is our pre-occupation. Everything else fits into it! This is not easy. We have to learn to allow Jesus to stand over the top of everything and become the conscious continuum of our lives.

Being a disciple of Jesus is an all-consuming endeavor. It is an 'either-or'. Either we are disciples, or we are not. For

16

this to work, it must be our consuming passion. Being a disciple is the greatest commandment personified. It is loving Jesus with all of our heart, soul, strength, and mind. It is recognizing our position and His position. It is understanding that we were bought with a great price—His blood—out of the slave market of sin and that we now belong 100% to Him. It is committing our lives to listening to His direction and obeying His voice. It is putting Him above all else, including ourselves.

As kids, many of us played the game *Follow the Leader*. There was only one rule in this game: once a leader was chosen, we followed him or her, doing our best to mimic their every move and go wherever they led.

As a disciple, it is the same. There is only one rule— decide who we will follow and then mimic them every step of the way. We must make this decision hundreds of times each day. Every thought, every word, every deed, and every attitude requires a decision. Who are we following? Whose disciple are we?

This is a sobering thought. Too many of us go on autopilot each day. We get into our routine or schedule and just *do*. We don't stop and consider. We just do. It is easy to just do. It is natural to just do. It is hazardous to just do.

Jesus calls us to stop *just doing* and start *doing what He wants us to do*. Jesus calls us to consider His way in all things. He longs to lead us step by step, like our own personal cloud by day or pillar of fire by night. And, as with the Israelites during the Exodus, we have to learn to follow Jesus in this manner. When the cloud or fire moves, we move. When it stops, we stop. We linger as long as it lingers. We move as long as it moves. We keep pace with it, fast or slow. Yes, Jesus longs to lead us, and He wants us to follow Him.

What is the alternative? We walk according to our flesh

instead of by His Spirit, and we listen to the whispers of Satan's demons in our ears.

There is no middle ground here. In any given moment, we are either following Jesus or we are following Satan. We are listening to Jesus or we are listening to Satan's demons. We are obeying Jesus or we are obeying those same demons. We are being used to accomplish things for Jesus or we are being used to advance the purposes of Satan.

This is a challenging thought, but it is truth.

For those of us who tend to be strong-willed or self-sufficient, this is a tough concept to own. We have to slow down, look, and listen for Jesus. We need to discern if what we are hearing lines up with the truths and principles of the Scriptures—if it is really Jesus' voice. And we have to begin with the little things. As we master the basics of listening for, recognizing, and obeying the voice of Jesus, it becomes easier and forms a lifestyle.

Following Jesus is really a matter of learning to hear His voice.[6] Most of us have spent a lifetime listening to other voices. Think about it. How messed up are our lives? How messed up are our relationships? If we had been listening to Jesus, would we really have these issues? No! We have listened to the many voices of Satan through his demons and the false philosophies of the world instead of listening to Jesus. We know the voice of these demons better than we know Jesus' voice. Now, we need to learn to recognize the voice of the Shepherd of our souls. Then, we need to obey Him.

For some, this will be too difficult, too restrictive, or too radical. Well, each must decide his path. Each must decide if his salvation experience was the beginning of living—really living—for Jesus, or if it was an event of minimal impact upon his daily life. Each must decide if he is going to be swept downstream with the popular religious notions

18

of the day, or if he is going to stand against the flow of complacency and error. Each must decide if he will go his own way or Jesus' way.

If we have a heart that yearns to know what Jesus wants us to do, He takes the responsibility upon Himself to communicate to us clearly and to direct our paths.

Let's each ask Jesus to teach us to hear His voice clearly. Ask Him to make Himself known to us intimately. Ask Him to help us listen for His voice, obey His commands, and follow His lead.

COUNT THE COST

Discipleship is a journey. The starting point is the place we find ourselves *today*. We may be a new convert or one of many years. We could have most of our life together or be about to lose it all. It does not matter. What is important is for each of us to understand where we are in our walk with Jesus and then consider the cost of following Him as His disciple.[7]

This is where many men fall. They blindly make an emotional commitment out of excitement or despair and then jump in line behind Jesus. After a while, when the emotional high or crisis has passed, when it becomes inconvenient, or when it does not fit into their lives as they envisioned following Jesus would—*when it costs them too much*—they fall away. That is when they give up. That is when they *un-decide* to follow Jesus as a disciple.

So count the cost.

All of us have habits to discard. Unbelief to overcome. Demons to contend with. Ourselves to die to. Our wills to lay down. These are hard things to do. The path is indeed difficult and few find it.[8]

Following Jesus is an adventure. One that few ever really experience.

◆◆◆ CHAPTER NOTES ◆◆◆

Knowing what Jesus wants is foundational to our lives as believers. There is much wasted time in the Christian community because we do not know what Jesus wants. There is much disillusionment because we do not know what Jesus wants. There is much hostility because we do not know what Jesus wants. There is much shallowness because we do not know what Jesus wants.

1. The Great Commission

(Matthew 28:19-20) "Go therefore and make disciples of all the nations, baptizing them in the name of the Father and of the Son and of the Holy Spirit, teaching them to observe all that I have commanded you. And behold, I am with you always, to the end of the age."

Jesus gave the Great Commission before He ascended into Heaven. Its instructions are clear. We are to go to every people group and make disciples. How? By teaching them the things that Jesus taught us. It's not about programs to attract or entertain. It's not about facilities and amenities. It's not about soft-selling the Gospel so it isn't so offensive. It's about being Jesus to others and letting them see His power in our lives.

This is the great failing of the modern church. Many believers have no power to display to the lost because they never learned to follow Jesus *His* way so *His* power could flow through them. They are not disciples themselves, so they have little of value to offer to others. Because of this, 'church' degenerates into a consumer sales pitch for comparative shoppers. Fulfilling the Great Commission to make disciples begins with Jesus flowing freely through each of us—a real, live Jesus, full of power, truth, love, and mercy. This is the way of the disciple.

Three things are required in order to make disciples. First and foremost, those we are discipling must desire to be made into a disciple. Secondly, those who are doing the discipling must be disciples of Jesus themselves. And last of all, it takes time—that crucial process of investing in others regularly so that they can learn firsthand.

Rarely are all three of these requirements met in today's local church fellowships. New converts often have no desire to do what is necessary to become disciples because they have been sold a cheap brand of easy Christianity, one that requires very little from the participants. Most Christians are not disciples of Jesus themselves and, therefore, have little to pass on to others. And finally, many are too busy with life to take the time to shepherd someone else and help them mature in the ways of Jesus.

2. Men Whose Hearts Are Truly His

Jesus is looking for men who are sold out to Him. He can do much through such a man.

(2 Chronicles 16:9a) For the eyes of the LORD run to and fro throughout the whole earth, to give strong support to those whose heart is blameless toward Him.

In order for *our hearts* to truly belong to Jesus, *we* must truly belong to Jesus. We must come to Him on His terms— not on our own or according to some religious doctrine. Salvation is not a feeling; it is a fact. It is not a belief; it is a conviction. It is not participation; it is commitment. Salvation is not some general idea originating in the mind that acknowledges Jesus as the Savior. It is a deep recognition of our sin and our need for the Savior Jesus to do for us what we cannot do for ourselves. We must be able to point to a specific time in our lives when we surrendered our heart to Jesus. See *Jesus the Redeemer* in the *Appendix* for more information.

3. Thirsting For God

(Psalm 42:1-2a) As a deer pants for flowing streams, so pants my soul for You, O God. My soul thirsts for God, for the living God.

4. Following Jesus

Many of us would say that we are following Jesus as His disciples. *But are we?*

To follow Jesus is to take Him at His word without question, believing that what He said about being our God and Lord and Brother is true and believing that what He said He wants from us as disciples is true. Our lives are a reflection of our beliefs. How we respond to Jesus and what He has said indicates our true level of commitment as a disciple of His. It is impossible for this to be otherwise. How we see Jesus in our lives—through our interactions with Him, in our relationship with Him, or in our responses to Him—points to our true level of discipleship, irrespective of what we say with our words.

If we say we follow Jesus in all He has said and is and wants from us, but we do not obey Him accordingly, do we really follow Him? This is the essential question found in the familiar Scriptural truth that faith without works is a dead faith. And even if we once followed Him closely with a holy desire, does this mean that we do so now...today? Isn't how we respond to Jesus' call to discipleship in our lives *today* the true indicator of what we actually believe about Him? We call Him 'Lord', but do we follow Jesus as our Lord and Master? Do we believe that He is Lord? Many of us profess to, but we do not, as indicated by our response to His call to deep discipleship.

That we do not *believe* what we profess to believe is proven by the fact that we do not *live* what we profess to believe. Being busy and doing good things in the context of a denominational religious structure does not constitute walking with Jesus as a disciple. Obeying Him in all things and thirsting after Him does.

The great commission tells us what it means to follow Jesus, to be His disciple. We are to do the things that He taught us. We can read the teachings of Jesus in the

Gospels to understand what He wants of us. There are some verses that shed light on how these things will be beyond what we would consider 'normal' obedience.

(John 14:12) "Truly, truly, I say to you, whoever believes in Me will also do the works that I do; and greater works than these will he do, because I am going to the Father."

Jesus said we would do the things that He did, and more. This is not a call to baby's milk Christianity. It is a call to the meat. It is not a signal for complacency. It is a summons to aggressiveness. It is not a call to safety. It is a challenge to risk.

(Matthew 10:1) And He called to Him His twelve disciples and gave them authority over unclean spirits, to cast them out, and to heal every disease and every affliction.

(Matthew 10:8) "Heal the sick, raise the dead, cleanse lepers, cast out demons. You received without paying; give without pay."

(Luke 9:1) And He called the twelve together and gave them power and authority over all demons and to cure diseases.

(Luke 10:19) "Behold, I have given you authority to tread on serpents and scorpions, and over all the power of the enemy, and nothing shall hurt you."

These verses give us some idea of the extent of the things that disciples can be called to do...even today. They are offered so we can see there is power in Jesus, and an expectation for us to walk in that power as His disciples. In order for Him to give us this power, He has to trust that we will use it properly. In order for Him to trust us, we have to know Him and how He wants such power used.

5. Followers Not Above Their Master

Following Jesus is not simple, basic, or peaceful. Jesus set our expectations for an easy Christian life aside. This is not to say that we all will suffer huge trials like imprisonment or martyrdom. But if we truly lay down our lives, we must be willing to follow Jesus to even these if necessary. Not all of our life will be a time of peace, but all of it is to be peaceful in Him.

(John 15:18-21) "If the world hates you, know that it has hated Me before it hated you. If you were of the world, the world would love you as its own; but because you are not of the world, but I chose you out of the world, therefore the world hates you. Remember the word that I said to you, 'A servant is not greater than his master.' If they persecuted Me, they will also persecute you. If they kept My word, they will also keep yours. But all these things they will do to you on account of My name, because they do not know Him who sent Me."

(Matthew 10:22a, 24-25) "And you will be hated by all for My name's sake...A disciple is not above his teacher, nor a servant above his master. It is enough for the disciple to be like his teacher, and the servant like his master. If they have called the master of the house Beelzebub, how much more will they malign those of his household!"

6. My Sheep Know My Voice

Jesus said that His sheep hear His voice so they can act on it by following Him.

(John 10:27) "My sheep hear My voice, and I know them, and they follow Me."

Jesus speaks to his sheep in many ways. He can speak directly to our minds and hearts. He can speak in dreams and visions. He can answer back when we pray. He can send other people to give us messages. He can communicate through the wonder of His creation. He can talk to us through His Word. He can speak through signs and wonders. He can use circumstances. He can even speak audibly to our ears.

Regardless of how He speaks, the Holy Spirit enables us to hear Him. We must earnestly seek to hear Jesus. We must learn to listen. And then we must act on what He has said. We are no different than Paul to whom it was told:

(Acts 22:14) And he said, 'The God of our fathers appointed you to know His will, to see the Righteous One [Jesus], and to hear a voice from His mouth.'

24

Three things block our ability to hear Jesus—our unbelief, our willfulness, and the demonic.

Unbelief causes us to discount who Jesus says He is and what He says He can do. This limits what Jesus will do in our lives.

(Matthew 13:58) And He did not do many mighty works there, because of their unbelief.

Our willfulness can cause us to go our own way, which is away from Jesus. Our willfulness causes us to sin, which breaks the free flow of our relationship with Jesus. When we draw back and away from Him or are aloof, why would He draw near to us so that we could hear Him?

(James 4:8) Draw near to God, and He will draw near to you. Cleanse your hands, you sinners, and purify your hearts, you double-minded.

(Zechariah 7:11, 13) But they refused to pay attention and turned a stubborn shoulder and stopped their ears that they might not hear…"As I called, and they would not hear, so they called, and I would not hear," says the LORD of hosts.

Demonic control in our lives can hinder our communication with Jesus. We can believe lies and become confused. We can have difficulty hearing Jesus or even wanting to hear Him.

(1 Timothy 4:1) Now the Spirit expressly says that in later times some will depart from the faith by devoting themselves to deceitful spirits and teachings of demons.

(1 Corinthians 14:33a) For God is not a God of confusion.

7. Count The Cost

It costs a lot to follow Jesus. Because of this, each of us must take pause and make sure we are willing to pay the price.

(Luke 14:26-33) "If anyone comes to Me and does not hate his own father and mother wife and children and brothers and sisters, yes, and even his own life, he cannot be My disciple. Whoever does not bear his own cross and come after Me cannot be My disciple. For which of you, desiring to

build a tower, does not first sit down and count the cost, whether he has enough to complete it? Otherwise, when he has laid a foundation and is not able to finish, all who see it begin to mock him, saying, 'This man began to build and was not able to finish.' Or what king, going to encounter another king in war, will not sit down first and deliberate whether he is able with ten thousand to meet him who comes against him with twenty thousand? And if not, while the other is yet a great way off, he sends a delegation and asks for terms of peace. So therefore, any one of you who does not renounce all that he has cannot be My disciple."

8. The Path Is Difficult

(Matthew 7:13-14) "Enter by the narrow gate. For the gate is wide and the way is easy that leads to destruction, and those who enter by it are many. For the gate is narrow and the way is hard that leads to life, and those who find it are few."

Abundant life in Jesus is found on the more difficult path. Many people refuse to trade their present problems for future possibilities with Jesus (even if these possibilities are to be wonderful) because they are comfortable where they are and their circumstances are familiar to them. Such people have decided that they do not want to travel on a different path with Jesus, even if it is a better path. They would rather live with what they have in their lives or for their lives than risk walking with Jesus into the unknown.

Jesus is looking for men whose hearts truly belong to Him. Men He can use to further His Father's plan here on earth. Jesus is looking for disciples.

1) Look up the definition of *disciple* and write it down.

2) List as many characteristics of a disciple of Jesus as you can think of.

3) Think back to a time when you bought something that cost a lot of money. When you were trying to decide to spend the money, what thoughts went through your mind?

4) Have you ever decided to <u>not</u> buy something that cost a lot?

5) What was the determining factor(s) in your decision to <u>not</u> buy it?

6) Following Jesus costs each of us a lot—our hearts, our wills, our affections, our time, our resources, etc. When you think about following Him, what thoughts go through your mind?

7) What feelings do you feel?

8) Read **Mark 12:30** below. What does this verse mean to you?

(Mark 12:30) "And you shall love the Lord your God with all your heart and with all your soul and with all your mind and with all your strength."

9) If a disciple had this kind of love, what would he be willing to do for Jesus?

10) What do you think about the statement that there are no neutral decisions?

11) Do you believe that every time we make a decision, one of two kingdoms is advanced—Jesus' or Satan's kingdom?

12) We make hundreds of decisions each day ranging from the most basic to the more serious. Make a list of as many decisions that you can remember making in the past 48 hours.

As you look at the list, what was the basis of each of the decisions? Was it your own wants and desires? Was it the desire of someone else? Did you ask Jesus what He wanted? Did you do what He wanted or what you wanted?

13) If these decisions were used to determine whom it is you are following, who would it be?

14) Read **Numbers 9:16-23** below. What do these verses say to you?

(Numbers 9:16-23) So it was always: the cloud covered it by day and the appearance of fire by night. And whenever the cloud lifted from over the tent, after that the people of Israel set out, and in the place where the cloud settled down, there the people of Israel camped. At the command of the Lord the people of Israel set out, and at the command of the Lord they camped. As long as the cloud rested over the tabernacle, they remained in camp. Even when the cloud continued over the tabernacle many days, the people of Israel kept the charge of the Lord and did not set out. Sometimes the cloud was a few days over the tabernacle, and according to the command of the LORD they remained in camp; then according to the command of the LORD they set out. And sometimes the cloud remained from evening until morning. And when the cloud lifted in the morning, they set out, or if it continued for a day and a night, when the cloud lifted they set out. Whether it was two days, or a month, or a longer time, that the cloud continued over the tabernacle, abiding there, the people of Israel remained in camp and did not set out, but when it lifted they set out. At the command of the Lord they camped, and at the command of the Lord they set out. They kept the charge of the Lord, at the command of the Lord by Moses.

15) Jesus said that His sheep know His voice. Note all the ways that Jesus speaks to *you* from the list below.

Through His Word

To your mind or heart

Through others

In dreams and visions

Through His creation

Through prayer

Through signs and wonders

Through circumstances

Audibly

JESUS IS CALLING

Every man has a calling on his life.[1]

If we belong to Jesus, our calling is holy, it is to further God's plan for us, and it was given before the world began. Our calling is not about meeting the expectations of life—being a good husband or father or provider or protector. Our calling is not necessarily about our vocation, although what we do for a living can be a part of it. Our calling is that one overriding thing that God has given us to do to fulfill the purpose for our life. In this way, our calling is the means to our destiny.

Some callings are high profile. Most are not. Some callings are radical. Most are not. It doesn't really matter. What matters is that we understand we are all created to fulfill some portion of God's plan for mankind and that we listen to Jesus when He reveals to us our part in this plan.

Every calling comes with a price to pay.[2] It is not just business as usual. There is sacrifice involved, self-sacrifice. There is the requirement to put other things aside. Things we would rather not put aside. Things we cherish. Our idols. There is an investment to be made. Time. Money. Effort. Callings take us out of our comfort zones. They surround us with the unfamiliar. They stretch us, sometimes to the point of breaking. All of this drives us back to the One who called us—Jesus. He called, so He will equip.[3]

The Bible is full of such callings.[4] Noah was called to save a remnant of mankind and animal kind in a boat. Abraham was called out from his people and homeland to

31

follow God and become a mighty nation unto Him. Joseph was called to prevent the beginning generations of this nation from perishing in a famine and to provide them a place where they could flourish into a mighty nation. Moses was called to deliver these people from slavery. Gideon was called to deliver them from oppression. David was called to be a king over them. Josiah was called to bring this nation back into a true worship relationship with God. Samuel, Samson, the prophets, the apostles—all of them had specific callings from Jesus on their lives. Callings based on His purposes in the world. Callings based on His Father's plan.

BUSY-NESS FOR GOD OR ABOUT GOD'S BUSINESS?

Life comes at us fast these days. We all suffer at some degree from 'requirement fatigue'. There are so many things to take care of, so many things to pay attention to. They all come at us at the speed of *now*. And on top of it all, we have our local church obligations—well-meaning pastors and teachers challenging us to give more time and more money, to be involved in this, to go and do that, to participate, to be more committed. And as we sit there and listen, we sink a little lower in our seats with each new challenge. Our hearts want to do what is right, but there is a part of us that pushes back, that shuts down, that *rebels*. We don't *want* more requirements put on us. We don't *need* more requirements put on us. There are already too many things we are not doing.

Most of us have been there. We have shared the corporate guilt of failure, of not being and doing and going and participating as much as we have been challenged to do, as much as other men are doing. But have we lost our way here? Is this guilt really valid? Has the leadership in our church bodies forgotten that our primary responsibility is to follow the lead of Jesus as *individuals* first? That all of us are not called to participate in the next activity or program or event? That the world will not go to hell any faster if we are not involved in everything, or any slower if we are?

Are all of us really called to do all of these things?

The answer is 'yes', and 'no'.

Yes, because, as Christians, we are commanded to do many things that are good things.[5] We are commanded to worship God. We are told to study His word. We are given the responsibility to take the Gospel to the world. We are instructed to serve our fellow believers. We are commanded to make disciples. Some of these commands are personal, and some include corporate participation with other believers. The corporate part requires planning, preparation, practice, and our time.

No, because we are not necessarily called to the same tasks, or methods, or ways as those of other men.[6] A local church body is not the only mechanism for doing these good things. At the end of our lives, we will not stand before Jesus in judgment with our local group of believers (or the greater Church Body of Christ for that matter). We will stand alone. We will not be judged according to what any church group or denominational body required of us. We will be judged according to what Jesus required of us.[7]

It is not in the doing. It is in the obedience of doing what we are *to be* doing. What we are to be doing is tied to our calling. This is the crux of the matter.

Jesus is not merely calling us to do things, even if they are good things. He is calling us to do specific things. Isn't this where most of us get off track? We as an individual or a local church body or a denomination get an idea to do something 'good' in the name of Jesus, and we go off and start doing it. Then we ask Jesus to catch up to us and bless our efforts. It seems very backwards and out of step with Him. Why should He bless it? Because it was something 'good'? If it wasn't something He called us to do, why would we expect Him to bless it? In the best case, we are wasting precious time in our doing. In the worst case, we are likely sinning in the disobedience of our doing.

Remember, Jesus is our Commander. He has specific things for us to do and specific things He does not want us doing. He also has specific reasons for both the doing and not doing. Wouldn't we all rather be in step with Him in obedience than be busy doing 'good' and trying to save the world by our own design and on our own strength?

And so we waste time. And we toil on. And we get burned out. And we do not want anything else to do—even the things that Jesus truly wants us to do. And Satan wins.

Wouldn't it be better for us to be about God's business than our busy-ness?

WHO WILL GO FOR US?

Our calling is much more than being busy for Jesus. It is about being *effective* for Jesus. It goes beyond the mere day-to-day and reaches out to the very heart of our destiny. It is unique to us individually, but can be a common part of the larger sequence of events that Jesus is orchestrating corporately around the world. It is not *primarily* based upon our desires, our abilities, our talents, or our place in life, but these can be used to fulfill it. Our calling *is* based on how we were spiritually gifted from the moment of salvation and how Jesus wants us to use these gifts to fulfill our purpose.

It has been said that all men die, but very few truly live. How can we live our lives if we have nothing that is worth dying for? We can't. We can exist, but we can't live. We can survive, but we can't thrive. We can only get by, day-to-day, week-to-week, year-to-year, and then we die. We can do some good things. We can be better than others. But in the end, what did we accomplish? Why did it matter? Was Jesus pleased with us? Or did we waste what He gave to us like the wicked, lazy servant in the Parable of the Talents, burying it in the trivialities of life and never investing it to further Jesus' plans through our calling as He intended?[8]

A calling is worth dying for. It is worth laying our lives down daily for. It has everlasting consequences. It leaves a legacy to those who come after us, generation after generation.

Jesus calls each of us to do something specific for Him that He uses to glorify His Father. He asks, along with the Father and the Holy Spirit, 'Whom shall I send, and who will go for Us?'[9]

HERE I AM! SEND ME

If your phone rang right now and the Caller ID said 'Jesus', what would you do? Would you let it go to voicemail? Would you answer it? Would you cut the conversation short, telling Him you were busy at the moment and would get back to Him?

All who hear their call will respond in some way, but not all will accept it, walk into it, and take ownership of it. Some will deny it. Some will ignore it. Some will explain it away. Some will blatantly reject it.

How can this be?

Well, some of us are just plain lazy. We are not interested in anything that we don't feel like doing at the moment, especially if it requires effort. And we know it will require effort.

Many of us are complacent. We don't want to be challenged out of our steady-state lives. We are comfortable right where we are...very comfortable. We do not want the risk involved or the exposure to the unknown.

For the others, it is because we feel we are already maxed out. We already have as many requirements placed on us as we can handle. We can't take another.

Most of us feel inadequate. We are not sure if we are up for the task. We are afraid to try because we have already failed enough in our Christian walk and we don't want to fail at something else.

All of these are real reasons. But are they valid reasons? Look at them—laziness, complacency, being uncomfortable, overload, and inadequacy. None of them are. Each is self-imposed. Laziness is a choice. Complacency is a life style. Comfort is an escape. Overload is misplaced priorities. Inadequacy is believing the lie that God can't work through and strengthen our weaknesses. Each one feels very real to us, and we use them quite effectively to justify our own will in things. But in the end, they are just excuses. And we all know it.

The good news is that Jesus gave us a few things at salvation to help us overcome these excuses.[10] He gave us the Holy Spirit. He gave us spiritual gifts. He gave us His power over sin. These were beginning points, like the talents of His parable. They were not intended as ending points. It is up to us to walk into them and to progress from there, giving Him a return on these investments and furthering His plans.

WHY THIS IS IMPORTANT

There is a stirring upon the face of the earth today. A stirring by the Spirit of God. A challenging of hearts. An invitation to a close fellowship with the Creator of all things. As part of this stirring, Jesus is quietly raising up an army of warriors whose hearts are fully His. He is calling these few to that pure place of total surrender—that rarified state of complete and total belief and faith in Him. He desires to confound the world by demonstrating His awesome power

36

through this troop, 'turning the whole world upside down' as the early believers did.[11] He will use these dedicated warriors to work mightily in their families, raising Godly generations after them. He will use these fearless soldiers to change their world by confronting the forces of evil head on and by helping those who heed the same call to walk in true power and freedom through this fallen world.

Jesus is singling out the few. Those who will die to themselves. Those who will truly live for Him.

Will we answer the call? Will our cry be, 'Here we are! Send us'? Or will it be, 'We have to think about that. We're kind of busy right now, Jesus. Can we get back to you'? Or maybe, 'Sorry, Jesus, but I think you have the wrong number'?

Jesus is calling. Will we follow where He leads?

♦♦♦ CHAPTER NOTES ♦♦♦

We are all called to something greater than our wants, our plans, and ourselves. We are called above the futility and vanity that surrounds us. Jesus calls us to Himself, His desires for us, and His plans for our lives.

(Romans 1:6) Including you who are called to belong to Jesus Christ.

1. Calling Versus Purpose

Our calling is different than our purpose. Our *purpose* is the reason we were created and exist. All believers share one common purpose—to glorify God through Jesus.

(1 Peter 4:11b) In order that in everything God may be glorified through Jesus Christ.

(Isaiah 43:6b-7a) Bring My sons from afar and My daughters from the end of the earth, everyone who is called by My name, whom I created for My glory.

(1 Corinthians 10:31) So, whether you eat or drink, or whatever you do, do all to the glory of God.

Our *calling* is the way that Jesus wants us to live out and fulfill our purpose of glorifying God while on earth. It is our long-term mission. It is the accomplishment of our part in our Father's plan for mankind.

(Colossians 4:17b) See that you fulfill the ministry that you have received in the Lord [your calling].

This long-term mission is made up of many short-term assignments. The short-term assignments are stepping-stones that move us along the way of the overriding call on our lives. Many of us can see and understand the short-term aspects of our calling—the specific leadings by Jesus to do one thing for a season and another for a different season. But have we caught the vision for Jesus' overall call on our lives? Do we understand what it is? Are we pressing forward toward this goal every day?

(Philippians 3:12-14) Not that I have already obtained this or

38

am already perfect, but I press on to make it my own, because Christ Jesus has made me His own. Brothers, I do not consider that I have made it my own. But one thing I do: forgetting what lies behind and straining forward to what lies ahead, I press on toward the goal for the prize of the upward call of God in Christ Jesus.

Our calling is closely related to our spiritual gifting. Each of us is given different gifts according to Jesus' plan for us. We are to recognize, understand, and use these gifts because they enable us to fulfill our calling. We are to literally walk through these gifts into our calling.

(Romans 12:4-6a) For as in one body we have many members, and the members do not all have the same function, so we, though many, are one body in Christ, and individually members one of another. Having gifts that differ according to the grace given to us, let us use them.

Our calling leads to a life of significance in the service of Jesus, which in turn leads to the fulfilling of our destiny.

Like each of us, Jesus had a purpose and a calling. Like us, Jesus' purpose was to glorify His Father. And like us, Jesus had to fulfill His purpose by fulfilling His calling.

(John 17:4) "I have glorified You [God the Father] on earth, having accomplished the work that You gave Me to do."

Jesus' calling was to come into the world in human form in order to bring the good news of God's reconciling salvation to man.

(Luke 4:18-19) "The Spirit of the Lord is upon Me, because He has anointed Me to proclaim good news to the poor. He has sent Me to proclaim liberty to the captives and recovering of sight to the blind, to set at liberty those who are oppressed, to proclaim the year of the Lord's favor."

2. The Price Of The Calling

That which does not cost us anything is prone to be held in disdain. It costs us to follow Jesus. We must lay aside everything that does not bring glory to Him—everything that slows us down and everything that causes us to sin.

For any of us who have run races competitively, we know it is all about being light, sleek, and unencumbered. Anything that is bulky, causes wind resistance, or is heavy, is cast aside for the sake of the race.

(Hebrews 12:1) Therefore, since we are surrounded by so great a cloud of witnesses, let us also lay aside every weight, and sin which clings so closely, and let us run with endurance the race that is set before us.

The race set before us is our calling. The weights are the things of the world in our lives that slow us down and hinder the accomplishment of our calling.

3. Jesus Equips Us For Our Calling

Jesus always supplies what we need to fulfill our calling. The primary and most essential thing He supplies is our spiritual gifting through the Holy Spirit. It is our responsibility to understand what gifting He has provided and to use it for His glory to fulfill our calling.

(1 Peter 4:10-11) As each has received a gift, use it to serve one another, as good stewards of God's varied grace: Whoever speaks, as one who speaks the oracles of God; Whoever serves, as one who serves by the strength that God supplies—in order that in everything God may be glorified through Jesus Christ. To Him belong glory and dominion forever and ever. Amen.

Most of us receive these gifts at the moment of salvation when we are baptized into the body of Christ.

(1 Corinthians 12:13a) For in one Spirit we were all baptized into one body.

It is also clear from Scripture that we can receive additional spiritual gifts later on after our salvation experience. Timothy received a spiritual gift when he was ordained.

(1 Timothy 4:14) Do not neglect the gift you have, which was given you by prophecy when the council of elders laid their hands on you.

Likewise, Paul tells the Corinthian believers to desire the

40

best gifts, indicating that additional gifts could be given after salvation.

(1 Corinthians 12:31a) But earnestly desire the higher gifts.

Spiritual gifts are different from natural abilities or skills. Natural abilities are talents or capabilities we are born with. Skills are acquired through environmental conditioning or training. Spiritual gifts are a manifestation of the Holy Spirit living inside us. They are supernatural.

(1 Corinthians 12:7) To each is given the manifestation of the Spirit for the common good.

4. Bible Callings

(Genesis 6:13-14) And God said to Noah, "I have determined to make an end of all flesh, for the earth is filled with violence through them. Behold, I will destroy them with the earth. Make yourself an ark of gopher wood. Make rooms in the ark, and cover it inside and out with pitch."

(Genesis 12:1-3) Now the LORD said to Abram, "Go from your country and your kindred and your father's house to the land that I will show you. And I will make of you a great nation, and I will bless you and make your name great, so that you will be a blessing. I will bless those who bless you, and him who dishonors you I will curse, and in you all the families of the earth shall be blessed."

(Genesis 50:19-20) But Joseph said to them, "Do not fear, for am I in the place of God? As for you, you meant evil against me, but God meant it for good, to bring it about that many people should be kept alive, as they are today."

(Exodus 3:4, 10) When the LORD saw that he turned aside to see, God called to him out of the bush, "Moses, Moses!" And he said, "Here I am"..."Come, I will send you to Pharaoh that you may bring My people, the children of Israel, out of Egypt."

(Judges 6:11-12, 14) Now the Angel of the LORD came and sat under the terebinth at Ophrah, which belonged to Joash the Abiezrite, while his son Gideon was beating out the wheat in the winepress to hide it from the Midianites. And the Angel of the LORD appeared to him and said to him, "The LORD is with you, O mighty man of valor!" ...And the LORD

turned to him and said, "Go in this might of yours and save Israel from the hand of Midian; do not I send you?"

(1 Samuel 16:12-13a) And he sent and brought him in. Now he was ruddy and had beautiful eyes and was handsome. And the LORD said, "Arise, anoint him, for this is he." Then Samuel took the horn of oil and anointed him in the midst of his brothers. And the Spirit of the LORD rushed upon David from that day forward.

(2 Kings 22:1a, 23:25) Josiah was eight years old when he began to reign, and he reigned thirty-one years in Jerusalem...Before him there was no king like him, who turned to the LORD with all his heart and with all his soul and with all his might, according to all the Law of Moses, nor did any like him arise after him.

5. Basic Christian Duties

As we serve, we are called to the basics.

(Matthew 4:10a) Then Jesus said to him, "Be gone, Satan! For it is written, 'You shall worship the LORD your God, and Him only you shall serve.'"

(2 Timothy 2:15) Do your best to present yourself to God as one approved, a worker who has no need to be ashamed, rightly handling the word of truth.

(Mark 16:15) And He said to them, "Go into all the world and proclaim the gospel to the whole creation."

(Hebrews 13:16) Do not neglect to do good and to share what you have, for such sacrifices are pleasing to God.

(John 13:34a) "A new commandment I give to you, that you love one another."

(1 Timothy 5:3) Honor widows who are truly widows.

(Matthew 28:19a) "Go therefore and make disciples of all the nations."

6. The Church Is The Body

Everyone who is saved has a specific part to play in the plan of God. Some might be called to a solo mission. Others could be called to mighty collaborations. We are not all called to the same thing, the same way. Jesus has a specific calling for each of us.

The Church is the Body of Christ on earth.

(Colossians 1:24) Now I rejoice in my sufferings for your sake, and in my flesh I am filling up what is lacking in Christ's afflictions for the sake of His body, that is, the church.

The body is composed of many different members. Just as in the human body, there are hands for grasping, joints for bending, skin for covering, etc. Each part has a specific primary function, but each can work in concert with the other members. God set all in place according to His plan.

(1 Corinthians 12:12, 18) For just as the body is one and has many members, and all the members of the body, though many, are one body, so it is Christ...But as it is, God arranged the members in the body, each one of them, as He chose.

God gives the different members different functions. These functioning parts give the church everything it needs to accomplish its mission and to do so in a positive manner.

(Ephesians 4:11-12) And He gave the apostles, the prophets, the evangelists, the shepherds and teachers, to equip the saints for the work of ministry, for building up the body of Christ.

Every part of the body does its share to contribute to the good of the whole. Different parts are called to do different things. Though different, each part makes a vital contribution to the benefit of the whole.

(Ephesians 4:16) From whom the whole body, joined and held together by every joint with which it is equipped, when each part is working properly, makes the body grow so that it builds itself up in love.

Jesus is the Head of the body. The Greek word for 'head' is very specific. It signifies that Jesus is the 'source'. The source of what? Power. Jesus provides the necessary power to all members through their spiritual gifts. This allows each to fulfill their purpose the way they were called to fulfill it. Because of this empowerment, the church as individuals and as a whole can accomplish Jesus' plan to the glory of His Father.

(Ephesians 4:15b) We are to grow up in every way into Him who is the head, into Christ.

7. The Judgment Seat Of Christ

Each of us will answer only to Jesus for what we have done with everything He has given us here on earth—spiritual gifts, talents, knowledge, revelation, means, and opportunities. We will stand alone. We will not answer to any man, only to Jesus.

(2 Corinthians 5:10) For we must all appear before the judgment seat of Christ, so that each one may receive what is due for what he has done in the body, whether good or evil.

8. Parable Of The Talents

We are called to use what Jesus has given to us in this life to further our calling for His purposes. The objective is to obey Him and give Him a return on His investment in us. Jesus looks unfavorably on anyone who fails to do so.

(Matthew 25:14-30) "For it will like a man going on a journey, who called his servants and entrusted to them his property. To one he gave five talents, to another two, to another one, to each according to his ability. Then he went away. He who had received the five talents went at once and traded with them, and he made five talents more. So also he who had the two talents made two more. But he who had received the one talent went and dug in the ground and hid his master's money. Now after a long time the master of those servants came and settled accounts with them. And he who had received the five talents came forward, bringing five talents more, saying, 'Master, you delivered to me five talents; here, I have made five talents more.' His master said to him, 'Well done, good and faithful servant. You have been faithful over a little; I will set you over much. Enter into the joy of your master.' And he also who had the two talents came forward, saying, 'Master, you delivered to me two talents; here I have made two more talents more.' His master said to him, 'Well done, good and faithful servant. You have been faithful over

a little; I will set you ruler over much. Enter into the joy of your master.' He also who had received the one talent came forward, saying, 'Master, I knew you to be a hard man, reaping where you did not sow, and gathering where you scattered no seed, so I was afraid, and I went and hid your talent in the ground. Here, you have what is yours.' But his master answered him, 'You wicked and slothful servant! You knew that I reap where I have not sown, and gather where I scattered no seed? Then you ought to have invested my money with the bankers, and at my coming I should have received what was my own with interest. So take the talent from him and give it to him who has the ten talents. For to everyone who has will more be given, and he will have an abundance. But from the one who has not, even what he has will be taken away. And cast the worthless servant into the outer darkness. In that place there will be weeping and gnashing of teeth.'"

9. Here I Am

With all that Jesus has provided to us, shouldn't we be willing to make our lives available for His use as He sees fit?

(Isaiah 6:8-9) And I heard the voice of the Lord, saying, "Whom shall I send, and who will go for Us?" Then I said, "Here am I! Send me."

10. Things Given At Salvation

At salvation we are given some basic things so that our new life in Jesus can be successful.

Foremost, we were given the Holy Spirit to live in us.

(Ephesians 1:13-14) In Him [Jesus] you also, when you heard the word of truth, the gospel of your salvation, and believed in Him, were sealed with the promised Holy Spirit, who is the guarantee of our inheritance until we acquire possession of it, to the praise of His glory.

Additionally, each of us is gifted to do the work that Jesus intended for us to do. These spiritual gifts are essential to our fulfilling our calling and are specific to us.

(1 Corinthians 12:4-6) There are varieties of gifts, but the

same Spirit; and there are varieties of service, but the same Lord; and there are varieties of activities, but it is the same God who empowers them all in everyone.

(Romans 12:4-6a) For as in one body we have many members, and the members do not all have the same function, so we, though many, are one body in Christ, and individually members one of another. Having gifts that differ according to the grace given to us, let us use them.

And lastly, we were given our freedom.

(Romans 6:6-7) We know that our old self was crucified with Him in order that the body of sin might be brought to nothing, so that we would no longer be enslaved to sin. For one who has died has been set free from sin.

11. Turned The Whole World Upside Down

The early church operated in the power of Jesus through the Holy Spirit. These people had discovered a great truth—when they decreased, Jesus increased. When they died to themselves, He lived through them. This was the key to their power. This is the key to our power.

(Acts 17:6b) These men who have turned the world upside down have come here also.

1) Every man has a purpose and a calling. What is the difference?

2) How do purpose and calling work together in a man's life?

3) Do you believe that you have a calling from Jesus? If so, do you know what it is? (*Write it down*)

4) How does your calling fulfill your purpose?

5) If you know what your spiritual gifts are, list them.

6) How do these specific gifts relate to your unique calling?

7) What do you believe is your destiny?

8) What short-term assignments have you completed in your long-term calling?

9) What have you sacrificed to fulfill your calling?

10) What else do you believe Jesus is telling you to sacrifice?

11) How willing are you to give Him what He asks?

12) When you think of fulfilling your calling, what feelings come alive in you? List them.

Look at each feeling on your list. Which ones are positive? Negative? Put a 'plus' (+) beside the positive feelings and a 'minus' (–) beside the negative feelings on your list.

13) Do you have any negative feelings? If so, why do you think you have these negative feelings?

14) Busyness is rampant in our society. How many hours a week on average do you spend on your calling?

15) How many hours a week on average do you spend on other church-related activities?

16) When you compare the numbers, what *specific* adjustments do you need to make?

17) Many times we are busy with "good" things but they are not "God" things. Can you think of a time when you decided to do—or actually did—something good and *then* asked God to bless it? What was it?

18) Do you think that He should have blessed it? Why or why not?

19) What things in your life are worth dying for? Make a list.

20) Did you include your calling on the list above? Why or why not?

ANSWERING THE CALL

Many of us have experienced what we would describe as the *leading* of God in our lives. But have we sensed Jesus' *calling* in our lives?

Many times the calling comes when we least expect it. We may be fully engaged in life at the time. It may come even though we are not seeking any divine intervention in our circumstances. It might be an outgrowth of something we are already involved in. It could also be totally disconnected from anything we ever thought possible.

When we get the calling, we will know it. It will sear itself like a brand upon our heart. There may be an adrenaline rush. Our hearts may pound with fierceness in our chests. It may produce tears in our eyes when we begin to understand its full implications in our lives. Our heads may spin with a thousand thoughts as we try to process everything it involves. But we will know it is our calling. And we will know it is from Jesus.

This, then, leaves only our response. What will it be? Will we take the call and own it? Or will we put the call on 'hold' while we get back to the busy-ness of our plans?

THE CALL ON HOLD

Why would we ever put the call of Jesus in our lives on 'hold'? What would cause us to do such a thing?

Some of us might not understand that it is a calling. We may see it only as a suggestion. We may have only heard of this sort of thing happening to others. We may not fully appreciate the gravity of the situation. We may feel it is something for another time and place in our lives. Or we may not want to do what we are being called to do.

Some of us might not be at the place where we will answer that call—not from the place of our circumstances, for Jesus knows all that is going on in our lives—but from the place of our heart. Our heart may be hard and its soil, rocky. We may have issues. Issues that are large. Issues we have not yet dealt with or do not know how to deal with. This rockiness may have prevented the calling from sinking in very far. It may have withered and dried out before it could get much root in our heart.

Some of us may be too busy with living life. Children, bills, jobs, promotions, houses, moves, more bills. Laughter, tears, love, hate, victory, defeat, agreeing, disagreeing, closeness, distance, satisfaction, disappointment. Churches, teachings, doctrines, approaches, serving, sitting, more churches, more doctrines. Visions, deaths of visions, passion, disillusionment, doing, waiting, knowing, wondering. And sinning. These can choke out the calling like a thicket of weeds, slowly but surely.

And so we don't pursue the calling. We don't try to understand it. We don't ask more questions. We just put the call on 'hold'.

In all of these, the root issue is the condition of the soil of our heart.[1] It is hard and weedy and dry.

So we put Jesus on 'hold'. We waste years of our lives in the process. Years that could have been spent in preparation. Years that could have been spent in pursuing. It is heartbreaking. Time wasted. Opportunities lost. Blessings missed. All the while, we drag our family along. Sometimes, we try to make some progress on our own against the weeds and dryness. But it proves to be impossible. Only Jesus can break apart the hardness of our hearts and make them soft so that our calling can take root and flourish. Only He can purge us of the root causes of the hardness—our willfulness, our sinfulness, and our sense of entitlement. Only He can heal the wounds of our past. Only He can set us free from those things that hold us captive. Only He can repair the damaged relationships. Only He can bring clarity to all that is in our lives.

What we have to do is yield to the work of Jesus in our lives.

SPADE WORK

With any agricultural pursuit, there is much work to be done preparing the soil so that crops can grow, leading to a harvest. Left to itself, soil will not produce an abundance of crops. Weeds, yes, but not crops. The soil must be turned and broken apart. On a farm, this means plows and other soil-tilling equipment. In the garden, it means using a shovel.

Shoveling is hard work. In fact, it is backbreaking work, producing ample amounts of sweat, sore muscles, and huge blisters. That is the essence of spadework. Without properly prepared soil, there is only a minimal crop.

Soil preparation takes time. Shovel full by shovel full. Area by area. Digging and turning and breaking apart. Making all ready for new growth. For new seed. For a profitable crop.

So it is with answering the call. We are where we are. Irrespective of that place—good or bad—it is the beginning point of our great adventure with Jesus. It is time for preparing the soil of the heart. If it is stony and hard, it must be broken apart. If it is full of weeds, they must be pulled out and cast aside. If it is dry and parched, it must be watered and made soft.

How do we do this?

Only through Jesus, by the power of the Holy Spirit. He must do the work in our heart. We cannot do this on our own. We have tried and we have failed. Jesus will prepare our heart to accept His great calling if we ask Him and we allow Him.

PREPARED TO ANSWER

The initial cleanup work is just the beginning. There is an investment of time to be made as we begin to walk into our calling. Noah spent years planning, building, and fitting out the ark. Abraham waited years for God to give him the promised son from whom would come those descendants as numerous as the stars in the sky. Joseph was dropped in a hole in the ground and spent time in prison before he was elevated to rule over Egypt. Moses lived 40 years in obscurity as a fugitive before he was sent back to Egypt to confront the new Pharaoh. Gideon took months growing in obedience and faith before he confronted the invading enemy armies. David invested years in the fields tending sheep and later endured many years fleeing for his life before he became king. Josiah had to grow in age before he was ready to purge the Baals from the nation and reinstate worship as prescribed in the Book of the Law. The prophets had to be spoken to over time. One even had to be chased down and swallowed by a great fish.[2] The apostles had to be taught, scattered, and anointed.

None of these men were ready to step into their calling on day one. They each had to be prepared.[3] They had things they needed to do. They had things they needed to work out. They had things they needed to learn. They had things they needed to unlearn. For Noah, it was standing alone when no one believed him about the coming judgment. For Abraham, it was waiting on God's timing instead of his own. Joseph had to learn humility before he could assume a position of greatness. For Moses, it was emptying himself of the many capabilities he had acquired in the palace of Egypt and relying on God alone. Gideon had to learn to do more with less so God would get the glory. For David, it was learning to lead people God's way. Josiah had to come to a mature understanding of God and what His holiness required. The prophets were challenged with learning to persevere in the face of hostile, stiff-necked people. For the apostles, it was overcoming their fear of the religious leaders of the day. All of them had to learn the faithfulness of Jesus and His promises. Each had to be prepared for the tasks ahead. All had to walk through this preparation and into their calling.

And so it will be with every one of us.

♦♦♦ CHAPTER NOTES ♦♦♦

Once called, each man can exercise his will in deciding whether to answer his calling or to ignore it. If we understood that our calling was the one thing on earth that would fulfill us and bring true significance to our lives, would we not be eager to answer?

1. Parable Of The Sower

This parable could be aptly named *The Parable of the Soils* because it speaks to the condition of the soil of men's hearts. It is not speaking about salvation. It is speaking about the spiritual health of a heart at any given time. How is yours?

(Matthew 13:3b-9, 18-23) "A sower went out to sow. And as he sowed, some seeds fell along the path, and the birds came and devoured them. Other seeds fell on rocky ground, where they did not have much soil, and immediately they sprang up, since they had no depth of soil, but when the sun rose they were scorched. And since they had no root, they withered away. Other seeds fell among thorns, and the thorns grew up and choked them. Other seeds fell on good soil and produced grain, some a hundredfold, some sixty, some thirty. He who has ears, let him hear...Hear then the parable of the sower: When anyone hears the word of the kingdom and does not understand it, the evil one comes and snatches away what has been sown in his heart. This is what was sown along the path. As for what was sown on the rocky ground, this is the one who hears the word and immediately receives it with joy; yet he has no root in himself, but endures for a while, and when tribulation or persecution arises on account of the word, immediately he falls away. As for what was sown among the thorns, this is the one who hears the word, but the cares of the world and the deceitfulness of riches choke the word, and it proves unfruitful. As for what was sown on good soil, this is the one who hears the word and understands it. He indeed bears fruit and yields, in one case a hundredfold, in another sixty, and in another thirty."

2. Jonah

Many people do not believe the account of Jonah being swallowed by a sea creature. They think it is preposterous. But Scripture is full of the preposterous, and Scripture is clear. Jesus (the LORD) made a special preparation of a 'great aquatic animal'. What type of sea creature it was, we do not know. But Jesus was clearly in control. He prepared the creature and He commanded it to swallow Jonah and spit him out three days later.

(Jonah 1:17, 2:10) And the LORD [Jesus] appointed a great fish to swallow up Jonah. And Jonah was in the belly of the fish three days and three nights...And the LORD spoke to the fish, and it vomited Jonah out upon the dry land.

Jesus Himself referred to this event, validating its truth.

(Matthew 12:40) "For just as Jonah was three days and three nights in the belly of the great fish, so will the Son of Man be three days and three nights in the heart of the earth."

3. Bible Characters' Preparation

Each person called must undertake a season of preparation in order to fulfill their calling. As it was for these great men of the faith, so it will be for each of us.

(Genesis 7:11) In the six hundredth year of Noah's life, in the second month, on the seventeenth day of the month, on that day all the fountains of the great deep burst forth, and the windows of the heavens were opened.

(Genesis 21:1-2, 5) The LORD visited Sarah as He had said, and the LORD did to Sarah as He had promised. And Sarah conceived and bore Abraham a son in his old age at the set time of which God had spoken to him...Abraham was a hundred years old when his son Isaac was born to him.

(Genesis 37:23-24; 39:20) So when Joseph came to his brothers, they stripped him of his robe, the robe of many colors that he wore. And then they took him and threw him into a pit. The pit was empty; there was no water in it...and Joseph's master took him and put him into the prison, the place where the king's prisoners were confined, and he was

there in prison.

(Acts 7:30, 34b) "Now when forty years had passed, an angel [the Angel of the LORD-Jesus] appeared to him in the wilderness of Mount Sinai, in a flame of fire in a bush...'And now come, I will send you to Egypt.'"

(Judges 7:2, 7a) The LORD [Jesus] said to Gideon, "The people with you are too many for Me to give the Midianites into their hand, lest Israel boast over Me, saying, 'My own hand has saved me.'"...And the LORD said to Gideon, "With the 300 men who lapped I will save you and give the Midianites into your hand."

(1 Samuel 16:19, 19:10) Therefore Saul sent messengers to Jesse, and said, "Send me David your son, who is with the sheep."...And Saul sought to pin David to the wall with the spear, but he eluded Saul, so that he struck the spear into the wall. And David fled and escaped that night.

(2 Kings 22:1a, 3a) Josiah was eight years old when he began to reign...In the eighteenth year of King Josiah...

1) When was the first time you heard Jesus giving you your calling? Describe it.

2) Have you fully embraced your calling? Why or why not?

3) If you have embraced your calling, what hindrances in terms of thoughts, feelings, circumstances, etc., did you overcome in order to do so?

4) If you are denying your calling in any way, what is causing you to do so?

5) Read the *Parable of the Sower* (**Matthew 13:3-9, 18-23**). Why could it just as aptly be named the *Parable of the Soils*?

(Matthew 13:3-9,18-23) And he [Jesus] told them many things in parables, saying: "A sower went out to sow. And as he sowed, some seeds fell along the path, and the birds came and devoured them. Other seeds fell on rocky ground, where they did not have much soil, and immediately they sprang up, since they had no depth of soil, but when the sun rose they were scorched. And since they had no root, they withered away. Other seeds fell among thorns, and the thorns grew up and choked them. Other seeds fell on good soil and produced grain, some a hundredfold, some sixty, some thirty. He who has ears, let him hear...Hear then the parable of the sower: When anyone hears the word of the kingdom and does not understand it, the evil one comes and snatches away what has been sown in his heart. This is what was sown along the path. As for what was sown on rocky ground, this is the one who hears the word and immediately receives it with joy, yet he has no root in himself, but endures for a while, and when tribulation or persecution arises on account of the word, immediately he falls away. As for what was sown among thorns, this is the one who hears the word, but the cares of the world and the deceitfulness of riches choke the word, and it proves unfruitful. As for what was sown on good soil, this is the one who hears the word and understands it. He indeed bears fruit and yields, in one case a hundredfold, in another sixty,

and in another thirty."

6) What is the *soil* in this parable?

7) How is answering your calling tied to the condition of your heart?

8) Just as soil has to be prepared to accept the seed, our hearts and our lives must be prepared in order for us to walk fully into our calling. As you consider your calling, what preparation work do you see that Jesus will need to do in your heart and life? Be specific.

9) As you look at this list of preparations, write down how Jesus will accomplish each one through you. *(Ask Him)*

❧ PART 2 ☙
THE PROBLEM

Let's face it. We have problems. Big problems.

We thought that making a commitment to Jesus would be the solution, but what happened? Why do we live lives of quiet desperation? Why do we struggle so much against the darkness of our flesh? Why do we slink through life on the fringes of our salvation and not come fully into the light? Why do we look into the mirror and not like what is staring back at us?

These are all questions we have asked ourselves, we are asking ourselves, or we should be asking ourselves.

If Jesus is the answer, why do we still have these questions?

All of us have things in our lives that slow down our progress. Like speed bumps on a road, these do not allow the free flow of our lives as a disciple. Each impediment taken alone hinders our walk. Taken as a group, they can stall all forward progress or even cause us to fall back.

Some of the things that hinder our walk are obvious. Others are not. All must be examined under the microscope of truth and eliminated from our lives one by one.

This section explores the most common impediments to our walking with Jesus as His disciples—hindrances many have not considered; those that trip us right out of the gate and stall our progress along the way.

SHALLOW MEN IN DEEP TROUBLE

Walk into any church today and what will we see? We will see men. We will likely see more women than men, but we will see men. If we look carefully into the eyes of these men, what will we see? Much of the time, we will see varying levels of deadness.

How can this be? How did we get to this place? How did the flicker of life go out in our eyes? How did that warrior spirit get slowly strangled to death? How did all of those hopes and dreams and expectations we had for life get put aside and replaced by hopeless resignation? How did we come to the place of accepting mediocrity around us? Or even in us?

How did we become so shallow?

Jesus is challenging us here. He is calling into question some of the basics of our manhood. He is touching that place deep down inside us that longs to make a difference; that place created to be the antithesis of shallowness, where the conqueror in us is supposed to dwell; that place that longs to be significant.

Significance is not about being successful as the world around us defines success. It is not about *having*—money, possessions, or otherwise. It is not about *achieving*—a position at work or some personal best. Such things are illusions, places where we can hide our true selves.

Significance is not about self-centered, self-seeking, or self-aggrandizing thoughts or actions. That is the way of popular culture today—to be concerned only with one's own wants and desires; to crave to be noticed; to be larger than life; to be famous; to be infamous; to become an idol to the adoring public. Such things only stroke our egos. They make us hollow—a shell of a man with no core.

Significance is not about being a hero. Many men are confused about this and have fallen victim to the cult of hero worship that is prevalent today. They long to be a hero—*the hero*. But this desire is just another manifestation of being self-centered and self-seeking. It is another type of false significance.

Significance is not about being dutiful or following an accepted formula for the ideal Christian man. As men, we have duties that God has given us to fulfill, and He expects us to do so. But most of us have been over-domesticated. We have had too much of our wild heart tamed.[1] We no longer dream, we endure. The hope of accomplishing something great for God has been replaced by a reluctant acceptance of all that will never be in our lives. The flicker of the possible in our eyes has been replaced by the deadness of the impossible. We do what we need to do. We go where we need to go. We move through the motions of being a husband, a father, and a church member. It is a familiar rut that we plod, like a mule in the traces.

Still, the longing of a man's heart is to become truly SIGNIFICANT in a deep way. To somehow be part of something greater than himself. To spend the days of his life to the benefit of something that is worthy, something worth dying for. To fully respond to his calling. To put his heart completely into his interactions with his spouse, children, grandchildren, and others in his life. To own Jesus' vision for his life, and to impart that vision to his family. To get back the *why not?* approach to life instead of the *no way* approach he has adopted.

Jesus put this desire for significance deep within us. But not for ourselves. For Him. We are to be His warriors. We are to conquer for Him. We are to follow Him as He kicks down the gates of hell. We are to be wild for Him. Not domesticated and laid back. Wild! And dangerous![2]

We are to take hold of our destiny and never be shaken from it.

So what happened? How did we become so shallow? So tame? So dead?

MASCULINITY LOST

Could the answer be that we allowed ourselves to become emasculated? Could it be that we allowed somebody or something to cut off the part of us that dreamed those dreams and hoped those hopes? The part of us that was confident in victory no matter the odds? The part of us that knew our place as men?

Yes, we have been emasculated.

And we allowed it.

We can't dodge this one. If we do, we might as well get back to our tame, purposeless, sinful, domesticated lives.

WE ALLOWED IT.

Strong words, but true words.

How?

It could have been a number of different things. Our culture is about emasculation. So is feminism or being politically correct. 'I'm okay and you're okay' is about emasculation. Something our parents, siblings, or our spouse said or did could have emasculated us. Ridicule from others or the intimidation of a bully could have emasculated us. A deformity, illness, or disease could have been the cause. It might have been abuse or an addiction that did it. Perhaps a boss or pressure to conform was the source. It could have even been the demonic. The list of possibilities is as long as the experience of man.

Whatever the cause, we allowed it to happen. We were created masculine. Deep within us we had the call to manhood—the call to rescue those in distress, the call to battle, the call to see the possibilities. We had it. And because we had it, it had to be taken from us. We can't shift the blame on this. We own it.

As a result, we have become shallow. And accommodating. And nice. And lazy. And false. We put on faces that say 'I'm okay'. We live places that say 'I'm okay'. We drive vehicles that say 'I'm okay'. We wear clothes that say 'I'm okay'. We spend money to say that 'I'm okay'. We fill our lives with experiences to feel that 'I'm okay'. We pursue relationships with minimal commitments so we can say to each other that 'I'm okay'.

But we are not okay. We look in the mirror and we see the deadness in our own eyes. The spark is not there. *We are not okay!* We turn to being busy with our trifles so we don't have to think about it. We chase after material things to try to feel better about it. We live a life of mobile devices, the Internet, and social media so we can distract ourselves from it. We lose ourselves in fantasy and entertainment and experiences so we don't have to face it. We check out through our addictions so we don't have to feel it. Even so, we are not okay.

And deep within us, there is a cry for help, a pleading cry. It is deep and mournful. It originates in the core of our being. It is filled with desperation and urgency. We know there is more than this to life. We long to be significant, to be equal to the fight, to be warriors, to be authentic, and to be deep. We long to achieve the destiny for which we were created. And as we continue to live in the shadows—on the sidelines of our true masculinity—we slowly lose all hope. We slowly come to the place of surrender. And we are taken a ready prisoner by Satan and his demons.

REGAINING OUR MASCULINITY

How do we get our masculinity back? We have to take it back.

We must take it back from those people, places, circumstances, or things that have taken it from us. We must take it by force, wresting it out of their clutches. We must reclaim our place as warriors. We must get out of the margins and back into the battle. We must stop being defensive and get on the offensive. We must get out of the shadows of despair and into the light of our destiny.

Regaining our masculinity is not easy. The world and everything in it does not want to give it back to us. It wants to keep us on the sidelines where we are not a threat, where we are not dangerous, and where we do not make a difference. It wants to keep us neutralized. It does not want us to band together with other warriors. It does not want us to raise warrior sons or daughters. It does not want us to count for anything in this life or leave anything behind at the end but a gravestone.

No. It will not be easy. Even within our church congregations we will face opposition. Many men there have grown comfortable without their manhood. It is safe that way—no waves to worry about; no unpleasantness to encounter; just go with the flow; don't make any sudden moves and nobody gets hurt. And when we begin to reclaim our masculinity, or start to question the current state of religious affairs within our local church bodies, or get excited about Jesus in all of His fullness, it is then that we will encounter resistance in the form of withering fire from those who are supposed to be on our side, as these same men try to brow-beat us off the field of battle to protect their own shallow complacency.

What will we gain when we take back our masculinity and begin to walk in it with Jesus? Significance. Authentic significance. We will lose our fear of the deep and swim out from the shallows. We will gain a satisfaction that can only come from knowing we are hot on the trail of our destiny. We will see real progress in our relationships. We will find our place in the line of battle. And ultimately, we will be able to own our masculinity in the way that Jesus intended.

Let us follow Jesus into our masculinity.

◆◆◆ CHAPTER NOTES ◆◆◆

Where are the men? What happened to them? We make excuses that our culture is changing and we have to change with it. We justify our fate as a member of the new global community where we have to accommodate everyone and everything, making sure no one feels uncomfortable with us. But in doing so, we have lost ourselves. We no longer know who we are and what we should do. We are confused. We have become uncomfortable with our masculinity and what it truly means to be a man. Very uncomfortable.

1. The Wildness Of A Man's Heart

The wildness in a man's heart is not the wildness of sin— the unrestrained lust to go our own way and do our own thing. It is the wildness for God. That overwhelming drive that does not ask, *'How much will this cost me?'* or *'How will this look to my neighbors?'* or *'What will my friends at church think?'* or *'Where will this lead?'* or *'How long will this take?'* It is a heart that is intentionally abandoned to Jesus. It is a heart given fully to Him for His purposes. It is a heart that does not hesitate at the crucial moment. It is a heart that moves in step with our Creator to fulfill His plan for us.

Jesus had a wild heart. He never did things 'kind of'. He pursued everything with a fullness that defied the religious conventions of the day. He had a drive to fulfill His calling. He allowed nothing to deter him—not well-meaning friends, not public opinion, not armies of temple guards, not the religious elite, not His own family, and not even the sure pain and suffering that was to come. Jesus did not have much materially, yet He lived a life so abundant that it interrupted history itself.

We are to have this same type of wildness in our hearts as men. We are to guide our families with this wildness of purpose. We are to impact our world by turning this wildness loose under the direction of our Commander as we fulfill our calling.

2. Dangerous Men

Jesus likes dangerous men. Men who will take hold of the fullness of their salvation and possess it. Men who will storm the gates of hell on the heels of their Commander with the same violence as an army taking the walls of an enemy fortress. Men who have burned their ships of complacency on the shores of enemy territory with no option of turning back. Men who have sold out to the cause of their Lord. Men who will fight to the death for the lives of their wife, their children, and their future generations. Men who recognize that they have absolutely nothing left to lose in this life and everything to gain in the next.

Dangerous men.

Being dangerous means taking risks. Having faith requires us to take risks as well. Living a life of faith is to live dangerously in the hands of Jesus, putting it all on the line for Him as He directs.

1) When you think of the word *shallow*, what comes to mind?

2) Look up the definition of *significance*. When applied to your life, what do phrases such as 'having meaning', 'having an effect on the surroundings', and 'having importance' mean to you?

3) Think of the self-centered meaning of *significance* in the popular culture today. How is this a counterfeit of the significance Jesus wants our lives to have?

4) The world worships heroes. Many men desire to be a hero. How is this desire just another manifestation of counterfeit significance?

5) Since your calling is Jesus' vision for your life, what is the relationship between this calling and achieving true significance?

6a) Emasculation takes away the essence of our manhood. Make a list of the times you were emasculated. Write only one per line.

6b) Look at this list. Who or what was involved in each instance of emasculation? Write these down beside each instance.

7) Look at your life today. What emasculates you today?

8) What does emasculation feel like to you? Describe it in detail.

9) How do you compensate for these feelings?

10) Look at the footnotes at the end of the chapter. What do you think it means to be 'wild for God'?

11) How do you think that Jesus wants you to take back your masculinity? *(Ask Him)*

12) Are you willing to forgive each person who has emasculated you as a first step to taking back your masculinity? Do so now.

13) When you think about regaining your masculinity, how does that make you feel?

† PRAYER THOUGHTS †

Ask Jesus to forgive you for your shallowness and complacency. Ask Him to help you get off the sidelines and back into the battle. Ask Him to help you walk fully into your manhood.

CREATING GOD IN OUR IMAGE

There is an old saying, *'familiarity breeds contempt'*. Things that become familiar to us tend to be looked upon as having little value. We take them for granted. They become common.

Could this be the case with our view of God?

We all know that the God of the Bible consists of three distinct persons, Father, Son, and Holy Spirit.[1] There are many irrefutable references to this fact found throughout the pages of Scripture beginning in the Genesis account of the creation of man. Jesus Himself clearly spoke about the Trinity in the Gospels. He spoke of Himself as the Son and He clearly claimed to be God. He spoke of His Father in heaven. He spoke of the Comforter, who we know as the Holy Spirit, who would come when Jesus ascended to His throne. Most of us know this as a fact from our past. And we know it to be true.

But if we were put on the spot in front of our wife, our children, our small group, our church body, or an unbeliever, how would we answer these questions: *Who is God the Father? Who is Jesus, really? Who is the Holy Spirit?*

Beyond our one or two-sentence answers, we may have only vague ideas. Who are these Persons of the Godhead? What is Their specific function in our everyday realities? How do we interact with each of Them? What do They want from us?

All of us have formulated some concept of who the Father is, or who Jesus is, or who the Holy Spirit is, and

71

that concept is so familiar to us that we have put Them all in a tidy box, stamped the word 'God' on it, closed the lid, and put it on the shelf. *There, that is settled.*

And we moved on.

When we think about it this way, are we not acting as though God is below our true consideration? Are we not looking down our intellectual noses at Him and dismissing knowing Him more fully in our shallowness? Have we become so busy with our religiosity, our serving, our weekly church routines, and with life in general that we don't give knowing God a second thought?

Have we ever stopped to consider this? For most of us, the truth is we never thought it was important to ponder God deeply, to find out who He really is and what He really does. We did not find it worth our time. We merely formulated an opinion about Him and moved on. Then we wonder why He feels so distant, so separate from our lives.

In our lack of desiring to know God, we have disrespected Him. That is contempt, pure and simple.

GOD THE FATHER

God the Father is the head of the Trinity.[2] God the Son and God the Holy Spirit, though equally God, defer to Him in hierarchy. The Father is perfect. This means He is flawlessly righteous, holy, and just. His righteousness demands that He act in accordance with His divine purity. His holiness demands that He be set apart from all that is unholy. His justice demands that He establish laws, rules, and rights based upon His perfection. These attributes separate Him from all that is *not* perfect, righteous, holy, or just. Man in and of himself is none of these. This creates a problem for man—a gulf between what is perfect and what is not.

No man has seen the Father physically at any time but

Jesus. In his flesh, man could not look upon the perfection of the Father and live. It is only through Jesus' death and atoning blood that man can come before the Father and call upon Him as 'Abba'—'Daddy'. As believers, we have access to the Father, but we must first be made presentable through the righteousness, holiness, and perfection of Jesus to satisfy the just requirements of the Father on our behalf. Then we can be introduced to the Father as an adopted son.

God the Father is the original planner of creation.[3] It is He who has established the plan of history for His creation. This plan is being executed within the realm of creation and within the confines of time, space, mass, and relativity. He has given authority to execute this plan to Jesus the Son and to the Holy Spirit working on behalf of the Son. Unredeemed men cannot deal directly with the Father because of His holiness. Redeemed men can deal directly with the Father through the finished work of Jesus, but it is Jesus who deals with most men as He executes His Father's plan in the lives of those men.

What does the Father want from us? Complete holiness through Jesus.

GOD THE SON

Jesus is the Son of God.[4] That is the short answer. But that is where the simplicity ends. Jesus is God. He was the means by which God the Father created all things—the instrument of creation, the Creator. It was not the Father or the Holy Spirit who performed the very act of creation. It was Jesus. Creation came by the Word spoken by Jesus as He executed the perfect will of the Father in collaboration with the Holy Spirit. He is the One who created each of us.

Jesus is the person of the Godhead who is most involved in the affairs of men. In His involvement, Jesus gets His hands dirty.[5] He engages sin and imperfection. He sets up kings and tears them down. He dispatches angels to do his bidding. It was He who sent a great fish to swallow a wayward prophet. He directed the building of a massive boat to save a remnant of mankind from drowning in His Father's judgment. He rained fire and brimstone down on evil cities. He is the means of our salvation—the solution to our really big problem with God the Father. All of His creation groans in anticipation of His return and the completion of His redemption. He directs our battle against the gates of hell. He does all of this to fulfill the will of His Father and to bring Him glory. Jesus is our Commander in Chief.

We know that Jesus was physically involved with man after He was born in Bethlehem. His adventures during that time are chronicled throughout the Gospels and into the Book of Acts. But most of us do not realize that Jesus was actively engaged with man from the moment He formed him from the dust of the earth. It was Jesus who appeared throughout the Old Testament as the Angel of the LORD.[6] He walked in the Garden of Eden with His creation, Adam and Eve. He wrestled with Jacob and made him look in the mirror at his self-absorbed life before He renamed him Israel. It was He who spoke from the burning bush and who gave Moses the Ten Commandments on Mount Sinai. He led the Israelites in the cloud and the pillar of fire. He was the Shekinah glory of God in the Tabernacle and Temple. He appeared to Joshua before the conquest of the Promised Land. He visited Abraham and promised him a son. He met with Gideon and accepted an offering from Him. Isaiah saw the length of the train of His robe as He sat on His throne in heaven. He spoke to and through the prophets. Jesus was physically involved in the affairs of men throughout the Old Testament and the New.

He still is. He is physically involved in our affairs today.

Jesus is not dead. He is very much alive. He is

Emmanuel, God with us.[7] He seeks to have a relationship with everyone who has called upon Him for salvation. It is not a long-distance relationship. He walks among us. He is here and He is here now. He knocks on the door of our hearts. Not just for salvation. He wants to fellowship with us. Today. He doesn't sit in heaven and watch our life's struggles from afar. He is active today in the affairs of men. In our affairs.

This is a big mistake that many make—seeing Jesus as far away and uninvolved. A far-away Jesus is not an intimate Jesus. A far-away Jesus is not an approachable Jesus. A far-away Jesus is not a connected Jesus. A far-away Jesus is not a relevant Jesus.

Jesus is very much alive, and He is very much here. He is intimate and approachable. He is connected and relevant. Correcting our view of Jesus' involvement in our lives is the key that unlocks what follows. Understanding the nature of Jesus and His desire for an active role in our lives is crucial to our becoming His disciples.

What does Jesus want from us? Our will.

GOD THE HOLY SPIRIT

The Holy Spirit is more of a mystery.[8] Many see Him as some kind of spiritual fog that rolls in and out of their lives. To others, He is the most important person of the Godhead. In fact, entire religious denominations have been built around over-emphasizing specific aspects of this Third Person of the Trinity. But who is He, really?

The Holy Spirit is distinct from the Father and the Son, and is fully God. He is not some vague cosmic vapor floating to and fro. He hovered over the face of the earth when it was void and without form. He is the promised Comforter according to Jesus. He restrains evil—He holds it back—in this very evil world. He is the down payment on our eternal redemption. He indwells the church by physically indwelling each believer. Along with the Father and the Son, He gives each of us supernatural gifts so Jesus can execute the Father's plan for our lives by enabling our calling. He convicts us of sin in concert with our conscience. He regenerates fallen man. He validates Jesus' call on our lives. He enables Jesus' will for our lives. He intercedes for us at the throne of grace as we pray, with a groaning that we cannot even hear. We can't see Him or touch Him. Sometimes we can feel Him. We must learn to listen very carefully to hear Him as He prompts us to action. He occupies our inner space—our spirit. He is called 'the Spirit of Christ' by Peter. Paul called Him 'the Spirit of His (that is God the Father's) Son'. Jesus said the Holy Spirit was another Helper, meaning one like Jesus.

One of the primary roles of the Holy Spirit living inside of a believer is to bear witness to all of the things of Jesus, about Jesus, and for Jesus, so that Jesus is glorified.[9] If Jesus is glorified, the Father can be glorified. And that is the ultimate objective of Jesus—to glorify the Father.

The Holy Spirit living in a believer allows that person to enjoy the fellowship of Jesus, because the Holy Spirit testifies to us about Jesus and guides us into all truth about Him. The Holy Spirit is our connecting point with Jesus. He allows us to hear Jesus' voice. He enables us to join with and receive the experience of Jesus as Jesus intended for us to experience Him. In this way, the Holy Spirit unlocks the mystery of who Jesus is to us and allows us to know Him. Really know Him.

What does the Holy Spirit want from us? Obedience to the call of Jesus in our lives.

THE ONE TRUE GOD

That is the primer on who God really is and the roles of each Person in the Godhead. Each Person is unique and distinct. Their positions are unique and distinct. Their roles are unique and distinct. Their attributes are unique and distinct. Nevertheless, they are each equally God.

Have we created God in our image, the way we imagined Him to be? Were we taught about God, but yet really don't know Him as He is? Has He become too familiar to us from our religious experience, and yet is He so far from what we *just know* Him to be that He is actually foreign to us? Have we sat in classes and services for years, hearing and singing about Him, and yet do not really know Him? Have we decided who we want Him to be, and in doing so have we happily settled for less than He truly is? Much less?

Are we guilty of this very sin?

If so, we have denied His power in our lives. We have limited His interaction to the basic rules of engagement we have defined, the conventions we have been taught. And then we look around and wonder why our lives do not convey His power? Why sin wins out? Why people are not attracted to the God we serve?

Isn't it time to understand who God is and start living like He was relevant to our everyday lives? Isn't it time to seek to know Him as He is? Isn't it time to allow Him to release His power in us?

We need to ask Jesus to show Himself to us. To teach us about His Father. To give us a clear view on the Holy Spirit. We have not because we ask not. Ask Jesus.

We cannot follow who we do not know.

◆◆◆ CHAPTER NOTES ◆◆◆

We do not fully understand the complexities of the Triune (three-Person) God we serve. The nature of God is such that the more we know about each Member of the Godhead, the more questions we will have. This should drive us to want to know even more.

Danger lurks when we stop trying to know or we simply don't care to know. For that is when we create a god of our own imagination, one with limits set by us.

1. The Trinity

The word 'Trinity' is not found in the Scriptures. Instead, it is a concept demonstrated in scripture. In these verses we see that God claims to be one God but yet He speaks of Himself in the plural sense. We see Jesus describing all three *distinct* persons as God—Father, Son, and Holy Spirit. The Trinity is not defined by the mathematical formula 1+1+1. It is defined by 1x1x1.

(Deuteronomy 6:4) "Hear, O Israel: The LORD our God, the LORD is one."

(Genesis 1:26a, 3:22a, 11:7) Then God said, "Let Us make man in Our image, after Our likeness"...Then the LORD God said, "Behold, the man has become like one of Us in knowing good and evil"..."Come, let Us go down and there confuse their language, so that they may not understand one another's speech."

(John 14:16-17a) "And I will ask the Father, and He will give you another Helper, to be with you forever, even the Spirit of truth."

(John 6:27) "Do not work for the food that perishes, but for the food that endures to eternal life, which the Son of Man will give you. For on Him God the Father has set His seal."

(John 1:1, 14) In the beginning was the Word, and the Word was with God, and the Word was God...And the Word became flesh and dwelt among us, and we have seen His glory, glory as of the only Son from the Father, full of grace and truth.

78

(Acts 5:3, 4b) But Peter said, "Ananias, why has Satan filled your heart to lie to the Holy Spirit and to keep back for yourself part of the proceeds of the land?...You have not lied to man but to God."

(Mark 14:61b-62) Again the high priest asked Him, "Are You the Christ, the Son of the Blessed?" And Jesus said, "I am, and you will see the Son of Man seated at the right hand of Power, and coming with the clouds of heaven."

(John 14:31a) "But I do as the Father has commanded Me, so that the world may know that I love the Father."

(John 15:26) "But when the Helper comes, whom I will send to you from the Father, the Spirit of truth, who proceeds from the Father, He will bear witness about Me."

2. God The Father

(1 Peter 1:16) Since it is written, "You shall be holy, for I am holy."

(Deuteronomy 32:4) The Rock, His work is perfect, for all His ways are justice. A God of faithfulness without iniquity, just and upright is He.

(Revelation 15:4a) Who will not fear, O Lord, and glorify Your name? For You alone are holy.

(Matthew 6:9) "Pray then like this: 'Our Father in heaven, hallowed be Your name.'"

(John 6:46) "Not that anyone has seen the Father, except He [Jesus] who is from God; He has seen the Father."

(John 1:18) "No one has ever seen God; the only God, who is at the Father's side, He [Jesus] has made Him known."

(1 Timothy 6:16a) Who alone has immortality, who dwells in unapproachable light, whom no one has ever seen or can see.

(1 John 4:12a) "No one has ever seen God."

(Exodus 33:20) "But," He said, "you cannot see My face, for man shall not see Me and live."

(Romans 8:15b) But you have received the Spirit of adoption as sons, by whom we cry, "Abba! Father!"

(Revelation 4:2-3, 5a) At once I was in the Spirit, and behold, a throne stood in heaven, with One seated on the throne.

And He who sat there had the appearance of jasper and carnelian, and around the throne was a rainbow that had the appearance of an emerald...From the throne came flashes of lightning, and rumblings and peals of thunder.

(Habakkuk 1:13a) You are of purer eyes than to see evil and cannot look at wrong.

(Matthew 5:48) "You therefore must be perfect, as your heavenly Father is perfect."

(1 Peter 3:18a) For Christ also suffered once for sins, the righteous for the unrighteous, that He might bring us to God.

3. God In Creation

God the Father planned and commanded creation. He used Jesus as the instrument of creation. In this sense, both are the creator. In the sense of the actual act, Jesus is the creator of all things.

(1 Corinthians 8:6) Yet for us there is one God, the Father, **from** *[emphasis added] whom are all things and for whom we exist, and one Lord, Jesus Christ,* **through** *[emphasis added] whom are all things, and through whom we exist.*

(Hebrews 1:1-2) Long ago, at many times and in many ways, God spoke to our fathers by the prophets, but in these last days He has spoken to us by His Son, whom He appointed the heir of all things, through whom also He created the world.

(Proverbs 8:29-30a) When He [God the Father] assigned to the sea its limit, so that the waters might not transgress His command, when He marked out the foundations of the earth, then I [Jesus] was beside Him like a master craftsman.

4. God The Son

(Isaiah 44:24a) Thus says the LORD, your Redeemer, who formed you from the womb.

(Mark 14:61b-62) Again the high priest asked Him, "Are You the Christ, the Son of the Blessed?" Jesus said, "I am, and you will see the Son of Man seated at the right hand of Power, and coming with the clouds of heaven."

(Colossians 1:15-16) He is the image of the invisible God, the firstborn of all creation. For by Him all things were created,

in heaven and on earth, visible and invisible, whether thrones or dominions or rulers or authorities—all things were created through Him and for Him.

(Psalm 139:13-16) For You formed my inward parts; You knitted me together in my mother's womb. I praise You, for I am fearfully and wonderfully made. Wonderful are Your works; my soul knows it very well. My frame was not hidden from You, when I was being made in secret, intricately woven in the depths of the earth. Your eyes saw my unformed substance; in Your book were written, every one of them, the days that were formed for me, when as yet there was none of them.

5. Jesus Gets His Hands Dirty

(Mark 2:15-16) And as He reclined at table in his house, many tax collectors and sinners were reclining with Jesus and His disciples, for there were many who followed Him. And the scribes of the Pharisees, when they saw that He was eating with sinners and tax collectors, said to His disciples, "Why does He eat with tax collectors and sinners?"

(Daniel 2:21b) He removes kings and sets up kings.

(Psalm 91:11-12) For He will command His angels concerning you to guard you in all your ways.

(Jonah 1:17, 2:10) And the LORD appointed a great fish to swallow up Jonah. And Jonah was in the belly of the fish three days and three nights...And the LORD spoke to the fish, and it vomited Jonah out upon the dry land.

(Genesis 6:13-14) And God said to Noah, "I have determined to make an end of all flesh, for the earth is filled with violence through them. Behold, I will destroy them with the earth. Make yourself an ark of gopherwood. Make rooms in the ark, and cover it inside and out with pitch."

(Genesis 19:24) Then the LORD rained on Sodom and Gomorrah sulfur and fire from the LORD out of heaven.

(Hebrews 9:27-28b) And just as it is appointed for man to die once, and after that comes judgment, so Christ, having been offered once to bear the sins of many...

(Matthew 16:18) "And I tell you, you are Peter, and on this rock I will build My church, and the gates of hell shall not prevail against it."

(John 4:34) Jesus said to them, "My food is to do the will of Him who sent Me and to accomplish His work."

(2 Timothy 2:3-4) Share in suffering as a good soldier of Christ Jesus. No soldier gets entangled in civilian pursuits, since his aim is to please the One who enlisted him.

6. Physical Manifestations Of Jesus In The Old Testament

Jesus has always been active in the affairs of men. It is easy to see this in the New Testament, but He was just as active in the Old Testament. Throughout history, Jesus was God manifest to man.

(Genesis 3:8a) And they heard the sound of the LORD God walking in the garden in the cool of the day.

(Genesis 32:24-30) And Jacob was left alone. And a Man wrestled with him until the breaking of the day. When the Man saw that He did not prevail against Jacob, He touched his hip socket, and Jacob's hip was put out of joint as He wrestled with him. Then He said, "Let Me go, for the day has broken." But Jacob said, "I will not let You go unless You bless me." And He said to him, "What is your name?" And he said, "Jacob." Then He said, "Your name shall no longer be called Jacob, but Israel, for you have striven with God and with men, and have prevailed." Then Jacob asked Him, "Please tell me Your name." And He said, "Why is it that you ask My name?" And there He blessed him. So Jacob called the name of the place Peniel, saying, "For I have seen God face to face, and yet my life has been delivered."

(Exodus 3:2a) And the Angel of the LORD appeared to him in a flame of fire out of the midst of a bush.

(Exodus 13:21-22) And the LORD went before them by day in a pillar of cloud to lead them along the way, and by night in a pillar of fire to give them light, that they might travel by day and night. The pillar of cloud by day and the pillar of fire by night did not depart from before the people.

(1 Corinthians 10:1-4) For I do not want you to be unaware, brothers, that our fathers were all under the cloud, and all passed through the sea, and all were baptized into Moses in the cloud and in the sea, and all ate the same spiritual food,

and all drank the same spiritual drink. For they drank from the spiritual Rock that followed them, and the Rock was Christ.

(Exodus 14:19-20) Then the Angel of God, who was going before the host of Israel moved and went behind them, and the pillar of cloud moved from before them and stood behind them, coming between the host of Egypt and the host of Israel. And there was the cloud and the darkness. And it lit up the night without one coming near the other all night.

(Exodus 31:18) And He gave to Moses, when He had finished speaking with him on Mount Sinai, the two tablets of the testimony, tablets of stone, written with the finger of God.

(Numbers 12:5-8a) And the LORD came down in a pillar of cloud and stood at the entrance of the tent and called Aaron and Miriam, and they both came forward. And He said, "Hear My words: If there is a prophet among you, I the LORD make Myself known to him in a vision; I speak with him in a dream. Not so with My servant Moses. He is faithful in all My house. With him I speak mouth to mouth, clearly, and not in riddles, and he beholds the form of the LORD."

(Joshua 5:13-15) When Joshua was by Jericho, he lifted his eyes and looked, and behold, a Man was standing before him with His drawn sword in His hand. And Joshua went to Him and said to Him, "Are You for us or for our adversaries?" And He said, "No; I am the Commander of the army of the LORD. Now I have now come." And Joshua fell on his face to the earth and worshiped and said to Him, "What does my Lord say to His servant?" And the Commander of the LORD's army said to Joshua, "Take off your sandals from your feet, for the place where you are standing is holy." And Joshua did so.

(Genesis 18:1-2, 10a, 22) And the LORD appeared to him [Abraham] by the oaks of Mamre, as he sat at the door of his tent in the heat of the day. He lifted up his eyes and looked, and behold, three men were standing in front of him. When he saw them, he ran from the tent door to meet them and bowed himself to the earth...The LORD said, "I will surely return to you about this time next year, and Sarah your wife shall have a son."...So the men turned from there and went toward Sodom, but Abraham still stood before the LORD.

(Judges 6:11, 21) Now the Angel of the LORD came and sat under the terebinth at Ophrah, which belonged to Joash the Abiezrite, while his son Gideon was beating out the wheat in the winepress to hide it from the Midianites...Then the Angel of the LORD reached out the tip of the staff that was in His hand and touched the meat and the unleavened cakes. And fire sprang up from the rock and consumed the meat and the unleavened cakes. And the Angel of the LORD vanished from his sight.

(Isaiah 6:1, 5) In the year that King Uzziah died I saw the Lord sitting on a throne, high and lifted up; and the train of His robe filled the temple...And I said: "Woe is me, for I am lost; for I am a man of unclean lips, and I dwell in the midst of a people of unclean lips; for my eyes have seen the King, the LORD of hosts!"

7. God With Us

Jesus is 'God with us' (present tense), not 'God who used to be with us a long time ago'. He is here among men right now, not in some distant place away from us.

(Isaiah 7:14) Therefore the Lord Himself will give you a sign. Behold, the virgin shall conceive and bear a Son, and shall call His name Immanuel.

(Matthew 1:23) "Behold, the virgin shall conceive child and bear a Son, and they shall call His name Immanuel" (which means, God with us).

8. God The Holy Spirit

(Genesis 1:2b) And the Spirit of God was hovering over the face of the waters.

(2 Thessalonians 2:7) For the mystery of lawlessness is already at work. Only He who now restrains it will do so until He is out of the way.

(Ephesians 1:13b-14) [You] were sealed with the promised Holy Spirit, who is the guarantee of our inheritance until we acquire possession of it, to the praise of His glory.

(1 Corinthians 6:19) Or do you not know that your body is a temple of the Holy Spirit within you, whom you have from God? You are not your own.

(1 Corinthians 12:4-7a) There are varieties of gifts, but the

same Spirit; and there are varieties of service, but the same Lord; and there are varieties of activities, but it is the same God who empowers them all in everyone. To each is given the manifestation of the Spirit for the common good.

(John 16:8-9) "And when He comes, He will convict the world concerning sin and righteousness, and judgment: concerning sin, because they do not believe in Me."

(Titus 3:5) He saved us, not because of works done by us in righteousness, but according to His own mercy, by the washing of regeneration and renewal of the Holy Spirit.

(John 16:13) "When the Spirit of truth comes, He will guide you into all the truth, for He will not speak on His own authority, but whatever He hears He will speak, and He will declare to you the things that are to come."

(Romans 8:26) Likewise the Spirit helps us in our weakness. For we do not know what to pray for as we ought, but the Spirit Himself intercedes for us with groanings too deep for words.

(1 Peter 1:10-11) Concerning this salvation, the prophets who prophesied about the grace that was to be yours searched and inquired carefully, inquiring what person or time the Spirit of Christ in them was indicating when He predicted the sufferings of Christ and the subsequent glories.

(Galatians 4:6) And because you are sons, God has sent the Spirit of His Son into our hearts, crying, "Abba! Father!"

(John 14:16-17a) "And I will ask the Father, and He will give you another Helper, to be with you forever, even the Spirit of truth."

9. Holy Spirit Testifies Of Jesus

(John 15:26) "But when the Helper comes, whom I will send to you from the Father, the Spirit of truth, who proceeds from the Father, He will bear witness about Me."

(John 16:14) "He will glorify Me, for He will take what is Mine and declare it to you."

(1 Corinthians 12:3b) And no one can say "Jesus is Lord" except in the Holy Spirit.

✦✦✦ STUDY GUIDE ✦✦✦

1) What does the saying *'familiarity breeds contempt'* mean to you?

2) Much of our knowledge and understanding of God comes from others and the traditions of men. Describe how much time and effort you have put into *knowing* God as He desires to be known—who He is, how He functions, how He interacts with you, and what He wants from you? What attitudes, circumstances, or thought patterns are keeping you from pursuing Him to know Him more fully?

3) How much of what you think you know of God is purely opinion and assumption? (%)

4) How much of what you think you know of God is merely traditional understanding that has been passed down to you by others? (%)

5) Have you treated *knowing* God with contempt? How so?

6) Write down the definition of *respect*.

7) Based on this definition, write down what it means to disrespect God.

8) Describe / define who God the Father is to you.

9) What do you think He wants from you?

10) Describe / define who Jesus is to you.

11) What do you think He wants from you?

12) Describe / define who God the Holy Spirit is to you.

13) What do you think He wants from you?

14) As you read the chapter sections on God the Father, God the Son, and God the Holy Spirit, what was the most striking revelation to you about each of them?

15) As you reflect on what you have learned, how have you created God in your image and according to your understanding? How have you limited the limitless and contained the uncontainable?

† PRAYER THOUGHTS †

Are you ready to free God from the box so you can really know Him? So that He can work mightily in your life? If so, ask Him to forgive you and help you walk fully into His intended relationship with you.

THE STATE OF OUR UNION

We are created in the image and likeness of God, or more correctly, *as* the image of God here on earth.

How many of us value this fact? How many of us see it as awe-inspiring? How many of us understand its implications for our lives? Or the possibilities?

Consider the high position this entails—that God would share Himself with us at such a level. Have we taken ownership of this? Have we embraced it? Have we walked into it? Do we live this as truth?

Perhaps not. But why not? Why don't we live like we are the image of God here on earth? Why don't we own it?

Again, is it not a question of holding God in contempt? Are we not each guilty of placing little value on this fact? Have we nonchalantly accepted the information, yet have not fully acted upon it? Have we put effort into knowing— intimately understanding and passionately pursuing—all that is gloriously inferred by this fact? Sadly, most of us have not. It is just another bit of spoon-fed knowledge that we take for granted, tuck away on the shelf beside our God-in-a-box, and leave behind as we go about our lives.

Let us take a closer look at what being created as God's image means for us.

MORE THAN SPECIAL

We know that God decided to create heaven and earth, the sea, sky, land, and all that is in them, and then man.[1] Jesus, as the creative agent of the Godhead, created mankind as both male and female. Since God is spirit and always refers to Himself as 'male', being created in His likeness and as His image must not refer to the physical because mankind is both male and female.

What then? Let us take a look at the rest of His creation.

The creation around us contains a plethora of different species or 'kinds' of animals, plants, invertebrates, and algae. Man has identified something short of two million distinct species. Humanity continues to explore God's creation and discovers new species every year. Estimates vary, but most scientists agree that we have identified fewer than half the species that exist on planet earth! But even when we look only at the known species in the creation, several things jump out that point clearly to the part of God's image we possess.

We have a creative ability that is unsurpassed by any animal. Look around. Mankind is creative...very creative. A simple picture drawn by a child contains a high level of innovation and imagination. Think of any form of technology or technology in general, or building construction, or vehicles, or the variety of consumer products. All of them are packed full of the genius of creativity. Man is driven to create. We cannot help ourselves. Animals do not possess the same level of creative genius. While some demonstrate a basic level of unique creative ability, most react and adapt to their situations out of their genetic pre-wiring and instincts. Man can create at a high level, as can the God who created man.

We possess the ability to reason, the ability for abstract thought. Each of us can ponder the questions that we face, connecting the dots until we have formulated an opinion or a solution. When we consider the abundance of God's living creation—all of the fish, birds, land animals, insects, and organisms—we see that they can learn some basic things and can adapt to new presentations of their surroundings.

But mostly, they just learn a response, one that is conditioned by their situation. They have personalities and even preferences, but they do not form high-level opinions of the world around them. They can bask in the warm sunlight of the day, but they don't ponder the relative beauty of today's sunrise versus yesterday's. Only man can reason at such an advanced level, just like the God who created him.

We have the ability to make moral judgments about right and wrong. Animals do not make moral distinctions. A dog cannot decide if we are morally right or if what we do is morally right. He can react if we are cruel or nice to him, but he can't judge. He can decide if he wants to bite or lick our hand, but he is not capable of processing the relative merit of either action beyond the reaction he receives from the act. He can even have feelings of affection for us, but he has no moral compass to direct those feelings. Dogs (and animals in general) do what they were created to do. Man can decide if something is right or wrong based on the internal conscience that God has given to each of us. Man possesses the knowledge of both good and evil, as does God.[2]

We possess a spirit that will live on after our physical death. This is our special connection to our Creator. It is the most important feature of all because it forms the basis for why we were created to begin with—to glorify God in worship and have fellowship with Him *forever*. We know that God is spirit and must be worshipped in spirit.[3] The fact that we can experience God and have a relationship with Him is a direct result of our having a spirit wrapped inside our soul (our mind, will, and emotions), which is wrapped inside of our body. The rest of the members of the living creation have no spirits (notwithstanding the angels and their demon counterparts, who *are* spirits). So, the rest of creation cannot have this relationship with their Creator.

We were given the role and the authority to rule over the earth and all of its fullness. This is the very essence of having been created as the image of God because it speaks to our function. We are to responsibly execute dominion while we are here—as God's representatives. This requires a close relationship with the Creator if we are to do this properly in His stead. No plant or animal or resource speaks for itself. Mankind is responsible to subdue, rule over, use, and maintain all that was given to us as we work under the direction of the Creator in compliant cooperation with His plan.

The insidiousness of the lie of Evolution has crept into the Church through the back door. The educational system has pounded the basic doctrines of this religion into the minds and hearts of multiple generations. Humanism—the belief that man is of prime importance in place of a supernatural god—has tried to drive out all vestiges of the divine God in our society using science as the whip. The creation around us is explained in terms of 'adaptations' and 'millions/billions of years'. These terms are thrown around in arrogant disregard for the Word of God, which states otherwise. This thought process has gone mainstream and is commonplace. Anyone who takes the view of Intelligent Creation is seen as ignorant of the obvious evidence around us and is openly ridiculed as being anti-science.

Most humans believe in some sort of evolutionary process. Some think that life began somehow in the primal soup of the earth (without regard for where this earth or this soup came from). Others think in terms of being planted by a super-human race and left to evolve from there. Others believe in an amalgamation of evolution and creationism where God jumped in and out of history over vast periods of time, providing the necessary sparks to take life to the next level. It is only a minority who believe the truth—that the creation account of Genesis is true and literal.

1. The Splendor Of Creation

Jesus' creation is marvelous in its variety and its forms. It points to one who is incomprehensible in His creativity, wisdom, and power. Mankind is the crowning glory of Jesus' creation, created to enjoy everlasting fellowship with the Triune Godhead. We are special. Very special.

(Genesis 1:26-28) Then God said, "Let Us make man in Our image, after Our likeness. And let them have dominion over

the fish of the sea and over the birds of the heavens and over the livestock and over all the earth and over every creeping thing that creeps on the earth." So God created man in His own image, in the image of God He created him; male and female He created them. And then God blessed them. And God said to them, "Be fruitful and multiply and fill the earth and subdue it, and have dominion over the fish of the sea and over the birds of the heavens and over every living thing that moves on the earth."

2. The Knowledge Of Good And Evil

(Genesis 3:22a) Then the LORD God said, "Behold, the man has become like one of Us in knowing good and evil."

3. Spiritual Connection

(John 4:24) "God is Spirit, and those who worship Him must worship in spirit and truth."

✦✦✦ Study Guide ✦✦✦

Many of us have not stopped to think about our being a special creation of God. Man is the only thing in all of creation that was made to bear the image of God. Nothing else was.

1) Take a moment to think about what it means to you to be created as God's image bearer on earth. Write down your thoughts.

2) How is your life reflecting this fact today?

3) What aspects or areas of your life need to change because of this fact?

4) How are you using the creative ability that God shared with you to enrich and bless others?

5) How are you using the gifts of reasoning and thinking that God gave to you?

6) How are you using the God-given ability to understand right from wrong to walk purely before your God?

7) How is the reality that you will share the gift of eternity with God playing out in the decisions you make each day and your life in general?

8) Looking back over the last four answers, have you *owned* fully the fact that you are special to God and have been created for a special relationship with Him? Write down some steps you can take to change your outlook and your relationship with Him.

† Prayer Thoughts †

Ask Jesus, your Creator, to forgive you for taking your existence for granted and for living below what He intended for you as His image bearer on earth. Ask Him to show you how to live as His special creation in a way that brings Him glory through your life.

Is God Our Hobby?

We don't talk much about having hobbies these days. We now have *activities*. We have *obsessions*. We have *diversions*. They are all similar. They are all activities outside our regular occupation. We engage in these things primarily for pleasure. They are supposed to have a calming effect on us. They usually satisfy a need within us.

Whatever we call them, these activities have some level of priority in our lives. We spend enough time on them to keep the interest alive. We work them into our busy schedules. But they do not have the highest level of priority. They can get delayed or cancelled by a more important, more immediate need, or by a circumstance.

Does this describe the place of a hobby in our lives? More importantly, does this describe our relationship with God?

The God of the universe, the Lord of all, our Creator, our Savior—our hobby?

PRIORITIES

It appears as if everything screams at us to be a priority today. We rush from one thing to another. We juggle. We calculate the trade-offs. We justify. The reality, though, is that a priority *is a priority*. It has to come first. It has to be most important. If a thing is not first or most important, it is not a priority.

The same is true with God. We say He is a priority in our lives. We want Him to be a priority in our lives. Many of us believe that He is a priority in our lives. But yet, He isn't. We can't seem to find the time in our busy day for Him. So we try to work Him in—a Bible chapter here, a devotional reading there—as long as it is convenient. We try different time slots—when we first rise in the morning, at our lunchtime break, right before we go to sleep. We try to make this time a priority—as long as there is not a schedule conflict or we are not too tired. But even as we work Him into our day, we are not consistent, and He is quickly relegated as a permanent entry on our *To Do* list. Time with God becomes another chore, another thing that we must get done today. When we think about His place in our lives, we get feelings of anxiety or impending condemnation instead of feelings of anticipation and desire that would be natural in a vibrant relationship.

For some of us, though, He has become enough of a priority that we work Him in regularly. We enjoy the time together. We feel fulfilled when we are finished. It settles our day. But when we are finished, we pack it all away—we pack Him away—and get back to the primary pursuits in our lives. We don't linger. We don't take Him with us. We don't walk with Him.

Is this how we are to interface with the God above all other gods? Is this to be the nature of our relationship with Him? With our Creator? Are we to try to fit Him into our schedule, or are we to fit into His? Are we to put Him into a nice box on a shelf when we are finished with our hobby for the day or week, or are we to acknowledge that He is un-containable and include Him every step of every day? Is He an add-on event in our lives, or are our lives integrated into His daily plan for us?

GOD'S LIST

Have we made all this too complicated? Let's look at our lives and try to order the things that compete for our attention and time, condensing everything down into the simple order of God's priority:

GOD

WIFE

CHILDREN

JOB

OURSELVES

EVERYTHING ELSE

Our first priority is God.[1] He is to be our primary occupation and not our hobby. He is to be our highest priority because He is pre-eminent. He is over all things. Nothing takes precedence over Him. Since His stated desire is for us to have a right relationship with Him,[2] nothing is more important in our lives than growing that relationship, whether we believe it or not, or do it or not. We are to be pre-occupied with Him and His plan for our lives.

Next is our wife. She was called along side us as our closest companion and equal helpmate in this life. We are responsible for her wellbeing before Jesus. Our marriage is to be the same type of relationship that Jesus has with His church.[3] That is a high standard to live up to for any of us. For this to be possible, the priority of our wife must be higher than any other priority but God, and our relationship with her has to mirror this level of importance.

Our children come after our wife. Both husband and wife are responsible for the nurturing of their children.[4] Even though we see them as more helpless and more needy, our children are not a higher priority than our wife in God's eyes. The same is true of our grandchildren.

Then comes our job or our career.[5] What we do for a living or what we have chosen as a career allows us to express our creativity, utilize our skills, and even use our spiritual gifts. Through our job, God blesses us with our daily bread, allows the means for our other activities, and provides our ability to financially further His work on earth.

Finally, we make the list. We would naturally like to be higher on the list because, let's face it, we are pretty important to ourselves. But this is not where God places us.[6] He has us as a lower priority. This is the essence of laying down our lives each day. Jesus clearly taught this by example. We are to do the same.[7]

Last on the list is everything else. Our pets. Our extended family. Our friends. Our sport or favorite sports team. Our vehicle. Our boat. Our activities. Our hobbies. Our busy-ness. Everything.

Most of us have our priorities confused. We have them out of order. Then we wonder why things don't run smoothly, why things feel out of kilter, why we are caught in the cords of our sin.

OUR LIST

If we were honest with ourselves, what would our list look like? How would it be ordered? Would this be our list?

OURSELVES

◆

EVERYTHING ELSE

JOB

WIFE/CHILDREN

GOD

For most of us, we are the priority every day and most minutes of every day. We have responsibilities, sure, but we mostly do what we want to do, how we want to do it, and when we want to do it. We say we don't put ourselves first, but our actions betray our words and the truth is found wanting. There is a space between this one and the rest of the list because that is how high many of us place our own importance above everything else in the scheme of things. We may not say this with words, but we certainly do with our deeds, attitudes, and actions. We love ourselves. We focus on ourselves. We take good care of ourselves. We put ourselves first in most things. Our life-long struggle is to take ourselves off the throne and put God on the throne where He belongs. This is not the way of the world around us where everything reflects self-absorption and all that goes with it—self-exaltation, self-gratification, and self-focus. But this is not where we are in God's design of things. We are way down on the list of His priorities for our lives. Besides, if we are at the top of the list, where is He? If we are on the throne, who really is our god? Let's endeavor to stay where we belong. We are not number one. God is.

Usually, our 'everything else' comes next on our list. This is a natural outgrowth of making ourselves the most important priority. This is where we nurture our wants, our desires, and our lusts. This is where we wrap them in toys and friends and relationships and activities. This is where we widow our wife and orphan our children. This is where we sacrifice their future so we can satisfy our present. The attitude that makes us and our personal desires the highest priorities is very dangerous. It is laden with entitlement. It is concerned only about the moment with little regard for future consequences. It can and will lead us to some very dark places. It may fill an immediate need or satiate a lust, but it does so at the expense of our wife, our children, and our relationship with God. Nothing on our 'everything else' part of the list is more important than the categories higher on God's list.

Our next priority is our job or career. Other than sleep, we spend the most time on this one thing each week. Many of us enjoy what we do. It makes us feel good to produce. We think about it. We plan around it. It occupies the better part of our day, the better part of our effort, and the better part of our heart. We lavish great amounts of time, effort, and passion on it. It meets many of our deepest needs—to be in control, to conquer, to achieve, to be recognized, to feel important, to belong. When we go down this path, our job or career becomes what defines us. It becomes our identity. That is why when we first meet someone in a social setting, we likely ask them, *'What do you do?'* What we do has quietly become who we are. And what we do is important to us. Now, we should not belittle the importance of having a job or a career. Most of us need to earn money to live and to support our families financially. But, because of this, we tend to see our job as the provider of the money. We forget that God provides. Not our job. And when we do, we give our job a higher priority than God.

Our wife and our children come next on our list. We say they are important, but they are not as important as we are, what we want, or our job. And they know it. Our wife becomes distant when she realizes that she is not as high on our list of priorities as she once was. She becomes resentful in the pain she feels. The marriage relationship stagnates. We begin to merely tolerate each other. This fuels our search for something else that is exciting; something else we can conquer or that meets our needs. The downward spiral becomes ever steeper. Our children fare no better. They know that they are not as important to us as they want to be. Wounds are made—deep, defining wounds that most will carry throughout their lives. Many children will replicate our behaviors in their own families or over-compensate to an extreme in the opposite direction. In either case, the next generation is weighed down with challenges that God never intended them to carry.[8] All because of us, our self-focus, and our wrong priorities.

Finally, at the end of the list, comes God. Our Creator. The One who died and purchased us. He is our lowest priority.

102

But it doesn't have to be this way. Through Jesus, we can change it.

God is a jealous God. He will not allow our pleasures, our jobs, our wife, our children or ourselves to remain a higher priority than He is. He will not tolerate any gods we put in His place.

If we have our priorities confused, we will never achieve what God has planned for us. We will never have a right relationship with Him or with others. We will never find peace and contentment.

Once we have our priorities in order, we will find time to spend on the others in their proper order, beginning with God. Our attitude and our approach will reflect this. It is a true principle.

Isn't it time for us to get our priorities straight? We may have to lose a little sleep, turn off the feed from our social media accounts, lose the TV remote, or set aside our mobile device. We may have to curtail our independent social activities. We may have to put some of our toys away. But whatever it takes, it will be worth it.

We need to ask Jesus to help us. Only He can show us what has to go, assist us in re-shuffling our day, and help us to integrate Him into all we do. He will teach us what to do, step by step. He created the universe out of nothing in six days. He can help us with our day.

Following Jesus is our priority.

◆◆◆ CHAPTER NOTES ◆◆◆

For too many of us, God is just a casual acquaintance. He is something that occupies our spare time. Sure, we may enjoy our time with Him, but it is not regular, deep, or anything beyond dutiful. It is a problem of laziness. It is a problem of taking our salvation passage to heaven for granted. It is a problem of misplaced priority.

1. God's Priority

Our God is a jealous God. He wants nothing to be higher in our esteem or affections than He is. This includes our wife, our children, our friends, our jobs, our activities, our possessions, our favorite vises, and even ourselves.

(Exodus 20:3) You shall have no other gods before Me.

2. A Relationship With God

To have an intimate relationship with God is our highest privilege.

(1 John 3:1a) See what kind of love the Father has given to us, that we should be called children of God.

3. A Relationship With Our Wife

Many of us have not treated our wife with the respect she is due. Many of us are not treating her well even now. Jesus expects us to give our wife the respect and honor that *He says* she deserves to receive from us.

Most of us are familiar with the verses from the Book of Ephesians that deal with the marriage relationship.

(Ephesians 5:22-33) Wives, submit to your own husbands, as to the Lord. For the husband is the head of the wife even as Christ is the head of the church, His body, and is Himself its Savior. Now as the church submits to Christ, so also wives should submit in everything to their husbands. Husbands, love your wives, as Christ loved the church and gave Himself up for her, that He might sanctify her, having cleansed her by the washing of water with the word, so that He might present the church to Himself in splendor, without

spot or wrinkle or any such thing, that she might be holy and without blemish. In the same way husbands should love their wives as their own bodies. He who loves his wife loves himself. For no one ever hated his own flesh, but nourishes and cherishes it, just as Christ does the church, because we are members of His body. "Therefore a man shall leave his father and mother and hold fast to his wife, and the two shall become one flesh." This mystery is profound, and I am saying that it refers to Christ and the church. However, let each one of you love his wife as himself, and let the wife see that she respects her husband.

There are many reminders in these verses regarding how each of us as men is to bless his wife. We are to love her the same way that Jesus loves us (His Church)—completely, faithfully, patiently, with kindness and understanding, esteeming her needs above ours. We are to give ourselves up *for* her. This means to lay down our life for her. This means to die daily to ourselves in relation to her—what we want, what we need, what we feel like we need to tell her. We are to do what is necessary to free her before God so she can fulfill her calling and destiny for Jesus. We are to help her to be perfect in every way (her sanctification), mainly by example—treating her as Jesus expects and not hurting her or provoking her. We are to love and care for her like we love and care for our own bodies—'cherish' is the word. We are to remember that becoming one flesh—becoming one before God—is the high purpose of marriage. This is to happen spiritually, emotionally, and then physically.

We are not to get caught up in or emphasize her submission to us or her need to respect us. That is her responsibility, and she stands before Jesus in these things. Instead, we should remember that we are commanded to submit to *one another,* which is exactly what is required in order for all of our above listed responsibilities to our wife to be possible.

(Ephesians 5:21) Submitting to one another out of reverence for Christ.

Peter gives us more information on this subject.

(1 Peter 3:7) Likewise, husbands, live with your wives in an understanding way, showing honor to the woman as the weaker vessel, since they are heirs with you of the grace of life, so that your prayers may not be hindered.

Peter tells us to understand our wife. He says we are to give honor to her. He says we are to treat her with gentleness and great care. He reminds us to keep things in perspective: we are heirs of the same promise of salvation— the one where God sees no difference between believers.

Paul echoes this same truth.

(Galatians 3:28) There is neither Jew nor Greek, there is neither slave nor free, there is no male and female, for you are all one in Christ Jesus.

And Peter ends with a specific warning that if the husband does not honor his wife and seek to deal with her in an understanding way, that man's prayers will be hindered. 'Hindered' refers to being resisted or interfered with. This means that we open ourselves up to demonic powers that will attack us and come between God and ourselves in our prayers if we violate these commands.

Jesus gave us some object lessons on how our wife is to be treated through His dealings with women. He respected the wishes of His mother even when it was not convenient or part of His original plan to turn water into wine at the wedding feast in Cana. He told men that lusting after a woman was the same as committing physical adultery with her. He convicted the men who were going to stone the adulteress that their sin was no less serious than hers. He treated prostitutes and diseased women with respect, love, and mercy. He honored the love and devotion that women had for Him throughout the Gospels.

As we seek to live with our wife in peace and harmony as one flesh, let us never forget that we must do so in His power. If we allow Jesus' power to flow through us, we can think, see, and feel what Jesus does. In doing so, we can love our wife perfectly.

(Philippians 4:13) I can do all things through Him who strengthens me.

4. A Relationship With Our Children

Our children are part of the heritage that we will leave behind on the earth when we die.

(Psalm 127:3-5a) Behold, children are a heritage from the LORD, the fruit of the womb a reward. Like arrows in the hand of a warrior are the children of one's youth. Blessed is the man who fills his quiver with them!

Our children are the arrows that are shot out into the world—arrows that can fly farther than we can go, arrows that can accomplish more than we can do, arrows that can be sharp in the hearts of God's enemies. Both husband and wife are responsible to properly feather these arrows and tip them with a sharp point. We are to deal with our children in the same love that Jesus has for them. We are to treat them with kindness, gentleness, and patience as a precious reward from God Himself.

(Colossians 3:21) Fathers, do not provoke your children, lest they become discouraged.

(Ephesians 6:4) Fathers, do not provoke your children to anger, but bring them up in the discipline and instruction of the Lord.

When necessary, we are to discipline them.

(Proverbs 13:24) Whoever spares the rod hates his son, but he who loves him is diligent to discipline him.

However, even when we do our best with Jesus to raise our children, they can decide to go their own way. It is here when we must allow Jesus to deal with them. He may have us stay close and woo them with His love, or He may have us stand aside, applying tough love and allowing the consequences of their decisions to work in their lives. Either way, we must make sure our children know we accept *them* unconditionally, but not *their actions.* Our heart's attitude must be to wait patiently for Jesus to do His work of drawing them back to Himself. If the relationship has been broken, we are to be ready to restore that relationship when Jesus tells us to do so. This is the message in the *Parable of the Prodigal Son.* For us, it is the *Parable of a Loving Father* who is in step with Jesus while dealing with his children.

5. A Perspective On Our Job Or Career

Many of us forget who provides for us and our needs. We come to believe that we do through our efforts and our ingenuity. But this is pride, pure and simple. We are only a heartbeat away from being unable to work—an illness, an accident, a layoff. It is necessary for each of us to leave the myth of self-sufficiency behind so that Jesus can bless us as He sees fit.

(Deuteronomy 8:17-18) Beware lest you say in your heart, 'My power and the might of my hand have gotten me this wealth.' You shall remember the LORD your God, for it is He who gives you power to get wealth, that He may confirm His covenant that He swore to your fathers, as it is this day.

This is not to say that we should not enjoy what we do for a living. If we have a job or career that brings us pleasure and contentment, this is a blessing from God.

(Ecclesiastes 5:18-19) Behold, what I have seen to be good and fitting is to eat and drink and find enjoyment in all the toil with which one toils under the sun the few days of his life that God has given him, for this is his lot. Everyone also to whom God has given wealth and possessions and power to enjoy them, and to accept his lot and rejoice in his toil— this is the gift of God.

The danger comes when we do not maintain these proper perspectives on what we do for a living. It is easy for us to fall into idolatry and to begin to worship success, recognition, prosperity, or even our simple ability to provide. These all will fade quickly when we die and then what will remain? What will define our heritage at that moment?

(Proverbs 23:4) Do not toil to acquire wealth; be discerning enough to desist.

6. God's Place For Us

We live in a world where being #1 is celebrated. Let us remember that this same world is a fallen world. Our flesh wants to be #1 in all things, but our new nature in Jesus allows us to be much more than #1. It allows us to be a servant and to put others before ourselves.

(Matthew 20:27-28) "And whoever would be first among you must be your slave, even as the Son of Man come not to be served, but to serve, and to give His life as a ransom for many."

(Romans 12:3a) For by the grace given to me I say to everyone among you not to think of himself more highly than he ought to think, but to think with sober judgment.

7. No Greater Love

Investing ourselves in God's priorities means a daily dying to our selfish priorities. This dying to ourselves is the greatest demonstration of love we can express. The rewards for doing so extend beyond our life to the lives of others and to eternity.

(John 15:13) "Greater love has no one than this, that someone lay down his life for his friends."

8. Generational Consequences

Our decisions matter—each day, each hour, and each minute. Our wrong thinking and sin have consequences that last beyond our short lives upon the earth.

(Exodus 20:5b) For I the LORD your God am a jealous God, visiting the iniquity of the fathers on the children to the third and fourth generation of those who hate Me.

✦✦✦ STUDY GUIDE ✦✦✦

We live in a world with mixed up priorities. It is a world of self-focus. It is a world where God gets pushed off and replaced.

1) Look up the definition of *activity*. Briefly, what is it?

2) Look up the definition of *obsession*. Briefly, what is it?

3) Look up the definition of *diversion*. Briefly, what is it?

4) Look up the definition of *hobby*. Briefly, what is it?

5) How are all of the above words related? What do they share in common?

6) When you think about your relationship with God, is it similar to any of the words above? Which ones? Why?

7) On a scale of one to ten, ask Jesus to show you where your relationship with God is right now and mark it.

Distant		Close
Detached	1<<————>> 10	Personal
Dead		Vibrant

8) How do you feel about your relationship as marked above?

9) Take a look at the six items below. Assign a number, 1 through 6, showing their *current* (and honest) priority in your life.

Job

Ourselves

God

Wife

Everything Else

Children

110

10) List them in their *correct* order of priority and briefly explain why each is to have that level of priority.

† PRAYER THOUGHTS †

Jesus knows what He wants changed in your life. He knows everything that is getting in the way of you embracing the priorities that will lead to a successful walk with Him. Ask Him what must be eliminated or changed in your life so that your priorities get in line with His. Make a list of all that is Jesus telling you.

RELIGION OR RELATIONSHIP

At its essence, religion is man's attempt to create God in his image—an image we can understand, an image we can comprehend, an image we can approach, an image we can manage.

The religions of the world are almost too numerous to count. There are twenty or so major religions, each composed of several distinct groups, denominations, or sects. Based on this, it is safe to say that man is a religious being. But what does this really mean? What exactly is religion? We throw the word around casually, almost without thought. Is religion a belief system? Is it based on a denomination or a sect? Does there have to be a god involved? What exactly is religion?

At the most basic level, religion is a set of beliefs concerned with the cause and purpose of the universe. A religion is usually composed of a shared worldview supported by a set of moral codes governing how the members involved in the specific religion should deal in the affairs of mankind. Its adherents usually share a common cause, with varying levels of religious commitment.

All religions are built around a belief system, even if that system is to not believe in any deity. Most entail an element of faith because the teachings and practices include the unseen and the un-experienced. Many involve traditions passed down from ages past.

Religion has been around for a long time. In fact, it was Cain who founded the first religion.[1] We may remember the familiar story. God had defined Himself and how He was to be approached in true worship. Abel understood this and obeyed with his sacrifice of a lamb from the flock—the substitutionary sacrifice of a life for a life. Cain decided to recreate God by defining the relationship in terms of the sacrifice he wanted to offer. His was the fruit of the cursed ground and the work of his hands—crops—instead of the prescribed life-blood sacrifice. He decided what would be acceptable to God and how God would be approached. In doing so, Cain created God in his image, and the first religion was born.

Mankind has been creating gods ever since.

With the resulting plethora of world religions comes every imaginable version of god. Each of these gods was created by man except one. There are big gods. Little gods. Cruel gods. Benevolent gods. Gods of poverty and necessity. Gods of opulence and wealth and health. Involved gods and ambivalent gods. Gods of inclusion. Gods who are exclusive. Defined gods. Ethereal gods. Personal gods and distant gods. Gods made with hands. Gods manifest as the world around us. Powerful gods. Impotent gods. Gods of peace. Gods of violence. False gods. Even men as gods. And then there is the one true God.

The consequences of mankind creating their own gods can be seen all around us. People go their own religious ways depending on their worldview, which is dependent on their god view. There is a cacophony of voices claiming to represent the truth. There are divisions and schisms. There is suspicion and misunderstanding. There is violence and hate. There is much evil perpetrated in the name of religion. There is much wasted time. There are many people going straight to hell.[2]

And all along, each of these religious participants feels justified in their actions, attitudes, and motives. They do not see that they are living lies and lives of sin or that they

114

have separated themselves from God. They do not see the need to come to the Creator on His terms. They do not want to see. They like their own terms better. Others are just ignorant of the truth, working their way through life according to the dictates and teachings of their religion, hoping for a better station in the next life. They are no less guilty, for the revelation of the true God is all around them.

And then there are those groups that call themselves by the name of Christ—the Christianized religions of the world. These can be split into 6 major groups with somewhere between 200 and 30,000 different sects or denominations around the world, depending on the criteria used to define them![3] And even while these groups hold up a banner bearing the name of Jesus, their view of who He is and how He operates is as varied as their imaginations and their traditions. To most, Jesus is merely the common currency of their religious system and activity. He is used only as a medium of barter by which they gain their religious ends. He is not real or alive, just used.

OUT OF FOCUS

If an uninformed stranger walked into one of our churches today, what would he see? More than any other time in history, he would see *busy* people. And what would they be busy about? Mostly *the program*—either in preparing, presenting, or participating.

But is this really what Jesus wants?

Is this is where we have lost focus? Have we begun to concentrate more on the method instead of on the message and the Man behind it? Have we focused more on the process instead of on the Person? Have we focused on what we, our church group or our denomination says is important, and discounted what Jesus says is vital? Have we worked harder at doing more—more attending, more participating, going more places, doing more things—than we have at knowing Him? Have we made Him common and spent Him as currency to accomplish our desires, goals, and objectives—individually, as a church body, or as a denomination? In doing so, have we stepped onto the slippery slope of our flesh instead of the solid ground of the Spirit? *Have we created our own religion?*

It is easy to get ensnared in the production that much of Christianity has become. It is so involved. We can spend countless hours doing things. We can divert vast sums of money to fund doing things. We can lavish great attention on preparing to do things. We can all feel the pressure to participate in creating and delivering the production.

BACK INTO FOCUS

How should we respond to this pressure to participate? How do we know what to say 'yes' to and when to say 'no'? Where is the balance between personal and corporate service to God?

Each of us should ask Jesus. *Jesus, what do You want me to do?* Only Jesus knows how He is going about executing His Father's plans here on earth. When He invites us to participate in His plan for mankind, it is His plan and not ours. Once we know where and how He wants us to serve, we can go full speed ahead with our participation so His purpose can be accomplished. Asking first provides us with an opportunity to see into the heart of Jesus and to understand Him more fully.

Jesus, how do You want me to do these things? What should my effort look like? What do I need to accomplish for You? Armed with the answers to these questions, our full creative power can then be applied to His tasks so that all can be accomplished. We are free to unlock the full potential of our contribution without fear or reservation. We will have the time and energy to accomplish all. We will know that our efforts are being spent in building a closer

116

relationship with Him instead of going off on a religious exercise of our own making.

Jesus' desire is for us to lift Him up so He can draw men to Himself.[4] Jesus' desire is for Him to be glorified in all things so that He can in turn bring glory to His Father.[5] His focus is on His relationship with believers and His potential relationship with those who have been called to believe.

Jesus may want us more involved with our local church body or He may want us less involved. Only He knows. At the end of our lives, we each shall be called to give an account to Him on how we used our time here on earth. No one from our church group will be standing with us. We will stand as individuals before Jesus.[6]

Busy-ness is a self-imposed trap. It has no place in the plan of God, and it serves no purpose. It is entirely our doing, and it ultimately glorifies Satan who wants to keep us occupied and unfocused.

Have we been guilty of being busy in our church families? Have we participated and volunteered without asking Jesus what He wanted and when? Have we just expected Him to bless whatever we were doing because it was 'good' and we waved His name over it? Have we been focusing more on our religion than our relationship?

If we have been operating our own religion, it is now time to come to our senses and stop. God has defined Himself— who He is, how He operates, and what He expects. Shouldn't we step away from our religion and get back into step with our relationship with Him?

If we have been trapped in the swirl of religious busy-ness, it is time to leave the peer pressure and our sense of duty behind and ask Jesus how He wants us to participate in our local church body and other ministry opportunities. It is time to find out what He wants us to do and how He wants it done. He will tell us. He has a plan.

Then, let us each repent of what we have been doing, and start doing only what He wants us to do.

Cain's religion did not work out well for him.[7] Ignoring Jesus and practicing our own form of religion will not work for us either.

We are not to be about our religion. We are to be about our relationship with Jesus.

Follow Jesus on His terms.

It is easy to get caught up in the trappings of religion. When we band together with others, there are always needs to be met, things to be done, places to go, schedules to keep, and people to help. None of these things are bad things. They are just secondary things. Our relationship with Jesus is the primary objective. When this is right, we will find balance in all other areas. We will be more effective as a church member. We will see results. We will be more fulfilled. It all begins with the relationship.

1. First Religion

We shake our heads at the audacity of Cain, but how many of us have done the same or are doing the same? How many of us know who God is and what He expects, but yet seek to 'improve' upon this by doing things our own way?

(Genesis 4:3-5a) In the course of time Cain brought to the LORD [Jesus] an offering of the fruit of the ground, and Abel also brought of the firstborn of his flock and of their fat portions. And the LORD had regard for Abel and his offering, but for Cain and his offering He had no regard.

2. Without Excuse

Scripture is clear that God has made His existence known to all men so that they are without excuse, regardless of the religion they have chosen to practice.

(Romans 1:18-20) For the wrath of God is revealed from heaven against all ungodliness and unrighteousness of men, who by their unrighteousness suppress the truth. For what can be known about God is plain to them, because God has shown it to them. For His invisible attributes, namely, His eternal power and divine nature, have been clearly perceived, ever since the creation of the world, in the things that have been made. So that they are without excuse.

(Romans 2:12-16) For all who have sinned without law will also perish without law, and all who have sinned under the law will be judged by the law. For it is not the hearers of the

law who are righteous before God, but the doers of the law who will be justified. For when Gentiles, who do not have the law, by nature do what the law requires, they are a law to themselves, even though they do not have the law. They show that the work of the law is written on their hearts, while their conscience also bears witness, and their conflicting thoughts accuse or even excuse them on that day when, according to my gospel, God judges the secrets of men by Christ Jesus.

3. Major Traditional Groupings Of The Christianized World

There are six major Christianized religious traditions: Anglican, Catholic, Pentecostal, Protestant, Orthodox, and Restorationists.

4. Drawing Men To Jesus

We do not have to work to draw people to Jesus. If we simply lift Him up in His full glory, He will draw people to Himself.

(John 12:32) "And I, when I am lifted up from the earth, will draw all people to Myself."

5. Jesus' Prime Desire

Jesus always deferred to His Father in heaven. He always sought to bring Him glory.

(John 8:29) "And He who sent Me is with Me. He has not left Me alone, for I always do the things that are pleasing to Him."

(John 17:4) "I glorified You [the Father] on earth, having accomplished the work that You gave Me to do."

If we bear fruit for Jesus, our Father is glorified. We do this by becoming Jesus' disciples.

(John 15:8) "By this My Father is glorified, that you bear much fruit, and so prove to be My disciples."

6. The Judgment Seat Of Christ

Each of us will answer only to Jesus for what we have done while here on earth. We will stand alone before Him. We will not answer to any man, for any man, or with any man.

(2 Corinthians 5:10) For we must all appear before the judgment seat of Christ, so that each one may receive what is due for what he has done in the body, whether good or bad.

7. Cain's Judgment

Cain ultimately killed his brother Abel in anger over Jesus' rejection of his religious efforts. Jesus judged Cain for this.

(Genesis 4:10-12) And the LORD [Jesus] said, "What have you [Cain] done? The voice of your brother's blood is crying to Me from the ground. And now you are cursed from the ground, which has opened its mouth to receive your brother's blood from your hand. When you work the ground, it shall no longer yield to you its strength. You shall be a fugitive and a wanderer on the earth."

Religion does not draw us to God. It does nothing to repair the broken relationship between God and man. Only the prescribed blood sacrifice does...the blood sacrifice of Jesus. It is all about the relationship.

Every religion defines who God is and how He relates to the universe. The Christianized religions of the world are no exception. Many Christian denominations and groups are bound by traditions that have been passed down from the past. These traditions, and the doctrines behind them, result in practices and pursuits that may be far removed from what Scripture has to say. In this way, these traditions, doctrines, and practices have become merely *religious* in nature.

1) Look up the definition of *religious*. Does the definition put more emphasis on *efforts* or *relationship*?

2) Find the definition of the word *religion*. Does it put more emphasis on *God* or on *systems of belief*?

3) Man's tendency is to be religious. Given the definitions you have just looked at, why do you think this is the case?

4) Why do you believe what you believe? Where did these beliefs come from? Were they passed down from others, or do you truly own them?

5) Have you ever stepped back from the traditions and doctrines of your denomination or local church and examined their scriptural basis with Jesus to see if they line up with His written word and His example?

6) Take some time and do so now. What did you find?

7) Think about the typical Sunday worship service in your local church body. When you look at the overall program, what is the basis for the types of activities that you see?

8) Look up the definition of *program* and write it down.

9) Find the word *performance* and write down the definition.

10) What do these two words (*program* and *performance*) have to do with building a personal relationship with Jesus?

11) Look at **John 12:32** below. What does this verse say to you in the context of any church service or Christian activity?

(John 12:32) "And I, when I am lifted up from the earth, will draw all people to myself."

12) How does this verse square up with the focus of your church body or the traditions of your denomination?

† PRAYER THOUGHTS †

Jesus came to free us from the bondage of religion. He came to bring us into a true relationship with Him as His disciples—one that is deep and personal. He did not come to be crowded out by religious activity. He came to be lifted up so He could draw all men to Himself. We do not have to entertain or put on a performance for the multitudes. We must simply lift Him up.

Jesus has a specific plan for you and your church focus. This may involve a change in your religious denominational affiliation. It may involve a change of your place of worship. It may involve a change in your level of participation and serving at your local church. Take some time before Jesus right now and jot down what He has to say on this subject.

My Will be Done

How many of us have a tendency to be stubborn? How many of us are always doing things our way...doing what we want to do, whether it was right or wrong, godly or sinful? As we look at our lives—past and present—is this a trademark we see? Is it *the* trademark?

The root of being stubborn is selfishness.

The root of selfishness is rebellion.

The root of rebellion is pride.

Pride is at the top of the list of sins that God hates the most.[1] In fact, it is the root of all sins. Unbelief, disobedience, and immorality—the list goes on and on—are all caused by man's pridefulness. Man believes he somehow knows better than God...that he somehow does not need God...that he somehow is God.

When we pause to think about this for a moment, aren't these basic thoughts and attitudes of self-elevation the foundation of all we struggle with in our lives?

But why? What in us drives us to go our own way against the clear commands and desires of Jesus? What makes us pridefully choose our own foolishness over the wisdom of our God? We know we have a new nature in Jesus, one no longer bound in slavery to sin.[2] We understand that this new nature is friendly toward God and not steeped in continuous struggle against Him. So why do we continue to sin willfully? Why do we lose the struggle against the natural tendencies and desires of our unredeemed flesh?

Each of us has a will we can freely exercise for good or for evil.

The human will is mankind's prerogative, not God's. We each own our will. God does not force His will on us or override our will. If this were not the case, Eve wouldn't have been deceived, and Adam would not have sinned. God would have controlled Adam and Eve's wills to prevent their sinning when He saw Satan coming along in the Garden. But God did not because He created mankind as free moral agents. Every man, woman, and child has the ability and the right to make their own decisions, to think their own thoughts, to do their own deeds, and to go their own way.

Man is the crowning jewel in Jesus' creation. Yet, (angels and demons aside) we are the only element of this creation that truly has a free moral will. The animals do not.[3] The plants do not. Nor do the rocks, mountains, seas, atmosphere, planets, stars, or galaxies. Each of them functions within the constraints set by God.

But not man.

We have a will. And we have a right to exercise that will as we wish. This is by God's plan and by His design. He does not cosmically take control of our will and force our obedience. We come to obedience on our own. We choose.

A MATTER OF THE HEART

Most of us believe that our will is the governing center of who we are. We think that all decisions are made from our will, which is a function of the mind. But Scripture teaches us that the essence of our will is found in the heart.[4]

For man to exercise his will, he must make a choice. Making a choice entails choosing one thing and refusing all others. Every choice involves a preference. Each preference is based upon the condition of that man's heart at that specific moment. So the heart is the prime driver—the seat—of each person's will. And out of the heart, we exercise our will.

Our problem lies with the fact that, because of its condition, our heart does not always point us to obedience. It can change minute by minute, hour by hour, and day by day as it is influenced by any of several factors—our conscience, our environment, the logic of our thoughts, the latest emotion, fleshly or godly desires, demonic powers, or God in the person of Jesus or the Holy Spirit. From the moment of salvation, our new nature *allows* us to make the right choices, but our heart *causes* us to choose according to what is in it. It really is a heart matter because the heart controls the will.

Jesus knows this. That is why He is always concerned with the heart. He knows that all of the issues of life flow out of the heart. And so His eyes search the earth for men whose hearts are truly His. Jesus knows that if He has a man's heart, He has that man's will.

Jesus' will for us is God-focused and perfect. Our will for us is self-focused and flawed. His plan for us is pure. Our plans are based on motives.

Even so, how many of us go our own way and are not in step with Him?

GOD'S SOVEREIGNTY VERSUS MAN'S WILL

God the Father is sovereign over all.[5] This means that He has absolute, final, and total say over everything that happens. God the Father has a plan for mankind wrapped in time and space that marches to its conclusion in His perfect timing.

But yet, we as men each have our own will, and we have the right to exercise that will as we desire.

How can this be? For God the Father to be sovereign, He must have supreme dominion and power over all else (omnipotence). He must also know everything—what has been done, what is being done, and what will be done (omniscience). But for man to have a will, he must have the ability to make moral choices. If God already knows what a man is going to do—what that man is going to choose—how does that man really have the freedom of his will—the freedom to exercise it as he sees fit?

Jesus showed us the answer when He was on earth two thousand years ago. He said that He did not come to do His will but His Father's will and that He could do nothing of Himself or speak anything on His own, except what came from His Father. In so doing, He made it clear that He was responsible for executing His Father's plans for mankind here on earth—both the overall plan of history and the individual plans for each man's life.

We know that God the Father has a plan for each man's life.[6] We know that Jesus does the will of His Father to further that plan in our lives according to what His Father has ordained. We also know that Jesus as God does not exercise predetermined control over our wills so that His Father's plans will be fulfilled.

If we control our will, how does Jesus execute His Father's plans?

Influence.[7] Jesus influences the exercising of our will according to the thoughts in each man's heart. This is a key point. While Jesus cannot control a man's heart (and therefore that man's will), He can influence it. These influences can be the circumstances of life, or thoughts placed in our hearts, or promises of consequences (good or bad), or the leading of the Holy Spirit in conjunction with the conscience, or even demonic workings. Additionally, His disciples experience His personal leading in their lives to the degree that they are willing to obey.

Jesus prepares His plan according to what His Father

desires. Once we act, He responds accordingly, always moving onward toward His Father's plan. In this way, God can be sovereign in history, knowing all and seeing all, and man can have his will to exercise in history while Jesus manages the outcomes of man's will for His Father.

THE CONSEQUENCES OF GOING OUR OWN WAY

Every time we don't cooperate with Jesus' will in our lives, we miss something He had planned for us. Whether time, money, relationships, quality of life, or opportunities, we have missed them. In His graciousness He may give us another chance, but it is not the same as His first chance. Things move on.

How much have we each missed of what was planned for us? And in doing so, how much have we caused our families to miss as well? What blessings have been passed by in our relationships? What have our children missed because of our sinfulness? How have we altered the trajectory of His plan for them? It is not just about us. We drag everyone along with our disobedient wills. This should be a sobering thought to us. And heart breaking.

God the Father has a plan, and Jesus wants to execute it in our lives to the glory of His Father. The plan ties to our calling, the destiny for which we were specifically created. Jesus may have to allow extra twists and turns in our lives or circumstances as His influencing power works on our hearts, but He is always moving us toward fulfillment of the Father's plan. He may have to switch to back up plans when we do not make the right choices. He may have to delay or cancel things in our lives. He may chasten us to try to get our attention when we go astray, but He is willing to set us back on His path when we repent. He may give us over to our wills, our vile passions, our stubbornness, and our rebellion for a season, but He waits at the end of the lane for the prodigal's return.

If we, as the prodigal, refuse to give up control of our life and remain on the path to destruction, Jesus will allow it. But, there is a limit to His graciousness toward us. We don't know where that line is in our lives, but Jesus knows. Once crossed, His judgment falls, the ultimate consequence being our death.[8] If we find this hard to believe, ask Nadab and Abihu about their profane fire. Ask Ananias and Sapphira about their deceptive gift. Ask the Corinthian church about the sick and dead from among them.

The challenge for us is to give our wills over to His; to conform to His purpose in all of our circumstances; to do what He says to do, whether we feel like it or not; to do it how He wants it done, whether we think our way is better or not; to do it for as long as He commands, whether we think we can endure or not.

We are talking about laying our lives down at His feet. Laying them down and not taking them back. Though we get weary or tired, we do not take them back. Though we are frustrated or impatient, we do not take them back. Though we are mistreated or maligned, we do not take them back. Though we feel like it or not, we do not take them back. This is an act of the will. It comes from a heart aligned to Jesus and operating in His power.

For most of us, this is the area of our greatest struggle, especially if we have had a lifetime of practice in exercising our will instead of bending it to His. It is natural to us. It is of the flesh. Only a heart yielded to Jesus will result in a will yielded to Jesus. Only a will yielded to Jesus will result in a life yielded to Jesus. And a life yielded to Him is a life of discipleship.

This is why we are commanded to love God with all of our heart, soul, mind, and strength. As we focus on doing this, our heart will come into alignment with His, and with our heart, our will.

Laying down our will is the basis for the rest of the steps to discipleship.

If we want to control our will, we cannot follow Jesus.

A man's will is a powerful force. The permission to exercise one's will is a basic right of man given by God. As with anything we possess, it must be consciously given back to Jesus. We must lay it at His feet and subject it to His perfect will.

1. Pride

While God hates all sin, the Book of Proverbs contains a short list of sins that God hates most.

(Proverbs 6:16-17) There are six things that the LORD hates, seven that are an abomination to Him: haughty eyes, a lying tongue, and hands that shed innocent blood, a heart that devises wicked plans, feet that make hast to run to evil, a false witness who breaths out lies, and one who sows discord among brothers.

Pride (haughty eyes) is a root sin. The Bible has much to say on the subject. Pride occurs when we forget our place before God. It is man's greatest tendency and man's greatest challenge.

It was pride that brought Lucifer down in his rebellion against God. His pride was displayed in his will to do things only reserved for God.

(Isaiah 14:12-14) How you are fallen from heaven, O Day Star [Lucifer], son of Dawn! How you are cut down to the ground, you who laid the nations low! You said in your heart, 'I will ascend to heaven; above the stars of God I will set my throne on high; I will sit on the mount of assembly in the far reaches of the north; I will ascend above the heights of the clouds; I will make myself like the Most High.'

His pride blinded him from seeing that it would all be folly before an omnipotent God. But yet, he rebelled, was judged by God, and became Satan.

(Isaiah 14:15-17) But you are brought down to Sheol, to the far reaches of the pit. Those who see you will stare at you and ponder over you: 'Is this the man who made the earth

tremble, who shook kingdoms, who made the world like a desert and overthrew its cities, who did not let his prisoners go home?'

Pride will likewise take us down. Pride will cause us to fall. Pride will cause us to be shamed. Pride will bring about our destruction.

(Proverbs 11:2a) When pride comes, then comes disgrace.

(Proverbs 16:18) Pride goes before destruction, and a haughty spirit before a fall.

2. Our New Nature

At the moment of salvation, we are given a new nature—Jesus' nature. We are freed from the bondage of sin and no longer have to keep on sinning.

(2 Corinthians 5:17) Therefore, if anyone is in Christ, he is a new creation. The old has passed away; behold the new has come.

(Romans 6:22a) But now you have been set free from sin and have become slaves of God...

3. Animals

Animals can make decisions, but there is no moral basis for these decisions. They do not innately know the difference between right and wrong. They can only learn a response to outside influences and act accordingly.

4. A Matter Of The Heart

The heart is the seat of our thoughts as a man. From it springs our true beliefs and attitudes at any given moment.

(Mark 7:21a) "For from within, out of the heart of man, come evil thoughts..."

(Proverbs 4:23-24) Keep your heart with all vigilance, for from it flow the springs of life.

5. Sovereignty Versus Will

God the Father is sovereign over all. He has a plan for human history that is being executed in His timing.

(1 Chronicles 29:11) Yours, O LORD, is the greatness and the

power and the glory and the victory and the majesty, for all that is in the heavens and in the earth is Yours. Yours is the kingdom, O LORD, and You are exalted as head above all.

(Acts 1:7) He said to them, "It is not for you to know times or seasons that the Father has fixed by His own authority."

6. The Father's Plan

There is a plan for each of us that was laid before the foundations of the earth (we were written in God's book).

(Psalm 139:16) Your eyes saw my unformed substance; in Your book were written, every one of them, the days that were formed for me, when as yet there was none of them.

7. Influence

Jesus utilizes many things to influence our hearts. Jonah had the prior circumstance of the great sea creature to motivate his obedience the second time Jesus commanded him to go to Nineveh.

(Jonah 1:1-3a; 3:1-3a) Now the word of the LORD came to Jonah the son of Amittai, saying, "Arise, go to Nineveh, that great city, and call out against it, for their evil has come up before Me." But Jonah rose to flee to Tarshish from the presence of the LORD...Then the word of the LORD came to Jonah the second time, saying, "Arise, go to Nineveh, that great city, and call out against it the message that I tell you." So Jonah arose and went to Nineveh, according to the word of the LORD.

Jesus uses the thoughts in the hearts of man—the thoughts of fear, hate, or rebellion. He can choose not to restrain these thoughts, allowing them to come to pass for His purposes. He sets other circumstances into place that give occasion to these thoughts (such as a large group of Jacob's people passing through another nation's territory, the rapid multiplication of the Israelites in the midst of the Egyptians, or a fugitive of low repute like Moses making demands of a mighty pharaoh).

(Genesis 35:5) And as they journeyed, a terror from God fell upon the cities that were around them, so that they did not

pursue the sons of Jacob.

(Psalm 105:25-26) He turned their hearts to hate His people, to deal craftily with His servants.

(Exodus 4:21) And the LORD said to Moses, "When you go back to Egypt, see that you do before Pharaoh all the miracles that I have put in your power. But I will harden his heart, so that he will not let the people go."

(Psalm 81:12) So I gave them over to their stubborn hearts, to follow their own counsels.

Jesus uses promises of consequences.

(Deuteronomy 11:26) See, I am setting before you today a blessing and a curse.

The Holy Spirit is used to lead us.

(John 16:13a) "When the Spirit of truth comes, He will guide you into all the truth."

Jesus even uses demons to influence men. The prophet Micaiah saw all of the angels assembled before Jesus (the LORD). He saw a demon step forward as part of this host of angels. This demon responded to Jesus' request and said he would go out as a lying spirit into King Ahab's false prophets (angels are not lying spirits—demons are). Jesus used a demon in this capacity to accomplish His will in the situation, and Ahab was killed in battle.

(1 Kings 22:19-22) And Micaiah said, 'Therefore hear the word of the LORD: I saw the LORD [Jesus] sitting on His throne, and all the host of heaven standing beside Him on His right hand and on His left; and the LORD said, "Who will entice Ahab, that he may go up and fall at Ramoth-gilead?" And one said one thing, and another said another. Then a spirit came forward and stood before the LORD, saying, "I will entice him." And the LORD said to him, "By what means?" And he said, "I will go out, and will be a lying spirit in the mouth of all his prophets." And He said, "You are to entice him, and you shall succeed; go out and do so."'

The disciples of Jesus have a special relationship that influences the thoughts of their hearts.

(John 10:27) "My sheep hear My voice, and I know them, and

they follow Me."

If we do not respond properly to Jesus' working in our lives and we go our own way, there are consequences.

(Deuteronomy 11:26-27a) "See, I am setting before you today a blessing and a curse: the blessing, if you obey the commandments of the LORD your God, which I command you today, and the curse, if you do not obey the commandments of the LORD your God."

8. Crossing The Line

Jesus does not stop working to fulfill His Father's plans for our lives. He will make provisions as we take our detours off His path so that Father God's plans get executed. He will do this until we cross the line where His judgment falls upon us.

John, writing to believers, tells us that there are sins that do not lead to death and there are those that do lead to death. He does not define what or where the line is, just that it exists.

(1 John 5:16-17) If anyone sees his brother committing a sin not leading to death, he shall ask, and God will give him life—to those who commit sins that do not lead to death. There is sin that leads to death; I do not say that one should pray for that. All wrongdoing is sin, but there is sin that does not lead to death.

Paul indicates that believers also suffer illnesses in addition to death because of their willful sinning. The fact that this is not talked about in our church experience today does not make it any less true.

(1 Corinthians 11:30) That is why many of you are weak and ill, and some have died.

Both the Old and New Testaments contain examples of this.

(Leviticus 10:1-2) Now Nadab and Abihu, the sons of Aaron, each took his censer and put fire in it and laid incense on it and offered unauthorized fire before the LORD, which He had not commanded them. And fire came out from before the

LORD and consumed them, and they died before the LORD.

(Acts 5:1-11) But a man named Ananias, with his wife Sapphira, sold a piece of property, and with his wife's knowledge he kept back some of the proceeds and brought only a part of it and laid it at the apostles' feet. But Peter said, "Ananias, why has Satan filled your heart to lie to the Holy Spirit and to keep back for yourself part of the proceeds of the land? While it remained unsold, did it not remain your own? And after it was sold, was it not at your disposal? Why is it that you have contrived this deed in your heart? You have not lied to man but to God." When Ananias heard these words, he fell down and breathed his last. And great fear came upon all who heard of it. The young men rose and wrapped him up and carried him out and buried him. After an interval of about three hours his wife came in, not knowing what had happened. And Peter said to her, "Tell me whether you sold the land for so much?" And she said, "Yes, for so much." But Peter said to her, "How is it that you have agreed together to test the Spirit of the Lord? Behold, the feet of those who have buried your husband are at the door, and they will carry you out." Immediately she fell down at his feet and breathed her last. When the young men came in they found her dead, and they carried her out and buried her by her husband.

The key to following Jesus successfully is to surrender our will to His. This is easy to say. After all, wasn't this what we pledged to do for Jesus in exchange for His salvation? Yet, how many of us have not kept our end of the agreement?

1) Write down a few descriptive words from the definition of *stubborn*.

2) Do the same for the word *selfish*.

3) And for the word *rebellion*.

4) And finally for the word *pride*.

5) In your own words and based on these brief definitions, trace the sin relationship from *stubborn*, through the words *selfish* and *rebellion*, back to the root of *pride*.

6) Why do you think that pride is the root of all other sins?

7) How would you define your will? What is it? Who controls it?

8) Why would God give you the right to exercise your will?

9) What is a preference?

10) How is the will governed by the preferences of the heart?

11) Can the preferences of the heart change?

12) What forces can influence the heart at any given moment? Make a list.

13) How do we bring our will into alignment with Jesus' will?

14) What keeps you from allowing Jesus to rule over your will?

15) How was your life during the times when Jesus ruled over your will? Give three examples.

16) How was your life during the times when you ruled over your will? Give three examples.

† PRAYER THOUGHTS †

Jesus sees all the way down to the hidden recesses of our heart. Ask Him to show you your pride. Ask Him to reveal your rebellion. Then confess these to Him and ask Him to change the preferences of your heart so that they match His. Lay your will down at His feet and ask Him to help you leave it there.

This is the essence of successful prayer—aligning our preferences and our wills to His.

IDENTITY FRAUD

In the past several years, we have all become familiar with identity fraud, a crime that affects millions of people worldwide. At its root, it's a crime where someone uses credible information to pose as someone else to the unsuspecting world in order to profit by way of deceit.

If we look up the words in a dictionary, the nature of this crime becomes clearer. Identity is the defining character or personality of an individual. It is who that person really is. Fraud is the intentional perversion of truth or an act of deceiving or misrepresenting. It is tricking or cheating someone else in order to gain something.

If any of us have been a victim of this crime, we know the shock of discovering that we have been taken advantage of in this manner. We feel violated in a very personal way as we are left to try to figure out the true nature of what we are dealing with. And we are angry that we have somehow allowed ourselves to be victimized when all we were doing was going about our daily business in trust.

When we think about the type of person who would be engaged in this activity, preying on the innocent and unsuspecting, what comes to mind? Anything good? Of course not.

So why do we do it?

One of the main reasons that men today have lost impact in their homes, communities, and churches is identity fraud—not as victims, but as perpetrators. We have assumed an identity, a persona, that is not who we really are. We have foisted this on the unsuspecting—our wife, our children, our friends, our co-workers, the members of our church body. Everybody. We have become the masters of deception. In doing so, we have deceived more than those around us. We have deceived ourselves.

But deep down, the reality of who we really are flickers across our mind, and our conscience protests our deceit. We know we are doing it. We know we shouldn't be doing it. We know we will continue doing it.

So, why is this the case?

FUGITIVES

We are on the run.

We are on the run from our present reality. We are on the run from our past. We are on the run from our failures. We are on the run from our wounds. We are on the run from ourselves. We are on the run from our sin.

When a man does not like who he is, he can become someone else. To become someone else, he has to run away from who he truly is. Once a man starts down this path, he has to stay on the run like an outlaw. Constantly in motion. Constantly adjusting to the situation. Constantly one step ahead of his reality. All so no one will suspect. So no one will see. So no one will know. So he can stand to look in the false mirror at himself—the one that changes his shape and his image into the counterfeit persona he has assumed.

And it is easy to do. Everybody is doing it. The whole world seems to be trying to be someone they are not. Mimicking famous people. Joining groups that have an image they want to assimilate. Doing things to be identified with others. Personas by association. We just slip right in line and join them. We decide who we want to be and strike the pose. We build a story line and we stick to it. We manage and manipulate the details so everything holds together.

142

And we keep running.

Most of us try to blend in. We want to fly under the radar. We want to remain undetected. We don't want to invite any scrutiny. Someone might see the inconsistencies. Someone might see the flaws. Someone might see the façade. Someone might start asking questions—awkward questions we don't want asked. Someone may take away our false mirror and replace it with a mirror of truth.

Others of us try to stand out. We forcefully fend off any scrutiny. We become a bombastic, larger-than-life personality. We go on the offensive. We become too successful, too loud, or too aggressive to even be approached. To even be questioned.

And we keep running.

FIG LEAVES

Regardless of our chosen defense mechanism, we try to appear to be what we think is expected by those around us—an attentive husband, a doting father, a workaholic employee, a pious church member. We hope that if we appear to be a certain way for a long enough period of time, people around us will accept it as truth. And we have at least a hope that we will actually become that person we are posing as.

So we imitate the hottest fads. We wear certain clothes certain ways. We walk or talk differently. We do our duties and perform as is expected for our audience. We live in special houses in the right neighborhoods. We drive specific cars. We go to certain places and do certain things. And in all of our doing, we sew on our fig leaves. We wear them and we hide behind them. We hope that they cover the reality underneath so nobody will see the real us.[1]

Meanwhile, we spiral down and down in our core being. Under those fig leaves lie our true identities. Our secret ones. The ones filled with our self-indulgence, our illicit affairs, our anger issues, our pornography, our poor relationships, our gambling, our homosexuality, our gender identity confusion, our irresponsibility, our over-eating, our alcohol or drug problem. Whatever the size of our fig leaves, the purpose is the same—to cover the lies in our lives. The ones we don't want others to see. The ones we do not want to face. The ones we do not want to deal with.

And we despise ourselves more and more. We sink deeper and deeper into the quicksand of hopelessness. We decide that we could never come clean. We are too far-gone. No one would ever understand what we have become or how we have sunk so low. At some point in the process, we even come to hate ourselves. This drives us to even more destructive behaviors as we seek to escape from those thoughts and feelings. And so the downward cycle continues. Slowly at first as we manage some control over it. But ultimately, we can't hold it back any longer and it takes on a life of its own, pulling us along as we lack the will to stop it.

Many of us have been there. We have felt the pain of failure. The hopelessness of a situation that we could no longer control. The fear of never being loved again if discovered. All of these feelings are lies, but we buy into them 100%. We give in to them. We use them as justification to keep doing what we are doing. Ultimately, we come to the point where we just don't care anymore. We don't care about our wife. We don't care about our children. We don't care much about ourselves. We certainly don't care about God. We just do what we want to do. This is the truth. Our lives are all about us.

We know we should stop deceiving ourselves. Unless our wife is deceiving herself, she knows something is wrong. Our children will not want to see it, but as they become adults, they will know. And God knows already. After all,

144

Jesus went to the cross because of these very things in our lives.

Yet, we think we can't let anyone know. Not our family, not our friends, not our co-workers, not other church members, not our pastor. What would they think of us if they found out that they had been duped for years? How could we explain who we really are, what we really think, what we really do when nobody is looking? How could we face ourselves, our past, our secret lives, our sins? How could we possibly tell our wife what has been and is going on?

So we keep on with the deceit. We refuse to deal with the problem. We die a little more each day. We have little or no impact for Jesus. We hide with our thoughts in our fear and our despair. *'But you don't know what I have done, what I have become. There is no way I can come clean on this. The hole is too deep. I have passed the point of no return.'*

Jesus understands this. He knows our fears. He can lead us out.

FREEDOM

In order for us to experience freedom from our problems, we have to make some decisions. We have to decide to turn and start down Jesus' path. If not, we will not arrive at freedom. Once we have decided to go there, we will not get there instantly. We might want to, but we cannot. It will be a journey. We will have to persist in that journey for as long as it takes to get to freedom. We have to keep walking with Jesus, keep making progress. If we stop, we will not make it. If we slow down, it will take longer to make it. If we take a detour, we might get lost and not find our way back.

Addictions of any nature are difficult to break. Cycles of evilness and every kind of related behavior have a gravitational pull that is very great. But freedom is just down the path. Jesus is pointing the way out to each of us right now. His way is the only way. We will never be free from anything to which we stubbornly cling. We must let it go. We must turn away. We must start the journey to freedom.

To authenticity.

It will not be easy. It is the second most difficult challenge we face, right behind laying down our will.

However, it is an essential step toward really walking with Jesus, the foundational step. He wants real men who have nothing to hide. He wants humble men who can acknowledge their past wickedness. He wants meek men, who have chosen to come clean. He wants men who are free to become His disciples for His purposes.

He wants men who have nothing to lose.

Know the costs.[2] We will have to tell our wife. We will have to explain it at some level to our children. Coming clean could cost us our marriage. It could cost us our families. These consequences are in the hands of Jesus. If we are obedient in what He is asking of us right here, right now, these potential disasters are His concern. If we initiate the confession, we will give Jesus a chance to work from our humble heart on the hearts of those we have deceived and hurt. We will see the miracles that only He can work in this regard.

Not coming clean will cost us a lot more. It will doom us to a life as a fugitive, living on the edge of the light. It will make us as a crust of bread in this life. When we are finally found out, we will likely lose it all. There will be eternal consequences in heaven as well in terms of our place and our rewards.

There is no one-way to do this. It starts with our resolve

146

to do it with the right attitude, to take full responsibility, to not shift blame. We must seek Jesus on this matter and see how He wants us to approach it. If we are open, He will direct us.

It will be a process. The journey to freedom always is. It will go as fast as we are willing to allow it and as fast as Jesus deems necessary. We might continue to struggle with urges to go back to our old ways and the habits of thought we have cultivated. No matter what, we must not go back!

If we choose to stay with Jesus, He will be there every step of the way, loving us, cleansing us, and carrying us.

This is a big step. It is a necessary step.

We must be authentic to walk with Jesus.

♦♦♦ CHAPTER NOTES ♦♦♦

'Who am I?' This is one of the great questions asked by mankind. Most people either do not want to know the answer to this question, or already know the answer and don't like what it is. In either case, man looks for something he can identify with and ultimately become, something he can live with. Then he changes his color like a chameleon so that he blends in with that identity. The true self never gets plumbed and falseness prevails.

1. Fig Leaves

(Genesis 3:7) Then the eyes of both were opened, and they knew that they were naked. And they sewed fig leaves together and made themselves loincloths.

We all have heard the story of Adam and Eve and their fig leaves. Yet, much can be learned from this verse. They had been naked since they were created. It was their natural state. What had changed? They were simply no longer innocent. Their guilt was exposed in their naked state. They were no longer who they once were due to their sin. They didn't want anyone to see their guilt. They needed to cover it up.

And see what happens next.

(Genesis 3:8) And they heard the sound of the LORD God [Jesus] walking in the garden in the cool of the day, and the man and his wife hid themselves from the presence of the LORD God among the trees of the garden.

They had to blend into their surroundings so no one would see. They had to hide the *real* them. If Jesus (God in the flesh who was walking in the garden) had not sought them out, they would have continued to hide and would have built a new lifestyle around their new personas.

And so it is with all who are not authentic. Jesus calls each of us out to authentic manhood. If we accept the call, it will allow us to build a deeper relationship with Him.

2. Coming Clean

Coming clean is difficult. It requires a humble heart. This may be tough after the years of posing as someone else, the years of running, and the years of hiding who we truly are because of the fear, anger, resentment, and bitterness that has built in our hearts. Jesus is the only one who can break our hard hearts.

Coming clean also requires that there be no blame shifting. Blame shifting is pointing fingers at other people or circumstances instead of at ourselves for our failures. This will not go over well or help the situation. It is a telltale sign of pride in our hearts. This is not a time to try to protect our wounds or ourselves. We must take the blame with sincerity of heart.

Ask for forgiveness. Allow Jesus to build our relationships anew.

◆◆◆ STUDY GUIDE ◆◆◆

Who am I? This is a core question for every man. Am I a product of my circumstances? Am I defined by my job or a title? Do my possessions or social status determine my identity? Am I known for my church affiliation? Or my social media presence? Is my identity found in the positions of authority that I hold—either in my home or in the public sector? Does my heart define who I am, or is it something else?

1) Look at the definition of the word *identity*. In your own words, write down what *identity* means to you.

2) People long to belong, to be accepted, and to be liked. We gravitate toward certain things and allow them to define who it is we want to be known as. List what you have used to define your identity.

3) Why have you gravitated toward this thing or these things to define your identity? *(Dig deep here and get down to the root causes.)*

4) Is the pose you have struck—the identity you have assumed—really you, or are you someone else? Are you someone in disguise?

5) Look up the definition of *fraud*. Look up the definition of *authentic*. Which one best describes the identity you have assumed—the one you show or display to the rest of the world? How so?

6) When a man does not like who he is, he changes his identity. There are many reasons why a man may not like who he really is—reasons that are enough to make him want to change his identity. A few of these are listed below. Carefully consider each item on the list and note any that you have difficulty accepting and owning.

Family (parents and siblings)

Birth order

Race / nationality

Basic physical features (looks)

Handicaps / infirmities

Mental capabilities

Physical capabilities

Time in history

Economic status

Sin / moral failures

Job or occupation

Consider the items you noted above. All but your economic status, your sin/moral failure, and your job/occupation are either things you *cannot* change at all or only by degrees. They have either been ordained or granted by God Himself in anticipation of His specific plan for you.

7) Over time, living the lie of a false identity causes a man to hate who he *really* is. Self-hate produces many feelings in a man. Below is a list of the most common. Note any you are experiencing in your life.

Self-criticism

Depression

Entitlement / indulgence

Envy

Hate / lack of love

Self-pity

Withdrawal / isolation

Anger

151

8) There are telling signs of self-rejection. Look at the list below and note any symptoms you see in your life.

Anger at God

Arrogance / superiority

Extravagance

Bitterness

Perfectionism

Comparisons to others

Not trusting in God

Lack of love

Look at everything you have noted on the lists above. All of them stem from a lack of understanding your *true* identity.

9) Read ***Philippians 1:21***. Paul tells us that living is Jesus and dying is more Jesus. From this passage, on what did Paul base his identity? What does this verse mean to you?

(Philippians 1:21) For to me to live is Christ, and to die is gain.

† PRAYER THOUGHTS †

Ask Jesus right now to help you accept the things you cannot change in your life. Ask Him to help you change the things you can change in your life. Ask Him to help you lay aside your false identity and put on your authentic one. Ask Jesus to help you find your true identity in Him.

WOUNDS

There is something deep within the heart of a boy that calls
him to adventure.[1] He is ever restless, ever moving.
Running, jumping, riding, climbing, rolling, and swinging—
this is what most boys do. The faster, the better. The
higher, the better. The steeper, the better. The more
dangerous, the better.

And then there are the by-products of being
adventurous. The cuts. The scrapes. The bruises. The
blood. The stitches. The scars.

If we take an inventory of our scars, we will find some
interesting things about them. They will likely be found in
various places on our bodies. They each will have a
different shape. They will be different sizes. Some will be
prominent and relatively fresh. Some will be subtle, faded
by time. Some will indicate a rather clean and quick
healing, while others will show evidence of a slow healing,
perhaps by being torn open more than once. Regardless of
their appearance, each of them is a mark from encounters
in our past. Each one has a memory attached to it.

Most of us have some physical markings from our past.
We remember them. They originated from a wound of some
sort—some minor, some not so minor. With these wounds
came pain. With the pain came a natural aversion to the
event that caused the pain. We remember. We tuck those
memories away. We try to avoid a repeat. We do not want to
experience the pain again. Only with time and proper care
will the wounds heal. But we are never the same. We have
scars, each one a reminder of a wound.

And then there are the invisible wounds and their scars, those of our inner being, our soul. These also have memories attached to them. Bad memories. Agonizing memories. Embarrassing memories. Angry memories. Sad memories. Painful memories. Memories that are always lurking, always haunting, always ready to spring up in response to some situation. Memories that drive our responses or our lack of responding. Memories that tend to define us even today.

UNHEALED

Most men carry wounds from the past. Many times these wounds have never healed properly, if at all. Some have scarred over with a rough, ugly protective covering. Some are still open, festering and full of putrid substances. All are painful deep down in our souls. They are wounds of the heart. We are driven by these wounds.

Wounds hurt. They do not heal on their own. They can hinder us for life, keeping us out of the battle.

Many wounds are caused by our fathers—our imperfect examples here on earth of our eternal Father. Some are caused by our mothers—the example of the nurturing part of God. Some are caused by our wives—the ones called to walk along side us and be part of us, and who have a greater sense of our vulnerabilities than anyone else. Others are caused by brothers, sisters, extended family members, friends, acquaintances, or even strangers.

Some wounds are caused by circumstances and happenings. A broken promise. Having too little. Doing without. A sickness, illness, or disease. Physical defects. Being physically or emotionally abandoned. Mental abuse. Physical abuse. Sexual abuse.

Some are caused by words. Cruel jokes at our expense. Being called names. Being made to feel worthless. Being made to believe that we have little if any value here in this life. The constant taunting and belittling by our tormentors. The unending reminders of our imperfections.

Whatever the source of our wounds, the result is always the same for a man. They produce a feeling of inadequacy.[2] They make us feel as though we are really losers after all. They make us feel that there is something wrong with us. They make us feel like we do not have, nor will we ever possess, what it takes to be a real man. They make us feel afraid. Very afraid.

What do we do as a result of our wounds?

We protect ourselves. We say in our hearts, *'Nobody is ever going to hurt me like that again!'* We build walls around our wounds. We hang heavy, reinforced gates on those walls. We prepare our weapons. We allow no one to come close to us, not even our wife. Especially not our wife. We do not share that intimate closeness in which anything can be discussed, that place where we become most vulnerable.

We run for cover. We live in the shadows. We are afraid to come out into the light. Someone might discover our wound and force us to reconsider it, to examine it, to get close to it once again. So we stay back under cover, allowing fear to control us.

We react. The wound becomes our master. It rules over us. We respond to the threat of more hurt. We pull away. We become distant. We make evasive maneuvers to lose the threat of repeated pain. All along, we are not in control. The wound is. Everything revolves around it—what we think, what we say, and what we do.

We go our own way. We take things into our own hands and try to control of our lives. We judge everything based on performance. On how we measure up. On how others compare. We love only on the condition that it will be returned in kind. Safe love. Controlled love. Love that cannot wound us again. For many, this path leads to deep emotional darkness.

But this is not all. In our attempt at self-preservation, we build our lives upon the faulty foundation of anger and resentment. We take shelter in unforgiveness and bitterness.

Our wounds make us angry. We are angry with those who have hurt us. We are angry with God for allowing it. Some of us can hide it and some of us can't. Those of us who can hide it outwardly seem like pretty stable people with an even keel who can sail through life. But deep inside, the anger smolders. Those of us who can't hide it, well, we make sure everyone knows we are angry. Over time our anger turns to hate. We hate those who have hurt us. We hate those who remind us of our hurts. We hate those who get too close to our wounds, who press in, who ask too many questions. Over time, we begin to hate ourselves. Sometimes, we may even come to hate God.

Hate is a strong word. But it is the truth. Long-term anger leads to hate if we are not careful. If we don't deal with the source of our anger. If we don't get some help.

And then there is resentment. It begins with the questions that roll around in our heads, the questions for which we find no answers. *'Why did that happen to me? Where was God when it happened? Why was I abused that way? Why did God allow these things? He could have prevented this! Why doesn't God heal me?'* These tormenting questions lead to a specific resentment toward the source of our wounds and a general resentment toward everybody and everything. Including God.

Next comes unforgiveness. We hold what has happened to us against those who caused it to happen. We cannot forgive them. We will not forgive them. We will not forgive

156

God. We will not forgive ourselves.

The result of this is bitterness. Bitterness is strong poison. It results in dangerous physical and spiritual problems. It is, in fact, the fertilizer that enables these problems to flourish. Bitterness is like an acid. It just keeps burning and burning until it burns all the way through our souls.

All of these emotions are real. Many of us have experienced them. We know that these emotions control us and we do not control them. They drive us toward a place of self-destruction. They open doors—spiritual doors—which we do not want opened.

We run for cover. We hide. We build walls. We protect ourselves from further hurt. That is what our unhealed wounds do to us.

R_x

How do we overcome our wounds?

There is only one answer to this question. There is only one cure. We must allow the Great Physician, Jesus, to heal them. We cannot do it ourselves. Most of us have tried. Others cannot do it for us. They can help, but they can't heal. Only Jesus can.

To begin our healing with Jesus, we must first admit that we have the wound. Most of us do not want to go anywhere near our wounds. We have had them for a very long time. They are infected and festering with anger, resentment, and unforgiveness. The stench of bitterness hangs over them as a foul-smelling cloud of rottenness. We would rather not deal with these wounds, so we instead choose to ignore them to the point of denying their very existence. But in this denial, we condemn ourselves to carry them unhealed for a lifetime. For a wound to be real, we have to be willing to see it as real. When we have spent years avoiding the reality of the wound, this is easier said than done. But it must be done. Each wound must be acknowledged and owned.

To further the healing process, we have to do what we would do if we went to the hospital. We must point out the wound. We have to answer questions about the wound. We have to allow Jesus to look at it, to probe it, to assess it. He may choose to call in an assistant to help us with the process, and, if so, they will need to do the same. We will have to revisit the history of the wound, to recount the events that led to the wound, and to acknowledge those who wounded us. Then the wound must be re-opened and all of the infection cleaned out. This means forgiving all involved—the person or persons who caused the wound, God, and ourselves.[3] Then, and only then, can it be bandaged and the healing process begun. Any shortcuts will cause the wound to remain unhealed.

Healing is a process and not an event. There may be times when Jesus simply takes it all away. Generally, though, just like a physical wound, these wounds of our soul take time to heal. They are sore for a while. They are a little touchy. If we don't work at getting them completely healed, they may become infected all over again.

Unhealed wounds are of great significance to us. They keep us out of the battle and on the sidelines. They marginalize our effectiveness in every area of our lives. The enemy knows this and does everything to keep us from dealing with our wounds. They threaten us with fear—of discovery, of embarrassment, of rejection. They continually hold the promise of more pain over our heads.

It is not good enough to just learn to live with our wounds, to limp slowly along through life. We have been trying that for years. Only when we deal with each and every wound and get them healed can we get back into the battle.

Let us each take our wounds to Jesus and lay them at His feet. Let us mourn and cry over each one. Jesus is waiting. He knows exactly what to do. He can heal them.

Unhealed wounds will hinder our walk with Jesus.

♦♦♦ CHAPTER NOTES ♦♦♦

Unhealed wounds are major forces in a man's life. Many of our actions and reactions, our behaviors and habits, and our thoughts and deeds can be traced directly back to unhealed wounds. Much of the time, we are not aware of the relationship between our wounds and our thoughts, emotions, or actions. We just know that something is not right.

Self-preservation is the strongest drive in mankind. Protecting our unhealed wounds is part of this self-preservation drive. The only way past this is healing. Healing is a process of honesty at any cost.

1. Adventurous Boys

Some men were not as actively involved in adventurous activities as others when they were boys. If we were not, it does not mean we are defective in some way. There are boys like Esau—rough and tumble, outdoor types. There are those who are more like Jacob—cautious, gentle homebodies. It matters not the temperament of a boy in this regard, the wiring is still the same. Boys seek adventure, whether in active engagements or in virtual realities, whether in action or in thought only. What goes on inside is the same. The need for adventure is there.

(Genesis 25:27) When the boys grew up, Esau was a skillful hunter, a man of the field, while Jacob was a quiet man, dwelling in tents.

2. Inadequacy

We were created in and as the image of God. We were created for lives of significance. Not that every man should be a ruler of a country, but every man should fulfill his destiny of a full, significant life for Jesus. Feeling inadequate or worthless is the opposite of feeling significant. Because these feelings keep us from our destiny, the causes of these feelings must be resolved. The wounds must be healed. Only Jesus can do this. This was His calling. To heal and set free.

(Luke 4:18) "The Spirit of the LORD is upon Me, because He has anointed Me to proclaim good news to the poor. He has sent Me to proclaim liberty to the captives and recovering of sight to the blind, to set at liberty those who are oppressed."

3. Forgiveness

Forgiving can seem like an insurmountable obstacle. We have grasped tightly to our unforgiveness for years. We have used it as justification for our pain. We have protected it and nurtured it. But the act of forgiving is essential to the wound-healing process. It is tough to forgive others who have hurt us. It is even tougher to forgive ourselves. After being forgiven by God, though, how can we not forgive ourselves? How can we not forgive others?

(Colossians 3:13b) As the Lord has forgiven you, so you also must forgive.

Wounds are evidence of inflicted traumas. They are reminders of unwanted intrusions.

1) When you think of a wound, what is the first word that comes to mind? Why?

Most men carry wounds from their past. Some wounds are of the body, but most are of the soul (mind, will, and emotions). These wounds can come from many sources— other people, situations, words, and even by the image in the mirror. Our tendency is to bury these wounds deep, salve them over with distractions, and try to ignore them.

2a) Make a list of your soul wounds from the past. Anything that hurt you deeply emotionally can qualify. Uncovering these wounds can be very painful. Remembering and reliving them can be agonizing. But they must be dug up and examined one by one. Ask Jesus to help you. Take your time and list each one. Use as much paper as necessary. It is important to recognize them all, no matter how painful.

2b) How many of the wounds on your list have you been denying? *Underline these.* It is important to face your unhealed wounds, and not shrug them off, seek to justify leaving them unaddressed, or avoid them.

2c) Look at the wounds on your list. Think of the people who hurt you. Write their names beside each wound. Which of these people have you not forgiven? *Circle these.* Confess your unforgiveness of each person to Jesus.

2d) Forgive each person who wounded you—even if you don't feel like it. Forgive them from your will, if you must. Forgive them like Jesus forgave you. Ask Jesus to help you. This breaks the power of each wound in your life so they can be healed—truly healed.

3) Many times we withhold forgiveness from ourselves, and we even refuse to forgive God Himself for what He allowed. In what ways have you not forgiven yourself?

4) In what ways have you not forgiven God?

† PRAYER THOUGHTS †

Forgive yourself and forgive God right now.

Cry out to Jesus over each wound. Weep over each one. Allow Jesus to clean out all of the poison—the bitterness, the hatred, the anger. Allow Him to heal each wound. Certain wounds may be tender and touchy for a while. Old reactions take time to stop and overcome. Let Jesus do His perfect work. He will heal them all.

Make a list of each person *you* have wounded. Purpose to seek them out and to ask them to forgive you. Let Jesus heal them as He has healed you.

INFESTED

Most of us understand at some level the reality of the unseen world around us. We know that God is spirit.[1] We understand that there are angels among us.[2] We at least recognize that there are also demons, those angels who were once with God until they rebelled with their leader, Satan, and were cast down to the earth.[3] Our Bibles tell us that this unseen world is a reality. But do we really believe it? Do we take it to heart? Do we understand this as fact? Do we ponder the implications?

Teaching on the spirit world around us is woefully missing in the modern church of the 21st century. Why is this the case? Maybe the reason is that we have become too sophisticated to think in terms that would be considered outdated, archaic, or superstitious by modern standards. Another possible reason is that the current generation of church leadership has not been properly taught on this subject themselves, and they have nothing of substance to share with their congregations. Either way, it is the responsibility of each of us to take the initiative and educate ourselves in the realm of the spirit world. It is not profitable for any of us to ignore this subject, expecting it to have no effect on our lives.

The Bible tells us clearly about this unseen world. It offers glimpses behind the thin skin that separates the visible physical world from the invisible spiritual world. There are approximately fifty references to demons in the New Testament and more than three times that number of references to angels. The subject is not isolated to a couple of accounts, but is a reoccurring theme of significant importance.

The angelic beings were created to serve God. Satan had a position of authority close to the throne of God. Satan's heart was lifted up in pride and he rebelled against God, along with one-third of the angels. The rebellion was crushed, and Satan and these angels-turned-demons were cast to the earth where they 'walk to and fro, seeking whom they may devour'. Although the earth and its kingdoms are subject to God's dominion, Satan became a squatting usurper, exercising influence over the peoples of the earth and its systems. Jesus called him 'the prince of this world', indicating a level of legal dominion over his (Satan's) followers in the world. Jesus defeated Satan through His blood on the cross and His resurrection from the dead.[4] Even though the war is lost, Satan and his forces battle on against God and His forces. Since his rebellion, Satan has maintained access to heaven where he accuses believers day and night before Jesus. During the Tribulation, Satan and his demons will be denied all access to Heaven forever more. They will continue to 'steal, kill, and destroy' on earth until they are thrown into the lake of fire at the end of this age.[5]

Both angels and demons are prominent in the Gospel accounts of Jesus' life and ministry on earth. The angel Gabriel announced Jesus' coming birth to Mary His mother. We know an angel appeared three times to Joseph, Jesus' earthly father, in dreams. We read that Jesus 'went around doing good and healing all who were oppressed by the devil'. We see Him casting demons out of people and healing them of their ills at the same time. We know that angels ministered to Jesus in His times of need.

Regardless of the Biblical testimony of the active spirit world around us, we humans ignore the majority of this unseen world in our day-to-day existence. We want to see things with our own eyes and touch things with our own hands. If we can't, we tend to disregard them and make

166

them less than real. While some will give credence to the presence of angels, many people discount the reality of demons. Even within the church, most give only a passing acknowledgement to demons and are ignorant of their ways because they have not had an encounter with the spirit world, or so they believe. In spite of man's view on the subject, one cannot believe the Scriptures and deny this otherworldly reality. The unseen world is all around us. It is real and it is purposeful. It has a great impact on each of us and our walk as disciples.

CHRISTIANS AND DEMONS

As Christians, we are in a battle against the spiritual enemies of Jesus—Satan and his demonic followers. Given this reality, it is a wonder why we are so ignorant of those against whom we battle. But this is the truth. And in this vacuum of knowledge, much confusion dwells among believers as to the realities of how our spiritual foes work among us and in us.

Man is composed of three distinct parts. We have the body—our physical being. We have the soul—our mind, will, and emotions. And we have our spirit—the everlasting aspect of our being. At the moment of salvation, God, the Holy Spirit, comes to live inside us as the down payment on our eternal life. He redeems our spirit, indwelling it as the place of His abode within us. The soul and body—the flesh—must yet be redeemed. It must be tamed. It must be brought into submission. This 'working out of our salvation' is a life-long endeavor.[6]

The trouble is that most of us are not just working against the desires of the flesh. We are working against demons that have infested our flesh.

This may be a new thought, perhaps even shocking. But it is truth—truth we will rarely hear mentioned today. Yet, Jesus confronted this reality in the people of His day. Why then should we be any different?

New Testament scriptures speak of two types of demonic influence in the life of a Christian—oppression and demonization.

When a person is 'oppressed', it means that demons are 'exercising power over' them. Oppression can be both external and internal in nature.

When a Christian is 'demonized' it means that they are 'influenced, controlled, or dominated by' demons. It is unfortunate that some translations for the Greek word used in this context have been rendered 'demon possessed'. This is an incorrect translation, and it is taken by most who read or hear it to mean 'owned'. A Christian is purchased and owned by Jesus.[7] A Christian cannot be owned by a demon. The proper translation is 'demonized'. This word is always used in the context of an indwelling spirit. If a person is demonized, they have a demon or demons dwelling in them, influencing, controlling, or dominating them in some way. Because the spirit of a Christian is the dwelling place of the Holy Spirit, the abode of demons in a Christian is their flesh (body and soul).

So, what is demonization about?

Oppression. Areas of control. Ground given over. Legal rights that have been forfeited.

GOD AND LEGALITIES

To fully understand how this works, we must first understand the nature of God the Father. He is holy and He is just. He is consistent in this. For this to be true, He has to demand strict adherence to the rules of engagement between good and evil—the legalities of the fight. Everyone engaged in the battle has certain rights bestowed upon them. Man has a right to his will. Believers have the right to use Jesus' name. Satan has the right to accuse believers before Jesus' throne and to petition Him for permission to infest them with his demonic horde. Satan and his demons have rights to 'ground' given in the human flesh due to iniquity and sin. Jesus has the right to establish judgments against sinful activity in families and individuals.

God the Father will not violate any of these rights. He cannot.

Rights come by way of permissions. We have to grant Jesus permission to work in our lives. If we do, Jesus has the right to work on us as He sees fit. Likewise, we have to grant the Holy Spirit permission to fill us. We do this granting consciously. It is an act of the will. For demons to infest a man, they must be given permission based on the rules of engagement. Once permission is granted, a legal right is established. When we answered the knock of Jesus on the door of our hearts and asked Him to be our Savior and Lord, He then established a legal right of ownership over our lives and us. When certain things happen, other doors are opened and demons are given legal rights to infest us and oppress us.

God the Father is sovereign over all. His rules of engagement stand. Demons cannot infest a believer whenever and however they desire. They must be given permission by Jesus personally based on the established rules and His holiness, justice, mercy, and love.[8] Demons then enter by permission through specific causational doorways.

DOORWAYS AND PERMISSIONS

How can demons come in? What are these doorways? Where do these permissions come from?

The most common doorway of entry comes in the form of a generational permissions.[9] Jesus grants the demonic permission to infest down bloodlines to the third and fourth generations in families because of the iniquity and sin of prior generations. Most of us were born with demons that came down our family lines. These demons were allowed to infest us at conception, in the womb, or later in life because of the permissions granted by previous generations.

Unforgiveness is the most common doorway that we open to the demonic through our actions.[10] Jesus stated this truth in the Parable of the Wicked Servant. We remember the story. The servant was brought before the king who demanded repayment of a debt. It was a huge debt that the servant could not possibly pay. In his mercy, the king forgave the man's debt. This same servant then came across someone who owed him very little compared to the debt he was just forgiven. He had the man thrown in prison until he could pay. When the king found out, he turned the wicked servant over to the jailers so he could be tormented. As believers, we have been forgiven much. When we refuse to forgive others who have hurt us, abused us, or wronged us, we open doors for the demons to torment us. How can we who were forgiven much by God refuse to forgive relatively little against others?

Another doorway is our own sin.[11] Every sin is rebellion against God—our pride, our anger, our lust, our covetousness, our addictions. Each of these sins, committed blatantly in the face of a holy God, can open doors and give permission for demons to enter. And they will. And they do. These infestations can begin new cycles of generational permissions that can be passed from us down our bloodlines for three or four generations.

Believing lies is a less obvious but equally effective doorway.[12] Lies about who we are. Lies about what we have done or have not done. Lies about what is going to happen to us. Lies about our impending demise by a family illness trait. Lies about our abilities or our inabilities. Believing lies leads to our acting upon them. When we do, doors can be opened.

Other door openers to the demonic are involvement in the occult (no matter how innocent we consider it to be), involvement in secret societies, involvement in hypnosis, and involvement with false religions.[13]

These are not meant to be exhaustive lists of possibilities, but are given only to allow us to see the commonplace permissions granted to infest a person's life.

At the moment of salvation the Holy Spirit possesses the spirit core of our being, but our flesh can, and usually does, contain varying degrees of demonic infestation from our past. They will not leave on their own.

WE WRESTLE NOT AGAINST FLESH AND BLOOD

We are in a war against a powerful enemy. On our own, we are no match for this enemy. We were created a little lower than them—we do not possess their power or their abilities.[14] They are more committed than we are because their eternity does not end well while ours does. They are persistent, they are resilient, and they are resourceful in their survival. They lurk in the dark places of our flesh.

The Bible tells us that we are not just wrestling against our flesh and blood or the flesh and blood of others.[15] We are wrestling against rulers—organized ranks of ruling demons set up as kingdoms. We are wrestling against authorities—spiritual powers placed in specific places of territorial authority (such as localities, cities, counties, states, nations, and continents). We are wrestling against cosmic powers of this present darkness—the spiritual forces of demonic rule in this time of darkness in the world. We are wrestling against spiritual forces of evil in the heavenly places—very destructive forces of wickedness placed over the earth. They are way beyond us as mere humans. We need help. Lots of help.

Jesus is our help. He has defeated them.[16] We must do our part. This begins with an acknowledgment that we most likely have demons embedded in our flesh. These demons are here to do as all demons do—steal, kill, and destroy. These demons will not leave on their own. We must follow Jesus' example and cast them out.[17] We cannot cast them out on our own. It is not that simple. There is much preliminary groundwork to do. All rights must be cancelled, all permissions revoked. Then we must get help from someone who is anointed to do this kind of spiritual deliverance work.

The preparation begins after the acknowledgment of our demonic infestation problem. We must be serious about being delivered from their clutches. We must examine our lives for their influencing and controlling manifestations. We must take inventory of probable doors that have been opened both generationally and by our own actions. There are *Deliverance Resources* in the *Appendix* to help with this.

Jesus wants us to be totally free. He wants to completely be the Lord of our lives. He wants us to walk in this freedom as His disciples. We cannot serve two masters.[18]

If we want to follow Jesus, the demons must go.

✦✦✦ CHAPTER NOTES ✦✦✦

The spirit world is a reality. If we could have our eyes opened to see this world, we would be shocked at its prevalence and its presence. We would see mighty armies of angels fighting vast armies of demons. We would find deep pockets of spiritual darkness where demons would be as thick as bats in a cave. We would find equal pockets of light where there would be a restraining of their evil presence. In all places, we would be astonished at the spiritual hierarchy, order, and sheer numbers.

1. God Is Spirit

God is spirit. His initial creation was spirit in the form of angels. When He created us, He made us essentially a spirit being. This allows us to worship Him and fellowship with Him. He wrapped our spirit in a temporary body made from the dust of the earth and gave it a soul so it could function, but our essence is spirit, like our Creator.

(John 4:24a) "God is Spirit."

2. Angels Among Us

God's angels are all around us. They are ministering spirits, doing His will.

(Hebrews 13:2) Do not neglect to show hospitality to strangers, for thereby some have entertained angels unawares.

(Psalm 91:11-12) For He will command His angels concerning you to guard you in all your ways. On their hands they will bear you up, lest you strike your foot against a stone.

(Hebrews 1:14) Are they not all ministering spirits sent out to serve for the sake of those who will inherit salvation?

Both Mary and Joseph were visited by angels regarding Jesus.

(Luke 1:26-27) In the sixth month the angel Gabriel was sent from God to a city of Galilee named Nazareth, to a virgin betrothed to a man whose name was Joseph, of the house of David. And the virgin's name was Mary.

(Matthew 1:20) But as he considered these things, behold, an angel of the Lord appeared to him in a dream, saying, "Joseph, son of David, do not fear to take to Mary as your wife, for that which is conceived in her is of the Holy Spirit."

(Matthew 2:13) Now when they [wise men] had departed, behold, an angel of the Lord appeared to Joseph in a dream and said, "Rise, take the child and his mother, and flee to Egypt, and remain there until I tell you, for Herod is about to search for the child, to destroy him."

(Matthew 2:19-20) But when Herod died, behold, an angel of the Lord appeared in a dream to Joseph in Egypt, saying, "Rise, take the child and his mother and go to the land of Israel, for those who sought the child's life are dead."

Angels proclaimed the birth of Jesus.

(Luke 2:13-14) And suddenly there was with the angel a multitude of the heavenly host praising God and saying, "Glory to God in the highest, and on earth peace among those with whom He is pleased!"

Angels also ministered to Jesus in His times of need.

(Matthew 4:11) Then the devil left Him, and behold, angels came and were ministering to Him.

(Luke 22:43) And there appeared to Him an angel from heaven, strengthening Him.

3. Demons Among Us

Likewise, there are demons all around us. Before he rebelled against God and was cast down to earth, Satan was named Lucifer, 'the shining one'. He held a high rank and was very beautiful.

(Ezekiel 28:12b-14) "You were the signet of perfection, full of wisdom and perfect in beauty. You were in Eden, the garden of God; every precious stone was your covering, sardius, topaz, and diamond, beryl, onyx, and jasper, sapphire, emerald, and carbuncle; and crafted in gold were your settings and your engravings. On the day you were created they were prepared. You were an anointed guardian cherub. I placed you; you were on the holy mountain of God; in the midst of the stones of fire you walked.

174

When Lucifer rebelled, he was judged by God and became Satan, 'the adversary'. Lucifer/Satan is a created being. He is in no way the equal counterpart of God. He is not omniscient (all knowing), omnipotent (all powerful), or omnipresent (everywhere at once). He is just evil personified.

(Ezekiel 28:15-17a) You were blameless in your ways from the day you were created, till unrighteousness was found in you. In the abundance of your trade you were filled with violence in your midst, and you sinned; so I cast you as a profane thing from the mountain of God, and I destroyed you, O guardian cherub, from the midst of the stones of fire. Your heart was proud because of your beauty; you corrupted your wisdom for the sake of your splendor. I cast you to the ground.

Jesus said He had seen (and was continuing to see) Satan's fall from his position in heaven.

(Luke 10:18) And He said to them, "I saw Satan fall like lightning from heaven."

One third of all of the angels rebelled with Satan and were likewise cast to the earth. 'Stars of heaven' refers to angels. They fell to earth as demons.

(Revelation 12:3-4a) And another sign appeared in heaven: behold, a great red dragon, with seven heads and ten horns, and on his heads seven diadems. His tail swept down a third of the stars of heaven and cast them to the earth.

Satan maintained his access to the throne of the LORD (Jesus) after his fall.

(Job 1:6) Now there was a day when the sons of God came to present themselves before the LORD [Jesus], and Satan also came among them.

When Satan comes into heaven and stands before Jesus, his main occupation is to accuse believers before Him.

(Revelation 12:10) And I heard a loud voice in heaven, saying, "Now the salvation and the power and the kingdom of our God and the authority of His Christ have come, for the accuser of our brothers has been thrown down, who accuses them day and night before our God."

175

Elsewhere we see this same thing occurring as Satan stood before Jesus to accuse a high priest named Joshua. Here, again, it is Jesus (the Angel of the LORD) who Satan comes before as the accuser ('one who opposes').

(Zechariah 3:1-5) Then he showed me Joshua the high priest standing before the Angel of the LORD [Jesus], and Satan standing at his right hand to accuse him. And the LORD said to Satan, "The LORD rebuke you, O Satan! The LORD who has chosen Jerusalem rebuke you! Is not this a brand plucked from the fire?" Now Joshua was standing before the Angel, clothed with filthy garments. And the Angel said to those who were standing before Him, "Remove the filthy garments from him." And to him He said, "Behold, I have taken your iniquity away from you, and I will clothe you with pure vestments." And I said, "Let them put a clean turban on his head." So they put a clean turban on his head and clothed him with garments. And the Angel of the LORD was standing by.

But Jesus is our legal advocate to His Father. As He took away Joshua's iniquity and covered his sin in perfected robes in the verse above, Jesus represents us and tells the Father, *'Their debt is paid in full.'*

(1 John 2:1b) But if anyone does sin, we have an Advocate with the Father, Jesus Christ the righteous.

In the Great Tribulation, Satan will be cast out of heaven permanently and have no further access to Jesus as the accuser of the brethren.

(Revelation 12:7-9) Now war arose in heaven, Michael and his angels fighting against the dragon. And the dragon and his angels fought back, but he was defeated, and there was no longer any place for them in heaven. And the great dragon was thrown down, that ancient serpent, who is called the Devil and Satan, the deceiver of the whole world—he was thrown down to the earth, and his angels were thrown down with him.

Satan is a usurper. He has no explicit authority over nations or kings, or over their glory. This authority was never delivered to him from Adam (because it was not

176

Adam's to give—it was never given to him by God) or from the Godhead. That God is sovereign is a fact presented in numerous verses in both the Old and New Testaments. It is God and God alone who owns the nations. He appoints their rulers, their times, and their boundaries. Satan has attempted to possess them as a usurper would—wrongfully and illegally in the place of their rightful owner, Jesus.

(Daniel 4:17b) To the end that the living may know that the Most High rules the kingdom of men and gives it to whom He will and sets over it the lowliest of men.

(Daniel 2:21b) He removes kings and sets up kings.

(Acts 17:26) And He made from one man every nation of mankind to live on all the face of the earth, having determined allotted periods and the boundaries of their dwelling place.

Satan does have a level of ownership over those who stand in rebellion to God, subject to the sovereignty of God. These people are found throughout the nations, and they operate the worldly systems that they have built around the globe. In this light, Paul calls Satan the 'god of this world'.

(2 Corinthians 4:3-4) And even if our gospel is veiled, it is veiled to those who are perishing. In their case the god of this world has blinded the minds of the unbelievers, to keep them from seeing the light of the gospel of the glory of Christ, who is the image of God.

Satan is the 'god' of all who stand in rebellion to God. Unbelievers follow his agenda against God, as he is the author of rebellion. So in this sense, Satan has authority over unbelievers. He acts on behalf of their master, sin. He leads them ever deeper into captivity through the working of evil in their lives.

Paul builds on this theme elsewhere. He reiterates that Satan works among those who are disobedient to God and His way—those who are children of wrath like each believer once was before they were saved.

(Ephesians 2:2-3) In which you once walked, following the course of this world, following the prince of the power of the air, the spirit that is now at work in the sons of disobedience—among whom we all once lived in the passions of our flesh, carrying out the desires of the body and the mind, and were by nature children of wrath, like the rest of mankind.

Paul calls Satan a 'prince'. The term 'prince' carries a spiritual connotation in the Bible that speaks of a hierarchy and structure. In a similar manner, Jesus calls Satan a 'ruler' three times, signifying his position in the spirit world.

(John 12:31) "Now is the judgment of this world; now will the ruler of this world be cast out."

(John 14:30) "I will no longer talk much with you, for the ruler of this world is coming. He has no claim on Me."

(John 16:11) "Concerning judgment, because the ruler of this world is judged."

Jesus said that Satan was the father of all who would not believe in Him.

(John 8:44-45) "You are of your father the devil, and your will is to do your father's desires. He was a murderer from the beginning, and does not stand in the truth, because there is no truth in him. When he lies, he speaks out of his own character, for he is a liar and the father of lies. But because I tell the truth, you do not believe me."

Satan and his demons now roam the earth, looking to keep people in darkness, to thwart anything that God has planned, and to generally cause trouble—especially for God's people.

(Job 2:2) And the LORD said to Satan, "From where have you come?" Satan answered the LORD and said, "From going to and fro on the earth, and from walking up and down on it."

(1 Peter 5:8) Be sober-minded; be watchful. Your adversary the devil prowls around like a roaring lion, seeking someone to devour.

Satan's powers of deception are great. Many times, it is he who is giving God's people direction—even to do 'good'

178

things. Ultimately, these 'good things' are purposed for a greater evil.

(2 Corinthians 11:14) And no wonder, for even Satan disguises himself as an angel of light.

Satan and his demons have a mission.

(John 10:10a) "The thief comes only to steal and kill and destroy."

4. Jesus Versus The Devil

Through His death and resurrection, Jesus has destroyed Satan's power.

(Hebrews 2:14-15) Since therefore the children share in flesh and blood, He Himself likewise partook of the same things, that through death He might destroy the one who has the power of death, that is, the devil, and deliver all those who through fear of death were subject to lifelong slavery.

(Acts 10:38) How God anointed Jesus of Nazareth with the Holy Spirit and with power. He went about doing good and healing all who were oppressed by the devil, for God was with Him.

5. The End Of Satan And His Demons

Ultimately, Satan and his demons are consigned to the lake of fire.

(Revelation 20:10) And the devil who had deceived them was thrown into the lake of fire and sulfur where the beast and the false prophet were, and they will be tormented day and night forever and ever.

6. Working Out Our Salvation

The idea of working out our salvation does not speak about works in relation to earning our salvation or somehow being worthy of our salvation. No. It remains subsequent to one's salvation event. It is really the practical everyday effort to walk closer to Jesus and become sanctified (set aside for holy purposes).

(Philippians 2:12-13) Therefore, my beloved, as you have always obeyed, so now, not only as in my presence but

much more in my absence, work out your own salvation with fear and trembling, for it is God who works in you, both to will and to work for His good pleasure.

7. Demons And Christians

Jesus owns us. For the true Christian, this is an indisputable fact.

(1 Peter 1:18-19) Knowing that you were ransomed from the futile ways inherited from your forefathers, not with perishable things such as silver or gold, but with the precious blood of Christ, like that of a lamb without blemish or spot.

(1 Corinthians 6:20a) For you were bought with a price.

But even though Jesus has bought us, we can be oppressed and in-dwelt by demons. Relieving this oppression was a large part of Jesus' ministry on earth.

(Luke 4:33-35) And in the synagogue there was a man who had the spirit of an unclean demon, and he cried out with a loud voice, "Ha! What have You to do with us, Jesus of Nazareth? Have you come to destroy us? I know who You are—the Holy One of God." But Jesus rebuked him, saying, "Be silent and come out of him!" And when the demon had thrown him down in their midst, he came out of him, having done him no harm.

(Matthew 17:18) And Jesus rebuked the demon, and it came out of him, and the boy was healed instantly.

(Mark 1:39) And He went throughout all Galilee, preaching in their synagogues and casting out demons.

But how do demons get into our flesh (body and soul) to oppress us? A few scriptures will help us understand the concept.

(Proverbs 25:28) A man without self-control is like a city broken into and left without walls.

Every city that wanted to be protected from raiding bands of thieves had a wall set about it with closely guarded gates. If a city's wall was broken down or compromised in some fashion, or if the gates were left open, anyone could come and go at will. When a man does not rule over himself and his affections or passions (he sins as he wishes, either in thought, word, or deed), he is, in effect, pulling down the very walls that protect him and opening the gates, leaving himself open to oppression by any band of thieves. They will come, and they will plunder.

Then there is the familiar account of Jesus cleaning out the temple. The temple was supposed to be a place of prayer and worship—and the very dwelling place of God— but the thieves had been given permission to come and set up shop in the outer courts (not the inner temple, or Holy of Holies, where God dwelled behind the veil). These thieves had to be driven out forcefully because they would never have left on their own.

(Matthew 21:12-13) And Jesus entered the temple and drove out all who sold and bought in the temple, and He overturned the tables of the moneychangers and the seats of those who sold pigeons. He said to them, "It is written, 'My house shall be called a house of prayer,' but you make it a den of robbers."

Our bodies are the temples of the Holy Spirit.

(1 Corinthians 6:19) Or do you not know that your body is a temple of the Holy Spirit within you, whom you have from God? You are not your own.

If we give permission for thieves to come and set up shop in our flesh (the outer courts), they will. They then have to be driven out.

The scripture below is the second half of the story of the paralytic man who was healed at the Pool of Bethesda. The man was lying by the pool, waiting for the water to be stirred for a healing. Jesus came along and healed him. Afterward, Jesus saw the man again and gave him a rather strong and peculiar warning—*Stop sinning or something worse may happen to you.* While it does not specifically say, evidently indwelling demons had caused the man's condition, and this condition was based on his past sins that had granted the demons permission to infest him. We know this because the act of sinning is not a physical cause of sickness. The man must have suffered from a spiritually imposed ailment.

(John 5:12-14) They asked him, "Who is the Man who said to you, 'Take up your bed and walk'?" Now the man who had been healed did not know who it was, for Jesus had withdrawn, as there was a crowd in that place. Afterward Jesus found him in the temple and said to him, "See, you are well! Sin no more, that nothing worse may happen to you."

The truth that Jesus was conveying in His warning is that whenever a man persists in his sinning, he gives up greater rights to his freedom by granting greater permissions over his life to the demonic world. In this way, a man is exposed to greater demonic forces (*something worse*). These demons may be granted permission to enter the man's flesh and infest him. This truth applies whether the man has been through a deliverance process or not.

8. God Grants Permission To Satan And His Demons

God must approve all demonic activity in our lives. His approval is a result of His omnipotence working in concert with His holiness, justice, and rules of engagement. Jesus (the LORD) executes His Father's judgment.

(Job 1:8, 12a) And the LORD said to Satan, "Have you considered My servant Job, that there is none like him on the earth, a blameless and upright man, who fears God and turns away from evil?"...And the LORD said to Satan, "Behold, all that he has is in your hand. Only against him do not stretch out your hand."

(Exodus 34:6-7) The LORD passed before him and proclaimed, "The LORD, the LORD, a God merciful and gracious, slow to anger, and abounding in steadfast love and faithfulness, keeping steadfast love for thousands, forgiving iniquity and transgression and sin, but who will by no means clear the guilty, visiting the iniquity of the fathers on the children and the children's children, to the third and the fourth generation."

(1 Corinthians 10:13) No temptation has overtaken you that

is not common to man. God is faithful, and He will not let you be tempted beyond your ability, but with the temptation He will also provide the way of escape, that you may be able to endure it.

9. Permission From Past Generations

Generational demons are given permission to move down our bloodlines and infest us by the decisions and actions of our prior generations. These demons are passed down according to God's rules of justice and not by anything we did to grant permission. These generational permissions to infest are not necessarily granted equally to our siblings and us—a brother or sister may have different types of demons and different levels of infestation. Sometimes certain generational demons will skip one generation and go to the next. All of this is done by the permission of God.

(Exodus 20:5b) For I the LORD your God am a jealous God, visiting the iniquity of the fathers on the children to the third and fourth generation of those who hate Me.

10. Permission From Unforgiveness

Most of us struggle with unforgiveness. It can be difficult to forgive others, God, or even ourselves. Yet, forgiveness is a key command from Jesus to every Christian. We are commanded by Him to forgive without limit. When Jesus said we are to forgive 'seventy times seven', He was saying 'however many times it takes'.

(Matthew 18:21-22) Then Peter came up and said to Him, "Lord, how often will my brother sin against me, and I forgive him? As many as seven times?" Jesus said to him, "I do not say to you seven times, but up to seventy-seven times."

Forgiveness does not depend on our emotions—whether we feel like forgiving or not. It is an act of the will. It is something that we must ask Jesus for the strength to do.

The tormentors in the story below are demons. A person's unforgiveness gives the demons access (they are delivered over to the jailers or tormentors).

(Matthew 18:23-35) Therefore the kingdom of heaven may be compared to a king who wished to settle accounts with his servants. When he began to settle, one was brought to him who owed him ten thousand talents. And since he could not pay, his master ordered him to be sold, with his wife and children and all that he had, and payment to be made. So the servant fell on his knees, imploring him, 'Have patience with me, and I will pay you everything.' And out of pity for him, the master of that servant released him and forgave him the debt. But when that same servant went out, he found one of his fellow servants who owed him a hundred denarii, and seizing him, he began to choke him, saying, 'Pay what you owe.' So his fellow servant fell down and pleaded with him, 'Have patience with me, and I will pay you.' He refused and went and put him in prison until he should pay the debt. When his fellow servants saw what had taken place, they were greatly distressed, and they went and reported to their master all that had taken place. Then his master summoned him and said to him, 'You wicked servant! I forgave you all that debt because you pleaded with me. And should not you have had mercy on your fellow servant, as I had mercy on you?' And in anger his master delivered him to the jailers [tormentors] until he should pay all his debt. So also My heavenly Father will do to every one of you, if you do not forgive your brother from your heart."

11. Permission From Our Sin

Our acts of rebellion toward God open doorways and grant permissions to demons.

(Romans 6:16) Do you not know that if you present yourselves to anyone as obedient slaves, you are slaves of the one whom you obey, either of sin, which leads to death, or of obedience, which leads to righteousness?

(Ephesians 4:26-27) Be angry, and do not sin; do not let the sun go down on your anger, and give no opportunity [ground or territory] to the devil.

(1 Samuel 15:23a) For rebellion is as the sin of divination, and presumption is as iniquity and idolatry.

(Proverbs 17:11) An evil man seeks only rebellion, a cruel messenger [demon] will be sent against him.

12. Permission From Believing Lies

We act upon what we believe. If we believe lies about God or who He is, lies about His love for us, lies about what He wants from us, or lies about how He sees us, we open ourselves to the power of the demonic. This happens because Satan is a liar. His demons constantly whisper words of deception in our ears. Believing these false ideas and acting on these wrong beliefs can open doors and grant permissions.

(John 8:44b) "When he [Satan] lies, he speaks out of his own character, for he is a liar and the father of lies."

(2 Corinthians 10:5) We destroy arguments and every lofty opinion raised against the knowledge of God, and take every thought captive to obey Christ.

(Ephesians 4:14) So that we may no longer be children, tossed to and fro by the waves and carried about by every wind of doctrine, by human cunning, by craftiness in deceitful schemes.

13. Permission From Occult Involvement (Occult, Secret Societies, False Religions, Hypnosis, Etc.)

We are warned many times in Scripture that while the occult is all around us, we are to stay away from it.

(Leviticus 19:31) Do not turn to mediums and necromancers [those who claim to communicate with the dead]; do not seek them out, and so make yourselves unclean by them: I am the LORD your God.

(Deuteronomy 18:10-12a) There shall not be found among you anyone who burns his son or his daughter as an offering, anyone who practices divination or tells fortunes or interprets omens, or a sorcerer or a charmer or a medium or a necromancer or one who inquires of the dead, for whoever does these things is an abomination to the LORD.

While some aspects of the occult are blatantly obvious to us, others are deceptively subtle or are made to seem harmless and even entertaining. Many movies and books contain themes of magic and sorcery. The rites of many secret societies (including fraternities and sororities) contain demonic elements in the form of curses and oaths. False religions are based on demon worship. Nevertheless, we should not forget that concealing the evil around us or making this evil look like something harmless, fun, or good is a common tactic of Satan and his demons.

(2 Corinthians 11:14) And no wonder, for even Satan disguises himself as an angel of light.

14. No Match For Demons On Our Own

Demons have power that surpasses our own. They are supernatural and we are not. We can only battle them with Jesus' power through His name.

(Psalm 8:4-5a) What is man that You are mindful of him, and the son of man that You care for him? Yet You have made him a little lower than the heavenly beings.

15. We Wrestle

Our true foes are not found in the physical world. Though people can and do cause us trouble in this life because of the corruptness of their flesh, we must remember that the true power behind the evil of this world and the hatred for Jesus lies in the demonic realm. This spirit otherworld is the source of much destruction and pain.

(Ephesians 6:12) For we do not wrestle against flesh and blood, but against the rulers, against the authorities, against the cosmic powers over this present darkness, against the spiritual forces of evil in the heavenly places.

16. Jesus Won The War

When we look at the world of evil around us, we sometimes forget that Jesus has already won the war. What we see is an enemy who, though ultimately defeated, has not given up. There are still battles to fight.

(Ephesians 1:20-21) [His great might] that He worked in Christ when He raised Him from the dead and seated Him at His right hand in the heavenly places, far above all rule and authority and power and dominion, and above every name

that is named, not only in this age but also in the one to come.

17. Demons Must Be Cast Out

Jesus gave us the truth about getting rid of demons in our flesh—He must cast them out by the power of His name.

(Mark 16:17a) "And these signs will accompany those who believe: In My name they will cast out demons."

18. Serving Two Masters

We can only have one master.

(Matthew 6:24a) "No one can serve two masters, for either he will hate the one and love the other, or he will be devoted to the one and despise the other."

♦♦♦ STUDY GUIDE ♦♦♦

The spiritual world is all around us. This unseen world affects our physical world every second of every day. It is organized, and it is against anything of God—including us.

1) Read **Ephesians 6:12**. What does this verse say to you about the involvement of the spiritual world in your life every day?

(Ephesians 6:12) For we do not wrestle against flesh and blood, but against the rulers, against the authorities, against the cosmic powers over this present darkness, against the spiritual forces of evil in the heavenly places.

2) According the book, *WATM?*, write down the meanings of the following words or phrases:

   a) Rulers

   b) Authorities

   c) Cosmic powers over this present darkness

   d) Spiritual forces of evil in the heavenly places

3) When you see the word *wrestle*, what comes to mind?

4) Like God, man is a triune (3-part) being. List the three parts of man.

5) Which one of these is the eternal part?

6) Which two parts make up the flesh?

7) What are the two types of demonic influence in our lives?

A *permission* given is an authorization given to someone. A *right* is a justified claim of entitlement to something. Sin gives permission to the demonic to work in our lives. Sin ultimately establishes demonic rights to inhabit our flesh.

8) As you consider your family bloodlines, what evidence or patterns of demonic influence, control, or dominion do you see coming down through the previous generations?

188

9) As you consider your life, what doorways have you opened in the following areas? Write them down.

Unforgiveness

Pride

Rebellion

Anger

Lust

Fear

Covetousness

Addictions

Believing Lies

The Occult

Secret Societies

Horoscopes

Hypnosis

Fortune Telling

False Religions

10) How did Jesus say we must get rid of the demons residing in our flesh?

Sanctification is the process of setting aside *each* area of our life to be used for God's purposes. Being controlled by the Holy Spirit is the means to sanctification. It is the process of getting all of our flesh under the control of Jesus.

11) In light of this, what does **Matthew 6:24a** mean to you?

(Matthew 6:24a) "No one can serve two masters, for either he will hate the one and love the other, or he will be devoted to the one and despise the other."

† PRAYER THOUGHTS †

Ask Jesus for help in this area. He is the supreme ruler
over all of creation. The demonic realm knows this and
trembles. Ask Jesus to show you the truth about yourself
and all that has come down your family bloodlines. Jesus is
the light of the world. Ask Him to lead you to the
deliverance minister that He has chosen to help you. Jesus
is the deliverer.

RELATIVITY

Everything that we have examined up to this point will have had an impact on our relationships. Our relationship with our wife. Our relationships with our children. Our relationships with our extended family. Our relationships with our friends. Our relationships with our co-workers. Our relationships with our local church family. Our relationship with our God. Each of these was marred by our lives as they have been. Every fault. Every challenge. Every hurdle. Every deficiency. Every sin. It is impossible for it to be otherwise.

It will be necessary to redeem our relationships by redefining them and by starting them over. But, there is to be no rebuilding in this process of redemption. Rebuilding implies that there was something there to begin with that could be rebuilt and was worth rebuilding.

This may strike a major chord of discouragement in us. We will want to put everything that has happened aside and move forward from today in each of our relationships.[1] But is this possible? Is what we had in these relationships something that we want to rebuild? How could it be? Before, our relationships had been built around us. They were built to accommodate our view of things. They were built to store all of the baggage in our lives, safe and dry. They had been built with extra rooms—secret rooms—to carefully isolate our sin areas from the rest of the relationship. They had been built with protective walls around our wounds—walls without doors or windows, designed to admit no one. They had been built with the help of the demons who infested us. This was never Jesus' intent for our relationships. We need to start over. We need a fresh approach. These relationships must be built around Jesus and not around our selfishness, our wants, our needs, our desires, or our lusts. We need these relationships to be built from the bottom up by the Master Carpenter from Galilee.

Once we can process this and accept it, the discouragement will begin to fade away and be transformed into excitement. We can have better relationships—much better. We can have relationships built around Jesus. Great relationships. Solid relationships. Relationships built upon what is best for others and not on what is best for us. True relationships. Trusting relationships.

This is very exciting. This is the chance to begin again.

THE LONG JOURNEY OF SANCTIFICATION

In order for this process of starting over to ever begin, we first must die.[2] All of who we have been must be killed and buried. It has to be dead. Really dead. Everything we were in those relationships has to die. How we looked at them has to die. What we thought of them has to die. All of the habits must die. All of the actions must die. Everything about them must be killed off.

What we are talking about here is sanctification, the process of being set aside unto a sacred purpose. Crucifixion in Jesus is the first necessary step.[3] Then, our new selves must be raised to life by Jesus.[4] But all is not perfect on the other side of our resurrection. Our flesh wants to come back to life. We have to deal with all of the situations of our former life along with the challenges of our new walk. We have old patterns that must be reprogrammed. We have situations to rectify. We have to unlearn ways of thinking and ways of doing. We have to unlearn old reactions to situations and learn new ways to respond with new attitudes. We must crucify our flesh daily.[5] We have to walk with Jesus in the power of His resurrection, step by step and day by day.[6]

We must also allow Jesus to finish His work in us. He may have some final dredging to do deep down in our hearts. He may have some final purging to do in our souls. He may have some surgery to perform. Many of these last vestiges of our past have been deeply ingrained in us. They have been so much a part of who we have been that we cannot differentiate between them and who we are today. The process of sanctification continues under the skillful hand of Jesus throughout our lives. Our responsibility is to continue yielding to it.

We will have to go through a different process of rebuilding with our wife than we will with each of our children. We will have to learn how to become the husband and father that they need us to be, the one that Jesus requires of us. And, as our journey continues with our wife, it will continue with each of our children at different levels and on different time frames. If we allow Jesus to work throughout this process, He will rebuild these relationships. They will be as He intended. They will be strong. They will stand the test of time.

At the same time, Jesus will build a new relationship with us. We will understand Him better as an individual Person of the Trinity. We will understand His role in our lives. We will understand our role in Him. We will see His plan for us and how we fit into it. We will love Him more deeply than ever before. We will feel His love for us more acutely than we ever thought possible. Deep and abiding. Our relationship with Him will no longer be on our terms, but on His. This will blossom into like relationships with God the Father and the Holy Spirit.

We will continue to struggle against our flesh, all of our weaknesses exposed. But the issues should not be as they once were. Sanctification is a life-long process. It is literally a step by step yielding to Jesus. It is integral to being a disciple of Jesus. It is part of our walk with Him.

Jesus will require that each relationship be built His way this time. Let us yield to Jesus and die to ourselves. Let us allow Him the freedom to dredge where He must dredge. Let us allow Him to raise us from death into a new life.

Resurrected men can walk with the resurrected Jesus.

✦✦✦ Chapter Notes ✦✦✦

We were created for relationships. This is a basic component of the human condition. That is why most people seek out others and band together in families, neighborhoods, cities, states, countries, groups, churches, and denominations. Family relationships tend to be our closest relationships with other humans. It is important that these be clean, pure, true, and honest.

1. Our Inclination To Rebuild

As men, we want to get right back to it. We want to put problems aside as if they did not happen or were of no consequence, and move on. We want to pick right up where we left off in our relationships. We are impatient to do so. Very impatient. Impatient with Jesus. Impatient with our wife. Impatient with the consequences of our actions.

But it is not that simple. We can't ignore the facts. Even if our relationships were started on solid foundations, we have done things to undermine them. If our relationships were built on faulty foundations, they were doomed to fall down from the beginning. In either case, our relationships have been condemned. They must be torn down and re-started. They must be built upon the solid rock foundation that is Jesus.

2. Dying To Self

Man does not speak of dying in glowing terms. To us, dying is a negative. However, to Jesus, dying is a positive. To Him, dying is just the beginning of living. And Jesus requires it of us as His disciples.

(Luke 9: 23-24) And He said to all, "If anyone would come after Me, let him deny himself and take up his cross daily and follow Me. For whoever would save his life will lose it, but whoever loses his life for My sake will save it."

3. Crucified With Jesus

At the moment of our salvation, our old man—the sin

nature we inherited by blood from Adam through our earthly father—was nailed to the cross and killed.

(Romans 6:6) We know that our old self was crucified with Him in order that the body of sin might be brought to nothing, so that we would no longer be enslaved to sin.

(Galatians 5:24) And those who belong to Christ Jesus have crucified the flesh with its passions and desires.

Our old sin nature was killed, and we received and became partakers of a new nature—Jesus' nature.

(Galatians 2:20a) I have been crucified with Christ. It is no longer I who live, but Christ who lives in me.

(2 Peter 1:4b) So that through them [the promises of Jesus] you may become partakers of the divine nature.

We become a new creation.

(Galatians 6:15) For neither circumcision counts for anything, nor uncircumcision, but a new creation.

The old sin nature of Adam has passed away. We have the new nature of Jesus.

(2 Corinthians 5:17) Therefore, if anyone is in Christ, he is a new creation. The old has passed away; behold, the new has come.

The nature of something defines its inherent character and basic constitution. The nature of something defines what it is and excludes it from being something else. The nature of something defines what is natural for it to be and to do.

Man can have only one of two natures. He can have the sin nature or the new nature of Jesus. Man is free to be what his nature allows him to be. This *being* takes no thought or energy. It is natural. Conversely, it takes a conscious effort for man to move outside the normal bounds of his nature. It is unnatural.

If a man is unsaved and still in his sins, his nature is sinful and is at enmity with God. Enmity means to be in a state of opposition with something. Enmity is a relationship of ill will and hatred. The man who has a sin nature is the man who stands in continual opposition to God. Such a man's natural tendency is to do only evil and sin. If he chooses *good*, it is not from a pure heart or from pure motives. Such a man cannot please God, regardless of how religious he may be or how good he looks in the eyes of the world. For him, it takes no effort to act within the bounds of his sin nature:

BARELY EVIL——TO——VERY EVIL

If a man is saved, his old sin nature has passed away—it has been killed and it is dead. He has a new nature—Jesus' nature. His sins have been forgiven. He is no longer at enmity with God, but is now a friend of God and has been adopted into His family. And because he is a friend of God, he can please God through his new nature. Although such a man can choose to sin, it is a choice and he now does not have to sin. The natural tendency of his new nature is now:

GOOD——TO——HOLY

4. Resurrected With Jesus

A resurrected life is a powerful life.

(Romans 6:4) We were buried therefore with Him by baptism into death, in order that, just as Christ was raised from the dead by the glory of the Father, we too might walk in newness of life.

5. Crucifying Our Flesh

We have a new nature—Jesus' nature. But yet, we can still sin. How can this be?

This new nature is spiritual. It is wrapped in our old body and surrounded by our soul (mind, will, and emotions). We have a new inside, but the same old outside—our flesh. Our spirit has been redeemed, but our flesh—our body and our soul—is still in the process of being redeemed. We have the first fruits of the Holy Spirit living in our spirit as the down payment on our redemption, but our body still groans to be redeemed.

(Romans 8:22-23) For we know that the whole creation has been groaning together in the pains of childbirth until now. And not only the creation, but we ourselves, who have the first fruits of the Spirit, groan inwardly as we wait eagerly for adoption as sons, the redemption of our bodies.

When we sin, it is a choice made in the corruption of the flesh. A sinful choice can be influenced by demons or remain just a choice of the flesh. Either way, we are responsible.

That is why we must crucify the flesh daily. Crucifixion is one of the most agonizing forms of killing ever devised. It is a slow, deliberate draining away of life. When we crucify our flesh, our flesh will want to stop the process and end the pain. Our self-centered passions and desires will scream out to be allowed to live. But they must be killed each day and every day for us to walk successfully with Jesus.

The call to discipleship is a call to walk the narrow path of sanctification. It is a call to take up the cross daily and to die every moment to our flesh and all of its selfish, sinful desires. That is the walk of sanctification. That is the walk of a disciple.

6. Spirit Walking

A powerful life comes by walking in the Spirit and not the flesh. It is making decisions influenced by the Spirit and not by the flesh. It is submitting to the Spirit and not to the flesh.

(Galatians 5:25) If we live by the Spirit, let us also keep in step with in the Spirit.

We were created for relationships. God created us for a special relationship with Him through His Son, Jesus. For this relationship to flourish, we must share a common nature.

1) When you think of the *nature* of something, what words come to mind?

2) Look up the definition of *nature* as it is used in this context. How is the nature of something described?

3) The Bible tells us that every man in Adam (every man with a human father) is born with a *sin nature*. With the above definition in mind, what does this tell you about such men?

4) Why do you think that Jesus was born *without* a sin nature? How was this possible?

When something is dead, it ceases to exist. Yet, it is commonplace to hear Christians explain away their sinful failings saying, '*it is just my old sin nature*'. This is not true. It is impossible for something that Jesus has made dead to be alive and working in us.

5) When a man is '*born of the spirit*', what does this man receive in place of his dead sin nature?

6) Since a true believer has received a new, living nature from Jesus (His nature), how can we explain why that same person can and does sin?

7) Scripture tells us that we must daily die to our flesh and all that is in the world. It tells us that the means of accomplishing this is by taking up our own personal cross and crucifying our flesh. In light of these thoughts, what does **Luke 9:23-24** mean to you personally? Be specific.

(Luke 9:23-24) And he said to all, "If anyone would come after me, let him deny himself and take up his cross daily and follow me. For whoever would save his life will lose it, but whoever loses his life for my sake will save it."

8) How does sanctification tie into your thoughts on **Luke 9:23-24** and how is sanctification related to following Jesus?

† PRAYER THOUGHTS †

Are you ready to build a great relationship with Jesus by following His lead in your life? Ask Him to show you the things that must be crucified in your life so that you can walk the narrow path of holiness with Him.

TAKING STOCK

Musical instrument builders have long recognized that most modern instruments don't have the same feel or quality of tone as those that were produced a few hundred years ago. They have discovered that the major difference is the quality of wood used to produce the instrument. Most modern wood is inferior, primarily in its density. Old growth trees produce a denser, heavier wood that new growth forests cannot. The contrast is amazing. There is a distinct difference in quality, in weightiness.

When working with this wood to produce the final product, the differences become even more distinct. The harder wood takes longer to cut and shape. It is tough. The harder wood is less susceptible to warping over time. It holds its shape. The harder wood takes a finish better. It shines with a beautiful luster. The harder wood can take the knocks of life better. It is durable.

WHAT ARE WE MADE OF?

We are at a point in our journey through this book where it is a good time for us to take stock. The challenges that we face to become a disciple of Jesus have been clearly laid before us.

When we look in the mirror and see the man looking back at us, what is that man made of? Is it solid, old growth wood, or is it modern-day particleboard? Are we tough enough to stand against the adversity to our new walk with Jesus, adversity that will want to cut us apart and grind us down? Or are we lightweight, butter knife soft with little resistance? Are we resilient and steadfast, remaining true to the work Jesus has already done in us? Or are we subject to being easily warped by the heat and moisture of our circumstances? Do we reflect the shine of our Savior? Or do we peel easily and fade with time? Can we take the kicks and nicks of life as a disciple and still fulfill our calling as an instrument of quality? Or do we look and sound as though we are beat up and ready to be relegated to some second-hand existence?

PRESSING ON

Do we want to know the heart of Jesus? Are we ready to overcome the difficulties and challenges in our lives that impede our walk as His disciple?

Then what holds us back?

Some of it could be learning to do what we have done precious little of before—laying down our will. Laying it down and not taking it back again.

More likely, though, it could be learning to trust Jesus. Trusting Jesus can be a struggle. In our heads, we know we can. But in our hearts, we are not so sure: *What if He fails us now? What if we don't hear Him correctly? Is He really going to come through on the finances so we can accomplish all He has asked us to do? Or should we make alternate plans and decide for ourselves the path forward?* The list of questions can go on and on. And Jesus will keep on stretching and stretching. Until we think we will snap. Until we learn to fully trust Him.[1]

Jesus will take us through the process of learning to trust Him as fast as we will allow Him to do so. He will be there every step of the way. He knows our hearts. He knows if we are sincere in our trust. He sees all the way down into the hidden recesses of our souls. He honors sincerity and will do mighty miracles in our lives to get us where we need to be.

So, how do we overcome all the obstacles we have discussed so far?

Perseverance. The word means 'continued effort to do or to achieve something despite difficulties, failure, or opposition'. That is where we are at this point. It is time to see what we are made of.

This is the last chapter in this section. We have looked at the challenges that stand in every man's way to becoming a disciple. Jesus calls each of us to persevere through these challenges. To become steadfast in our pursuit of Him. To go against the flow of the compromising culture around us in the world and the placating culture in our church fellowships.

The difficulties begin with our surrender. We must lay down our self-will and the pridefulness that keeps it alive. We have nothing to be prideful about. Apart from Jesus, we have nothing and we are nothing. Then comes trust. Complete trust that Jesus has our best in mind. Finally, we must persevere and push through each progressive barrier in our way.

Take another look at the man in the mirror. How does he look? Ready?

It's time to walk with Jesus.

◆◆◆ CHAPTER NOTES ◆◆◆

Every once in a while, it is good to stop and see how we are doing in every area of our lives. Jesus has given us things to accomplish so we can become His disciple. How are we doing?

1. Trusting Jesus With Everything

It is hard for self-sufficient men to let go. We like being the pilot, with God as our co-pilot. As long as we are driving our lives and making the decisions, we at least know where we are going, we have a pretty good idea of how we want to get there, and we feel like things are under control. When Jesus takes the wheel, well, that is an altogether different story!

Every time it is pointed out to us that we are not trusting Jesus with something, we automatically point out all of the things we do trust Him with. But truly trusting Jesus is like a binary toggle electric wall switch. It is either all 'on' or all 'off'. It is not a variable dimmer switch where we can continue to dial it up a notch. We either trust Him or we TRUST HIM. Trusting Him is not really trusting Him. TRUSTING HIM is.

While truly trusting Jesus is binary, the experience of learning to trust Him is like a variable dimmer-type light switch. It is a process that Jesus takes us through where He slowly 'turns it up'. As we learn to trust Him more, He requires more and tests us more. All until we stand in that place where He wants us to be—that place where we TRUST HIM with everything.

Your walk with Jesus is not free. It comes with a cost. As you have worked your way through the book, *WATM?*, you have seen the challenges you face in your quest for a vibrant relationship with your Savior.

1) List these challenges as you see them.

2) As you consider these challenges, what feelings are you processing? Be specific.

3) If you dig way down beneath each of these feelings, is the base question behind them, *'Can I really trust Jesus?'*

4) Look up the definition of *trust*. What does it mean?

5) When you think of Jesus and consider His character as God, do you think He is trustworthy? Why or why not?

6) When you look back on the fruits—the outcomes—of your life when *you* were in control, do you think the God of the universe could have done a better job if He had been in control?

7) How has your pride and self-will been in the way of trusting Jesus to lead you every day? Be specific.

† PRAYER THOUGHTS †

We, as men, have no basis of trusting ourselves to persevere through the many challenges we face while walking closely with Jesus as His disciple. Our only hope and our only course is to trust in Him for all we will need along the way. Ask Jesus right now to help you to trust Him. Ask Him to give you the courage to persevere through the costs of being His disciple.

❧ PART 3 ❧
THE PROBLEM

We have discussed many topics so far. We have looked at our misconceptions and our distortions of the Godhead—distortions caused by our lack of holy curiosity about the reality of each Member of the Trinity. We have examined the struggles and problems that we as men face and the challenges to aggressively following our Savior. We saw Jesus' concern for us and understood, maybe for the first time, His power waiting to be released in our lives.

Are there any lingering doubts in the back of our minds about these truths? Deep down inside does a fear remain? A fear of stepping out and acting on these things? A fear that somehow we will get out on a limb and it will break under the weight of all that we must do to become a true disciple and crash into the middle of our crisis of renewal? A fear that our faith may be proven to be a mere hope without substance or validity? That none of this will work and our latter state will be worse than our present one? A fear that we will start out of the darkness and that this Jesus we discussed will not be all we need Him to be, stranding us exposed in a place where we cannot move forward and we cannot go back?

Jesus knows our fears. He knows our doubts. He knows our hesitancy. He sees us lingering in the valley of shadows between our past dark wilderness and the bright and shining mountaintop of God. He watches as we crouch like a soldier who is cautious about advancing out beyond the covering fire of his unit and exposing himself to destruction. He knows we are wary about moving beyond the familiar cover we have relied on for our security. He looks upon us as the doubts whispered in our hearts form into questions expressed in our minds: *Can Jesus do all of this for me? Will*

He do all of this for me? Does He really understand all my problems? Will He help me, or is this His chance to punish me for all that I have been? What will happen if I trust Him and step out exposed?

This section will provide a fresh look at the completeness of Jesus—a glimpse into all that He is.

Jesus is the answer. He is the solution to each problem and challenge we face. After all, He is the Alpha and the Omega. The Beginning and the End.

That leaves a lot of room for each of us in between.

2000 Years of Misunderstanding

Once a year, the world pauses at Christmas time.[1] Most people can fathom at least some of the meaning behind what has become an increasingly secularized celebration of Jesus' birth. After all, mankind marks history according to the time before His birth and the time since His birth. But how many people really know what happened in that stable so many years ago? How many really understand the significance of it all? How many comprehend who Jesus was then and who He is now?

Most people did not understand who Jesus was when He walked the dusty lands between Galilee, Samaria, and Judaea. Most people throughout history did not have an accurate concept of the Jesus they heard about, whether through their cultures, their churches, or their religions. Most people today do not know Jesus, even in Christian circles. They do not truly know Him beyond the vague notions. Beyond the myths. Beyond the preconceptions. Beyond the misconceptions.

Perhaps, we are among those who do not know Him as He is? Even after church membership classes. Even after a lifetime of regular church attendance. Even after witnessing to others. Even after serving in a local church body. Even after hundreds of sermons. Even after reading through the Bible multiple times. Even after calling upon Him to save our souls from sure damnation.

What Is in a Name?

A person's name has significance. It speaks to who that person is. In the Bible, this is particularly so. Sons and daughters were named with a purpose, not just because the name sounded good or was unique.

The name 'Jesus' means 'God is my salvation', 'Savior', or 'Deliverer'.[2] That is significant. It adds value. It provides insight.

Here is a partial list of other names Jesus is known by in the Bible.[3] Each name and title contained in it has meaning. Each is significant.

Everlasting Father, Mighty God, Prince of Peace, Wonderful Counselor, Branch, Refiner, Purifier, Immanuel (God with us), Nazarene, Bridegroom, Son of Man, Friend of Sinners, Lord of the Sabbath, Christ, King of the Jews, Holy One of God, Carpenter, Horn of Salvation, Consolation of Israel, Master, Son of David, Word, God, Lamb of God, Rabbi (Teacher), Son of God, King of Israel, Bread of God, Bread of Life, Living Bread, Light of the World, I AM, Door, Good Shepherd, Resurrection and Life, Teacher, Lord, Way, Truth, Life, True Vine, Author of Life, Lord of All, Deliverer, Power of God, Wisdom of God, Wisdom, Righteousness, Sanctification, Redemption, Foundation, Our Passover Lamb, First Fruits, Our Peace, Cornerstone, Image of the Invisible God, Firstborn of all Creation, Head of the Body (the Church), Hope of Glory, King of the Ages, One Mediator between God and Man, Blessed and only Sovereign, King of Kings, Lord of Lords, Great God and Savior, Heir of All Things, Apostle and High Priest of our Confession, Great High Priest, Source of Eternal Salvation, Founder and Perfecter of our Faith, Mediator of a New Covenant, Great Shepherd, Lord of Glory, Lamb Without Blemish or Spot, Chief Shepherd, Advocate, Propitiation, Faithful Witness, Firstborn of the Dead, Ruler of Kings, Alpha and Omega, Who Is and Who Was and Who Is to Come, The Almighty, Holy One, True One, The Amen, The Faithful and True Witness, Lion of the Tribe of Judah, Root of David, Lamb, Faithful and True, The First and the Last, The Beginning and the End, The Root and the Descendant of David, Bright Morning Star.

Isn't this astounding?

Take another look at each of these names and titles. An entire book could be written on their meaning and significance. And they are significant, especially to us who seek to know Him better. How can we follow someone we do not know? How can we know Him if we don't appreciate those names and titles by which He is called? The names and titles that Jesus, as the Word of God, gave to Himself?

COMMON MISUNDERSTANDINGS

When Jesus walked the earth, He was misunderstood.[4] Many people thought Him to be nothing more than a good man. A surprising number thought He had demons! The rulers and religious elite of the day saw Him as a threat to their position and their power over the people. Many called Him a blasphemer. They wanted to stone Him or throw Him off of high places. Some thought of Him only as a temporal king. Many sought Him out merely as a healer of their infirmities and sicknesses. More than a few knew He could cast out demons and came to Him specifically for this reason. His own brothers sarcastically challenged Him to go to Jerusalem and show Himself, knowing that the religious authorities would likely arrest Him or worse. His disciples were little better. They claimed He was the Messiah, the Son of God, but many times they did not act like they believed this. They were devastated when the Romans killed Him, and they feared the same thing would happen to them. Even after He rose from the dead, some did not believe that He had done so. Less than thirty years after His death, false teachers, twisted in their misunderstanding of Him, led many astray. People who were called by His name did not walk closely with Him, making His sacrifice less than what it was meant to be in their lives.

Jesus was misunderstood then. And He is even more misunderstood two thousand years removed from that time and place.

Today, people follow Jesus on their own customized plan. They pick and chose what they will and won't believe. They decide what they will do and what is just too much for them. They even select how they will do what they have decided to do. They have their own customized Jesus. They decide how much power He will have over their lives. They decide how much time He will get. But it does not end there. People then decide what type of church or denomination or belief system they will take Jesus out to on Sunday. The rest of the week, they keep Him safely out of sight.

Let us look at the list of names and titles again. And let our hearts break before Him who made us. Let tears of shame and sorrow roll down our cheeks. Let us grieve over our shallowness. Our conformity. Our lack of wanting to know His heart.

We misunderstand Jesus. We don't know Him. We don't comprehend who He really is.

Oh Lord Jesus, how did we stray so far from You?

I AM THAT I AM

Jesus made it clear who He was.[5] He spoke the words that *affirmed* His calling. He performed the acts that *confirmed* His calling. The Old Testament foretold His coming four thousand years before He arrived. It contains over one hundred prophesies about His coming. There should have been no surprise when Jesus came to earth. Mankind had plenty of notice.

Jesus clearly stated his calling when He first began His ministry.[6] He came to preach the good news that a holy God was willing to be reconciled to sinful man, like a year of

212

Jubilee (the Israelite celebration every 50 years where slaves would be set free, debts would be cancelled, and family property returned). He came to heal. Body and soul. Physical infirmities and emotional wounds. He came to tell those held captive by Satan how they could be set free and how they could walk with Him. He came to give understanding to those devoid of understanding—spiritual understanding of who God is, spiritual understanding of the things around them and how they fit into His plan of time and space, spiritual understanding of each man's place in that plan. He came to free those who were oppressed by demons—true freedom from them, not accommodation of them. A freedom that begins with the understanding that demons are real and they enslave men. His message remains a clear message.

Jesus claimed to be God Almighty Himself. He did not hide it. Those around Him heard this. Those who wanted to believe this fact had ample opportunity by the witness of the miracles He performed, in all of the deeds He did, and in all of the words He spoke. John says in his Gospel that only a fraction of the things that occurred were written down because 'the world itself could not contain the books that would be written' if everything Jesus did was to be documented.[6] That is an important and sobering thought.

A NEW UNDERSTANDING

Most men are not aware of who Jesus is. Most have not taken the time to study the Scriptures to understand their description of Jesus and all that He did. If we would do so, we would catch a glimpse of Jesus the Son of God as the Man, the Warrior, the Deliverer, the Healer, the Master, and the Lover. We would start to see how He operated. We would begin to fathom His complexities as both God and man. We would see the different aspects of His personality on display. We would see that Jesus was complex in His humanity and not a two-dimensional visage of gentleness and decorum that we see in paintings. We would see His tenderness. We would see His stern side. We would see His wrath. We would see His love of us and His hatred of our sin. We would see His patience with our frailties and His disgust with our willfulness. We would see Him laugh with joy and weep in sorrow. We would see how He organized His followers into hierarchies and His use of the chain of command. We would see Him in times of exhaustion, and we would see Him in times of rest.

And even in all of this seeing, we would not have a complete picture because what we read about Jesus is only a very small fraction of what transpired during the thirty or so years that He walked on this earth. How many books would it take to fill the world? More than we can count! Yes, we have only a glimpse into all that Jesus did, said, and was.

Are we not guilty of creating Jesus in our image? It does not matter if that image is from our common culture or from our church or from our traditions or from our denomination. Have we all not done this? Have we allowed our familiarity to rule the day in contempt? Have we decided how much there is to Jesus? Have we placed limits on Him? Have we defined the rules of engagement between Him and us?

Have we put Jesus in a box built with human hands?

There is more to Jesus than most of us have seen. There is more to having a relationship with Him than the crumbs we have been eating from His feast table. Much more. And the great part is that every man can have as much of Jesus as he wants to have.

Let us explore. Let us come to know Him as He really is.

❖❖❖ CHAPTER NOTES ❖❖❖

1. Night Of Promises Fulfilled

Nobody knows the actual night that Jesus was born. There are a few theories on how the date was fixed to December 25th, but they are theories only. It really does not matter. It is the date that we celebrate His birth. There are four specific Old Testament prophecies surrounding Jesus' birth.

(Genesis 3:15) "And I will put enmity between you [Satan] and the woman, and between your offspring and her Offspring [Jesus]; He shall bruise your head, and you shall bruise His heel."

(Isaiah 7:14) Therefore the Lord Himself will give you a sign. Behold, the virgin shall conceive and bear a Son, and shall call His name Immanuel.

(Isaiah 11:1) There shall come forth a Shoot from the stump of Jesse, and a Branch from his roots shall bear fruit.

(Micah 5:2-3) But you, O Bethlehem Ephrathah, who are too little to be among the clans of Judah, from you shall come forth for Me One who is to be Ruler in Israel, Whose coming forth is from of old, from ancient days.

2. The Name Of Jesus

(Matthew 1:21-23) 'She will bear a Son, and you shall call His name Jesus, for He will save His people from their sins.' All this took place to fulfill what the Lord had spoken by the prophet: "Behold, the virgin shall conceive and bear a Son, and they shall call His name Immanuel" (which means, God with us).

3. His Names Are Wonderful

(Isaiah 9:6) For to us a Child is born, to us a Son is given; and the government will be upon His shoulder, and His name will be called Wonderful Counselor, Mighty God, Everlasting Father, Prince of Peace.

(Jeremiah 23:5) Behold, the days are coming, declares the LORD, when I will raise for David a righteous Branch, and He shall reign as King and deal wisely, and shall execute

justice and righteousness in the land.

(Malachi 3:3) He will sit as a refiner and a purifier of silver, and He will purify the sons of Levi and refine them like gold and silver, and they will bring offerings in righteousness to the LORD.

(Matthew 1:23) "Behold, the virgin shall conceive and bear a Son, and they shall call His name Immanuel" (which means, God with us).

(Matthew 2:23) And he went and lived in a city called Nazareth, so that what was spoken by the prophets might be fulfilled, that He would be called a Nazarene.

(Matthew 9:15a) And Jesus said to them, "Can the wedding guests mourn as long as the bridegroom is with them?"

(Matthew 11:19) "The Son of Man came eating and drinking, and they say, 'Look at Him! A glutton and a drunkard, a friend of tax collectors and sinners!' Yet wisdom is justified by her deeds."

(Matthew 12:8) "For the Son of Man is Lord of the Sabbath."

(Matthew 16:16) Simon Peter replied, "You are the Christ, the Son of the living God."

(Matthew 27:37) And over His head they put the charge against Him, which read, "This is Jesus, the King of the Jews."

(Mark 1:24) "What have You to do with us, Jesus of Nazareth? Have You come to destroy us? I know who You are—the Holy One of God."

(Mark 6:3) "Is this not the carpenter, the Son of Mary and brother of James and Joses and Judas and Simon? And are not His sisters here with us?" So they took offense at Him.

(Luke 1:69) And has raised up a horn of salvation for us in the house of His servant David.

(Luke 2:25-26) Now there was a man in Jerusalem, whose name was Simeon, and this man was righteous and devout, waiting for the Consolation of Israel, and the Holy Spirit was upon him. And it had been revealed to him by the Holy Spirit that he would not see death before he had seen the Lord's Christ.

(Luke 17:13) And [they, the ten lepers] lifted up their voices, saying, "Jesus, Master, have mercy on us."

(Luke 18:38) And he cried out, "Jesus, Son of David, have mercy on me!"

(John 1:1) In the beginning was the Word, and the Word was with God, and the Word was God.

(John 1:29) The next day he [John the Baptist] saw Jesus coming toward him, and said, "Behold, the Lamb of God, who takes away the sin of the world!"

(John 1:38b) And they said to Him, "Rabbi" (which means Teacher), "where are You staying?"

(John 1:49) Nathanael answered Him, "Rabbi, You are the Son of God! You are the King of Israel!"

(John 6:33) "For the bread of God is He who comes down from heaven and gives life to the world."

(John 6:35a) And Jesus said to them, "I am the bread of life."

(John 6:51a) "I am the living bread that came down from heaven."

(John 8:12) Again Jesus spoke to them again, saying, "I am the light of the world. Whoever follows Me will not walk in darkness, but will have the light of life."

(John 8:58) Jesus said to them, "Truly, truly, I say to you, before Abraham was, I AM."

(John 10:9) "I am the door. If anyone enters by Me, he will be saved and will go in and out and find pasture."

(John 10:11) "I am the good shepherd. The good shepherd lays down His life for the sheep."

(John 11:25) Jesus said to her, "I am the resurrection and the life. Whoever believes in Me, though he die, yet shall he live."

(John 13:13) "You call Me Teacher and Lord, and you are right, for so I am."

(John 14:6) Jesus said to him, "I am the way, and the truth, and the life. No one comes to the Father except through Me."

(John 15:1) "I am the true vine, and My Father is the vinedresser."

(Acts 3:15) And you killed the Author of life, whom God raised from the dead. To this we are witnesses.

(Acts 10:36) As for the word which He sent to Israel, preaching good news of peace through Jesus Christ (He is Lord of all).

(Romans 11:26) And in this way all Israel will be saved, as it is written, "The Deliverer will come from Zion, He will banish ungodliness from Jacob."

(1 Corinthians 1:24) But to those who are called, both Jews and Greeks, Christ the power of God and the wisdom of God.

(1 Corinthians 1:30) And because of Him you are in Christ Jesus, who became to us wisdom from God, righteousness and sanctification and redemption.

(1 Corinthians 3:11) For no one can lay a foundation other than that which is laid, which is Jesus Christ.

(1 Corinthians 5:7) Cleanse out the old leaven that you may be a new lump, as you really are unleavened. For Christ, our Passover lamb, has been sacrificed.

(1 Corinthians 15:23) But each in his own order: Christ the firstfruits, then at His coming those who belong to Christ.

(Ephesians 2:14) For He Himself is our peace, Who has made us both one and has broken down in His flesh the dividing wall of Hostility.

(Ephesians 2:20) Built on the foundation of the apostles and prophets, Christ Jesus Himself being the cornerstone.

(Colossians 1:15) He is the image of the invisible God, the firstborn of all creation.

(Colossians 1:18a) And He is the head of the body, the church.

(Colossians 1:27) To them God chose to make known how great among the Gentiles are the riches of the glory of this mystery, which is Christ in you, the hope of glory.

(1 Timothy 1:17) To the King of the ages, immortal, invisible, the only God, be honor and glory forever and ever. Amen.

(1 Timothy 2:5) For there is one God, and there is one Mediator between God and men, the Man Christ Jesus.

(1 Timothy 6:15) Which He will display at the proper time— He who is the blessed and only Sovereign, the King of kings and Lord of lords.

(Titus 2:13) Waiting for our blessed hope, the appearing of the glory of our great God and Savior Jesus Christ.

(Hebrews 1:2) But in these last days He has spoken to us by His Son, whom He appointed the heir of all things, through

whom also He created the world.

(Hebrews 3:1) Therefore, holy brothers, you who share in a heavenly calling, consider Jesus, the Apostle and High Priest of our confession.

(Hebrews 4:14) Since then we have a great High Priest who has passed through the heavens, Jesus, the Son of God, let us hold fast our confession.

(Hebrews 5:9) And being made perfect, He became the source of eternal salvation to all who obey Him.

(Hebrews 12:2a) Looking to Jesus, the founder and perfecter of our faith.

(Hebrews 12:24) And to Jesus the Mediator of a new covenant, and to the sprinkled blood that speaks a better word than the blood of Abel.

(Hebrews 13:20) Now may the God of peace who brought again from the dead our Lord Jesus, the great Shepherd of the sheep, by the blood of the eternal covenant...

(James 2:1) My brothers, show no partiality as you hold the faith in our Lord Jesus Christ, the Lord of glory.

(1 Peter 1:19) But with the precious blood of Christ, like that of a lamb without blemish or spot.

(1 Peter 5:4) And when the Chief Shepherd appears, you will receive the unfading crown of glory.

(1st John 2:1b) But if anyone does sin, we have an Advocate with the Father, Jesus Christ the righteous.

(1 John 2:2) He is the propitiation for our sins, and not for ours only but also for the sins of the whole world.

(Revelation 1:5) And from Jesus Christ the faithful witness, the firstborn of the dead, and the ruler of kings on earth.

(Revelation 1:8) "I am the Alpha and the Omega," says the Lord God, "who is and who was and who is to come, the Almighty."

(Revelation 3:7a) "And to the angel of the church in Philadelphia write: 'The words of the holy One, the true One.'"

(Revelation 3:14b) 'The words of the Amen, the faithful and true witness, the beginning of God's creation.'

(Revelation 5:5) And one of the elders said to me, "Weep no

more; behold, the Lion of the tribe of Judah, the Root of David, has conquered, so that He can open the scroll and its seven seals."

(Revelation 5:6) And between the throne and the four living creatures and among the elders I saw a Lamb standing, as though it had been slain, with seven horns and with seven eyes, which are the seven Spirits of God sent out into all the earth.

(Revelation 19:11) Then I saw heaven opened, and behold, a white horse! The One sitting on it was called Faithful and True, and in righteousness He judges and makes war.

(Revelation 22:13) "I am the Alpha and the Omega, the First and the Last, the Beginning and the End."

(Revelation 22:16b) "I am the root and the descendant of David, the bright morning star."

4. What People Thought Of Jesus

Solomon said that there was nothing new under the sun. What people think of Jesus today is not much different than what they thought of Him two thousand years ago.

(Luke 18:18) And a ruler asked Him, "Good Teacher, what must I do to inherit eternal life?"

(Mark 8:27-29) And Jesus went on with His disciples to the villages of Caesarea Philippi. And on the way He asked His disciples, "Who do people say that I am?" And they told Him, "John the Baptist; and others say, Elijah; and others, one of the prophets." And He asked them, "But who do you say that I am?" Peter answered Him, "You are the Christ."

(John 7:20a) The crowd answered, "You have a demon!"

(John 11:47-48) So the chief priests and the Pharisees gathered the council and said, "What are we to do? For this man performs many signs. If we let Him go on like this, everyone will believe in Him, and the Romans will come and take away both our place and our nation."

(Matthew 9:3) And behold, some of the scribes said to themselves, "This Man is blaspheming."

(John 10:31) The Jews picked up stones again to stone Him.

(John 6:15) Perceiving then that they were about to come and take Him by force to make Him king, Jesus withdrew again

to the mountain by Himself.

(Matthew 12:15b) And many followed Him, and He healed them all.

(Matthew 8:16) That evening they brought to Him many who were oppressed by demons [demonized], and He cast out the spirits with a word and healed all who were sick.

(John 7:3-5) So His brothers said to Him, "Leave here and go to Judea, that Your disciples also may see the works You are doing. For no one works in secret if he seeks to be known openly. If You do these things, show Yourself to the world." For not even His brothers believed in Him.

(John 20:24-25) Now Thomas, one of the Twelve, called the Twin, was not with them when Jesus came. So the other disciples told him, "We have seen the Lord." But he said to them, "Unless I see in His hands the mark of the nails, and place my finger into the mark of the nails, and place my hand into His side, I will never believe."

5. I AM

Jesus claimed to be the Son of God and God Himself. He did this plainly and emphatically.

(John 8:58) Jesus said to them, "Truly, truly, I say to you, before Abraham was, I am."

6. Jesus' Calling

(Luke 4:18-19) "The Spirit of the LORD is upon Me, because He has anointed Me to proclaim good news to the poor. He has sent Me to proclaim liberty to the captives and recovering of sight to the blind, to set at liberty those who are oppressed. To proclaim the year of the Lord's favor."

7. Many Things Not Written Down

There is more to Jesus than what we can read about in the Gospels.

(John 20:30; 21:25) Now Jesus did many other signs in the presence of the disciples, which are not written in this book...Now there are also many other things that Jesus did. Were every one of them to be written, I suppose that the world itself could not contain the books that would be written.

◆◆◆ STUDY GUIDE ◆◆◆

Most of the people groups on planet earth have heard something about Jesus. He may be more familiar or less familiar, but His name is firmly rooted in the history of mankind. But familiarity is fickle. It is convenient. And it can be very false.

1) Read **Mark 8:27-29**. If Jesus asked you this question, how would you respond?

(Mark 8:27-29) And Jesus went on with his disciples to the villages of Caesarea Philippi. And on the way he asked his disciples, "Who do people say that I am?" And they told him, "John the Baptist; and others say, Elijah; and others, one of the prophets." And he asked them, "But who do you say that I am?" Peter answered him, "You are the Christ."

2) Think about your understanding of who Jesus is. Number each category below, 1 though 10, indicating the volume of your knowledge about Jesus obtained through each source *(1 is little knowledge; 10 is much knowledge).*

Bible

Pastor

Jesus Himself

Books

Movies

Friends

Teachers

Denomination

Family

Seminars

3) On a scale of 1 to 10, rate your level of understanding about who Jesus really is.

Little Understanding   1 <<—>> 10   Great Understanding

4) Why did you give yourself that score?

5) Given your level of understanding about who Jesus is, how do you plan to get to know Him better?

† PRAYER THOUGHTS †

Jesus does not require us to know everything about who He is before we begin to follow Him. He only requires a surrendered will, a teachable spirit, and an obedient heart. If you really want to know Jesus, ask Him to begin to show Himself to you in a mighty way. And then be ready to learn, and do all that He says.

As you grow in your understanding of who Jesus is, you will see that He is the only true answer to the challenges you face.

JESUS THE MAN

Who is this Jesus? Do we understand? Do we have an answer?

At their core, these are questions of His relevance to us as humans on this little planet moving through the vastness of space. If we grew up on religiosity, Jesus might be to us this person who is far, far away. We might see Him as the God who dwells just beyond our outstretched arms. We might perceive Him as a figure that is larger than life—almost mythical and not quite relevant to the needs of our modern humanity. We might fear Him only because we believe He has the power to forgive our sins and would somehow limit His forgiveness toward us based on our actions of merit.

Would we realize that He was God? Yes. But our concept of Him could be blurred by the teachings of our churches and the accumulated theology from two thousand years of man's imperfect reasoning. Would we realize that He was a man? Well, that might be a little more difficult, for how could a powerful God become a mere man? How could divinity dwell with humanity in the same shell of earthly dust? While we could know this to be factual, we might not comprehend the fullness of this reality for our lives. And if this idea seemed vague in its reality to us, we might not take stock of the substance this should have in our lives. And Jesus being fully man is a substantial truth for all of us in our quest to walk with Him as a disciple.

Why? What bearing does Jesus' humanity have on our walk?

Jesus' humanity is significant both as the means of our salvation and our ongoing sanctification.

Jesus had to dwell on earth in fully human form so that the justice of His Father regarding the sin of mankind could be satisfied. God the Father's holiness required the sinless sacrifice of a perfectly lived life on earth to pay the price of redemption for our fallen humanity.[1] This is the means of our salvation. And Jesus had to dwell on earth fully as a man so we could see that it was possible to live a life of victory over sin...that we *could* successfully walk with Him regardless of our starting point. This is the means of our continuing sanctification—Jesus' power working in us through the Holy Spirit day by day.[2]

Jesus was a man when He came to earth—fully a man.[3] Of course, He was God as well, but He emptied Himself—He voluntarily accepted the limitations of being human, and He relied on His Father for any mighty power of God that would flow through Him—and became flesh and blood just like us. And He was like us in all things, except He did not sin.[4] This is a fact that our mind can accept at face value, but one it cannot comprehend from our human experience. Sin is intertwined in our lives from our earliest days. David said in the Psalms that we are conceived in sin.[5] Until Jesus saves us, sin is our master. After Jesus saves us, we have His power over sin.[6] Even so, we continue to struggle in our flesh against sin until the day we die.

Jesus dwelt with our humanness in all of its fullness. He experienced the same world around Him as we do around us. He had to overcome Satan in the same flesh as we have as regenerated believers so that no one could claim that God required an obedience that no man could produce. Yet, in all of this living as a human on earth for over thirty years, Jesus did not sin. He was tempted, but He did not sin. The scriptures are clear on this point. Jesus Himself said that Satan could find no way to get a hold on Him.[7]

Why is this important?

If Jesus wasn't fully man, how could He understand our inner most challenges? If He were somehow insulated from the struggles that we encounter in our lives, what would He have to offer to us in time of trouble? If Jesus did not experience the humanity around Him as a man would have experienced it, how could He relate to us and what we are experiencing?

Underneath all of these questions is the issue of 'trust'. If Jesus was not fully man, how could we ever trust Him with our humanity?

MORE THAN SUFFICIENT

Now that we know the path out of darkness and into light, now that we see we can finally walk with Jesus where He leads instead of groping in the darkness on the path of our choosing, now that we own the hope of escaping the chains holding us down, why do we hesitate? Why do we pause? Why do we vacillate?

Can we trust Jesus?

It may take a long time to learn to trust Jesus beyond the words and the superficialities. Maybe we are not sure we can trust Him. Perhaps we are not sure we want to trust Him. The ramifications of laying everything down at Jesus' feet swirl in our heads. We struggle to bring ourselves to the place of fully trusting Jesus. We have never trusted Him before like we need to trust Him now. We do not know how.

Our walk as a disciple is a matter of trust in Jesus.[8] Trust that He understands. Trust that He is completely sufficient. Trust that He has overcome what we face in our lives. Trust that He has walked on this same path with others. Trust that He has seen, even felt, the anguish of our hearts. Trust that He will do only what is for our good.[9] Trust that everything He does for us is done out of love and that everything He does not do for us is done out of love. Trust that Jesus is love.

Jesus sanctified His humanity by being filled with the Holy Spirit and fully surrendering His will to His Father in heaven. He used His sanctified life to defeat temptation and remain sinless. Even though God Himself, He didn't use His divinity to overrule His humanity. He lived in His humanity as we do. And because of this, He can relate to us. Fully. And we can trust in Him. Fully.

JESUS GOT HIS HANDS DIRTY

Jesus didn't stand around and watch the world go by two thousand years ago in order to remain sinless. He engaged it. He was not some iconic stained-glass window figure in a sterile white robe and halo that watched life with amused detachment.

Jesus was 100% boy when He was growing up. He crawled. He played. He ran. He jumped. He wrestled. He fell and scraped His knees. He climbed trees. He ate food and drank liquids. He breathed oxygen. He had chores to do around the carpenter shop. He even got sick at times.

Jesus grew up in a family. He had brothers and sisters.[10] Yet, He lived among His imperfect family members with His perfect compassion and His perfect responses to their fallen natures. He was the oldest son and the older brother. He fulfilled His role in His earthly family with wisdom, humility, and compassion.

Jesus was 100% man as well.[11] And as a man, He walked with other men. He mingled with those deep in sin. He ate with social outcasts. He dealt with every conceivable illness, disease, and infirmity. He touched those who were untouchable. He was present among the multitudes. He challenged the established religion of His day. He debated with the religious leaders about their misguided understandings, views, and actions. He dealt with the failings of His disciples—their wrong attitudes and views, their pride in themselves, and their ignorance of God.

Jesus had emotions, too. He wept. He laughed. He felt sorrow. He was filled with joy. He got angry. He was compassionate. He was full of zeal.

He even became weary at times—exhausted by the travel, tried by the bickering between His disciples, drained by the stubborn unbelief of the religious leaders and the merely curious, fatigued by the press of humanity upon His humanity. So, He would withdraw by Himself to commune with His Father.

Then He would get right back to His Father's business.

Yes. Jesus got His hands dirty when He walked on this earth.

But what about now? What about today, right here, right now, with us?

JESUS STILL GETS HIS HANDS DIRTY

Jesus is active in the affairs of men today. He works with men to fulfill the plans His Father has so that His Father can be glorified. He dispatches His angels to do His bidding. He wars against the forces of evil as the Captain of the angelic host.

And He deals with us. Mere men. Imperfect men. Sinful men.

When Jesus walked on the earth twenty centuries ago, He developed relationships. Some of these were close, while others were not. All were relationships of the heart, because Jesus always operates on a heart basis. He drew close to those who drew close to Him. A few special men formed a tight-knit group and walked with Him. They shared the commonalities of life together. The talked. They ate. They fellowshipped. Sometimes they were just quiet as they sat around a fire at night, perhaps watching the moon rising out of the evening mist over the hills. They traveled together. They sailed together. They fished together. They worked together. They weathered storms together. They were accepted as He was. They were persecuted as He was. They were rejected as He was.

If these things were true then, why would we think they are not today? If Jesus had close relationships with men of that day—shoulder to shoulder and heart to heart—why do we refuse to believe that the same would be so today? If He took the time to correct and teach His disciples of that time personally, why do we think He is more or less hands-off with us today? Is it because we reckon Him only as God and forget that He shared humanity with us? Or is it something else?

This concept of a personal Jesus without the up-close and personal involvement with us in our daily lives is a lie propagated by Satan and his demons.[12] But it is a common lie that is commonly believed—even though it is both illogical and does not line up with His call to discipleship.

Jesus is just as involved with men today as He was two thousand years ago. Man to man. Face to face. But as with the men of that era, He draws close to those who draw close to Him, those who are willing to have a relationship of the heart with their Creator.[13] These relationships are not arms-length relationships. They are not separated earth-to-heaven associations where we as men cannot quite reach to Him as God. No. They are every bit as real and personal as they were to Peter, John, and Paul.

Do we believe the lie that 'personal' means 'personal' except in the case of a relationship with Jesus where it does not mean 'personal'?

We can come to know better by way of His graciousness

toward us. As we seek Him, Jesus will reveal Himself to us. As we yield more of our life to Him and keep seeking Him, He will draw closer to us. He will teach us during these times together. He will show us the hardness of our hearts and the areas in our lives that need improvement.

As we continue our great adventures together, He will teach us what we need to learn. He will show us what we need to know. He will tell us what we need to do. He will lead us where we need to go. In all of these interactions, we must be seeking His presence and company. We must be inviting Him into the daily events of our lives. We can have as much of Jesus as we want.

These times with Jesus will not be figments of our imagination as some would claim. They will be real experiences, ones we cannot will into existence. Jesus will call us to them. Then, He will conduct and direct them. During these times together, Jesus will show us some of His great plans for our lives and those for our families. Through them, He may foretell some future events associated with our destinies.

The information we gain will be called extra-biblical revelation by some. We will be accused of adding to our understanding of Jesus things that are to be limited by the Scriptures. We will be told we are adding to His Word. They will tell us that we tread on very precarious ground because of this. Some may go as far as to neatly frame all of it as a known schism of the Faith and label it as false teaching. We should understand this and be prepared.

And then we should proceed undaunted.

Most of what Jesus will tell us during our times together will concern us, our families, and some of His plans. Additionally, He may speak or give us visions on other subjects, as He did in times of old. These times of revealing will enhance our understanding by way of explanation, but they will never contradict His written Word. This is how a real relationship with Jesus works. One that is akin to His relationships with the original disciples.

Jesus is real. He still gets His hands dirty. He deals with us both man to man and God to man. This relationship with Him is not unique to a few. It is open to all who are daily laying their lives down at His feet to follow Him as His disciples. It is open to all who seek Him with their whole heart.

The eyes of the Lord search diligently over the whole earth to strengthen those whose hearts are truly His.[14]

Jesus was fully human. This truth is a requirement for our salvation. He had to experience humanity in all of its fullness and overcome that humanity to perfectly fulfill the requirements of God's holy law. Most of us acknowledge Jesus' humanity and then quickly move on to His divinity. In doing so, we lose much of His essence. This does damage to our relationship with Him by removing the important element of His being a man. Just like us. Our relationship tends toward the *impersonal* as a result.

1. The Perfect Sacrifice For Sin

God's perfect justice demanded a perfect sacrifice. Jesus' sinless life as a man fulfilled the requirement. This perfect life was propitiation for our sin—it atoned, or paid the price for our imperfect lives before a holy God and brought us into favor with Him.

(Hebrews 2:17) Therefore He had to be made like His brothers in every respect, so that He might become a merciful and faithful high priest in the service of God, to make propitiation for the sins of the people.

(1 Peter 1:18-19) Knowing that you were ransomed from the futile ways inherited from your forefathers, not with perishable things such as silver or gold, but with the precious blood of Christ, like that of a lamb without blemish or spot.

(2 Corinthians 5:21) For our sake He made Him to be sin Who knew no sin, so that in Him we might become the righteousness of God.

2. The Source Of Jesus' Power

Jesus is the eternal God-man. He always existed in the form of a man and will so forever. He is both fully God and fully man. Though He was fully God, in order to be the perfect sacrifice for our sin, He had to voluntarily take on the limitations of humanity as He lived His perfect life twenty centuries ago. In other words, He had to empty Himself and then be filled with the Holy Spirit each minute of each day so that the Father's power could flow through Him. In doing so, He subjected His own will to that of His Father in heaven, doing only what His Father told Him to do and saying only what His Father told Him to say. He lived a sinless life through the power of the Holy Spirit, even though a man.

(John 8:28-29) Then Jesus said to them, "When you have lifted up the Son of Man, then you will know that I am He, and that I do nothing on My own authority, but speak just as the Father taught Me. And He who sent Me is with Me. He has not left Me alone, for I always do the things that are pleasing to Him."

3. Fully Man

Jesus dwelt on earth as a man. He experienced it as we do. That is why He can sympathize with us. That is why He is worthy of our trust.

(John 1:14a) And the Word became flesh and dwelt among us.

(Hebrews 2:17-18) Therefore He had to be made like His brothers in every respect, so that He might become a merciful and faithful high priest in the service of God, to make propitiation for the sins of the people. For because He Himself has suffered when tempted, He is able to help those who are being tempted.

(Hebrews 4:15) For we do not have a high priest who is unable to sympathize with our weaknesses, but one who in every respect has been tempted as we are, yet without sin.

4. Jesus Was Sinless

Jesus did not sin. He could sin, but He chose not to. He had to rely on the power of the Holy Spirit working in and through Him in all things. This was foretold by the prophet Isaiah and lived out by Jesus upon the earth.

(Isaiah 53:9) And they made His grave with the wicked and with a rich man in his death, although He had done no violence, and there was no deceit in His mouth.

(1 John 3:5) You know that He appeared in order to take

away sins, and in Him there is no sin.

(1 Peter 2:21-23) For to this you have been called, because Christ also suffered for you, leaving you an example, so that you might follow in His steps. He committed no sin, neither was deceit found in His mouth. When He was reviled, did not revile in return; when He suffered, He did not threaten, but continued entrusting Himself to Him who judges justly.

5. Conceived In Sin

The sin nature of man is passed down from Adam to all men and women through their earthly fathers at the moment of conception. Jesus did not come by way of an earthly father, but by God the Father Himself. Because of this, Jesus did not inherit a sin nature from a man. He had a sinless nature. Unlike Jesus, we were brought forth in sin and we do according to that nature until we are set free at salvation and are given a new nature—His nature. Then, sin becomes a choice for us.

(Psalm 51:5) Behold, I was brought forth in iniquity, and in sin did my mother conceive me.

6. Jesus Sets Us Free From The Slavery Of Sin

Every man is born a slave of sin until Jesus sets Him free at the moment of salvation.

(John 8:34, 36) Jesus answered them, "Truly, truly, I say to you, everyone who practices sin is a slave of sin...So if the Son sets you free, you will be free indeed."

7. Satan Could Not Find A Fault In Jesus

Because Jesus did not have a sin nature and chose not to sin, Satan could find nothing in Jesus to accuse Him of in order to negate the perfect sacrifice.

(John 14:30) "I will no longer talk much with you, for the ruler of this world is coming. He has no claim on Me."

8. Trusting Jesus

Trusting Jesus will likely be the biggest struggle of all we go through on the road to discipleship. It is because we are used to being in control. We like being in control and we depend on it. Even if things are not going well, at least we are in the middle of it all, trying to wrestle everything where we wish it to be. With Jesus in control, things are not that way. It is His program. It is His method. It is His timeline.

We may struggle to trust Him as we leave the falseness and posing behind to become an authentic man. The exposure without cover and the resulting vulnerability can be unnerving. We may struggle to trust Him with our feelings and our wounds.

But He is worthy of our trust. He was fully man Himself. He understands.

9. All Jesus Does Is For Our Good

(Romans 8:28) And we know that for those who love God all things work together for good, for those who are called according to His purpose.

10. Jesus' Family

Jesus grew up in an imperfect family. At times, they thought He was losing His grip on reality. His brothers did not believe He was God the Son until after He was killed and raised from the dead. Many of us did not come from a healthy family background. Jesus understands.

(Matthew 13:55-56a) Is not this the carpenter's son? Is not His mother called Mary? And are not His brothers James and Joseph and Simon and Judas? And are not all His sisters with us?

11. Jesus Was 100% Man

Jesus was a man. He experienced humanity. He spent real time with real people. He worked in the world among the multitudes. He was confrontational when it was required. His heart was broken more than once. He became indignant and angry. He had great compassion. He became tired. He needed to spend time with His Father

(Matthew 9:10-11) And as Jesus reclined at table in the house, behold, many tax collectors and sinners came and

236

were reclining with Jesus and His disciples. And when the Pharisees saw this, they said to His disciples, "Why does your Teacher eat with tax collectors and sinners?"

(Matthew 12:15b) And many followed Him, and He healed them all.

(Matthew 23:27-28) "Woe to you, scribes and Pharisees, hypocrites! For you are like whitewashed tombs, which outwardly appear beautiful, but within are full of dead people's bones and all uncleanness. So you also outwardly appear righteous to others, but within you are full of hypocrisy and lawlessness."

(John 11:35) Jesus wept.

(Matthew 23:37-38) "O Jerusalem, Jerusalem, the city that kills the prophets and stones those who are sent to it! How often would I have gathered your children together as a hen gathers her brood under her wings, and you were not willing! See, your house is left to you desolate."

(Mark 10:14, 16) But when Jesus saw it, He was indignant and said to them, "Let the children come to Me; do not hinder them, for to such belongs the kingdom of God"...And He took them in His arms and blessed them, laying His hands on them.

(Matthew 16:23) But He turned and said to Peter, "Get behind Me, Satan! You are a hindrance to me. For you are not setting your mind on the things of God, but on the things of man."

(Matthew 14:14) And when Jesus went out He saw a great multitude; and He was moved with compassion for them, and healed their sick.

(Mark 1:35) And rising very early in the morning, while it was still dark, He departed and went out to a desolate place, and there He prayed.

12. Our Own Personal Jesus

Either Jesus is a personal God or He is not. Either He has a personal relationship with believers or He does not. To have a relationship is to have something that connects the participants together. When something is personal, it is carried on between individuals directly. It is private. It relates to the people involved. So, having a personal relationship is not a casual matter that is generic in nature. It is not a group activity. No. It is a close kinship where nothing is held back. It is honest. It speaks of time spent together. It speaks of closeness. It speaks of a strong attachment. One to One.

Our personal relationship with Jesus will embody all of these characteristics, and more. It will be vibrant. It will be intense. We will spend quality time together face to face. This is a personal relationship with Jesus.

13. Draw Near To God

(James 4:8a) Draw near to God and He will draw near to you.

14. The Eyes Of The Lord Are Upon You

(2 Chronicles 16:9a) For the eyes of the LORD run to and fro throughout the whole earth, to give strong support to those whose heart is blameless toward Him.

The concept of Jesus being fully a man is difficult to grasp. Its significance has been lost across the years until the power it should unleash in our lives remains largely untapped. We have come to believe our words, *'Yes, Jesus was a man, BUT He also was God.'* And these words have become the excuse to crawl through a life of failure and spiritual impotence instead of running a victorious race.

1) Stop and think about how you see Jesus. Is He real? Is He far away? Explain.

2) Envision Jesus as a boy. What do you see?

3) Envision Jesus as a man. What do you see?

4) Make a list of your challenges and struggles as a man. Do you think that Jesus experienced the same things when He walked upon the earth as a man?

5) Make a list of the feelings you experience as a man. Do you think that Jesus was immune to these when He walked upon the earth as a man?

6) Scripture tells us that Jesus was faced with the same challenges as us as a man (not as God). How was it that He overcame these challenges and did not sin?

7) How can you apply the same principles in your life? Be specific.

8) Jesus desires to walk with you today. What keeps you from Him? Make a list of sins, wrong thinking, and wrong attitudes that are hindering your relationship with Jesus.

† PRAYER THOUGHTS †

Seek Jesus' forgiveness through true repentance. Ask Him to reveal Himself to you. And then look for Him. Listen for His voice. Draw near to Him and He will draw near to you.

Jesus the Warrior

Military history captures the imagination. Adventure. Heroes. Battles. Feats of bravery. Self sacrifice. Accolades for well-lived lives.

Contained in the pages of books on this subject are stories about common soldiers achieving uncommon success. In these stories we read about true leadership that enables this achievement—leadership that inspires men to willingly fight and lay down their lives for others, be they their wives, children, and families back home, or fellow soldiers with them in the line of battle. These leaders each share similar attributes. Their sense of honor, duty, valor, dedication, and determination take on regal splendor in light of the battles they conduct and the soldiers they lead. But they all share one common attribute, whether they are modern-era generals riding in command vehicles, or knights in armor mounted on horses hundreds of years ago.

They are all warriors at heart.

Our Commander

Few people today see Jesus as a Commander. Most see Him as a rather frail-looking nice guy carrying around one of the lost sheep. Instead of a helmet, they see Him wearing a halo. Instead of carrying a sword, they see a shepherd's crook. Instead of chainmail, armor, or camouflage, they see Him wearing a white robe. Instead of combat boots, they see brown sandals. Instead of leading vast armies of angels and men into battle, they see Him quietly tending a herd of sheep. Instead of kicking in the gates of hell, they see Him patting one of the lambs on the head. Instead of seeing Him in a council of war with His troops planning their next attack against the opposition, they see Him counseling the sheep to appease everybody. Instead of seeing Him turning the natural wildness of men's hearts loose to take the fullness of the kingdom of heaven by force, they see Him taming the male members of the flock and domesticating them.

Jesus is a Commander.[1] He is a Man of war. He is the Captain of the Host—the vast angel army. He is the victorious ruler, parading His defeated foes in chains through the streets of His kingdom as a spectacle to the cheering of thousands. He is the zealous warrior whose robe hem is stained with the blood of His enemies. A sword proceeds out of Him, inflicting great destruction on those who oppose Him. He rides a mighty battle horse as He leads the saints to victory. They rally under His banner. In His breast beats a warrior's heart. A heart bent toward the battle. A heart programmed for victory.

His mighty battle cry echoes in men's hearts across the centuries. Does it echo in our hearts today?

Yes. Jesus is our Commander.

THE FEW, THE CHOSEN

But what is a commander without warriors? We are called to be Jesus' warriors. Every man who is known by His name is called. Few respond and are chosen to go with Him. Those who do respond are trained personally by Jesus and by those He sends. The testimonies of their lives become their swords for the battle. He teaches them how to swing their swords for the Kingdom.

How many warriors are enough? The few who are sold out completely to Him. The few who have nothing to lose and everything to gain. The few who will lay their lives down for His cause, their wife, their children, and their future generations.

We few. We are enough because the battle belongs to Him already.

HIS WARRIORS

Warring for Jesus requires balance. As His warriors, we are to maintain the perfect balance for the battle. His balance. We are to battle for His sake and not for our own. We are to battle for His glory and not for our own. We are to battle for His cause and not for our own. We are to battle for His gain and not for our own. When He tells us to fight, we pursue the battle as if all depended on it. When He tells us to stop, we cease our pursuit and await His next directive. In all, we are to be under His control, following His lead. We are to be neither passive nor overtly aggressive in our warring.

Some of us tend to be passive. It takes a lot to push us 'too far'. We don't tend to make waves. We often look the other way or do not stand up for right against those who propagate wrong. We lose our nerve and justify our lack of action. Why do we do this? Some of it could be our wounds from the past. Some of it could be fear. Some of it could be laziness. All of it is wrong! Jesus calls this being 'luke warm'. He does not like this in a man. In fact, this trait makes Jesus physically sick. Under His training, though, we can learn to be more aggressive. We can learn to stand alone when required. We can learn to 'stick out' when the situation calls for someone to stick out. Jesus can help us.

Some of us tend to be too pushy or assertive. We are quick to take things into our own hands. We go off on our own. We display a disdain for those who we believe are not aggressive enough. We justify the rebellion in our hearts with our eager aggression. Why do we do this? Some of it could be our insecurity from the past. Some of it could be fear. Some of it could be our own base insolence and arrogance. All of it is wrong! Jesus sees into our hearts and calls out our haughty pridefulness. He hates pride and the impudence it creates in our hearts. He can teach us to put aside our brazenness and replace it with meekness, which is power under control. We can learn to appreciate what others bring to the fight. We can learn to follow His lead in concert with all who He has called to the battle.

Warring for Jesus is not done on our own strength or from our base natures as men. It is done on Jesus' power with His passion, and it is done out of love. The world is to see our great love for Him, and that love expressed in our concern for others. This love will cause us to emulate our Commander. As warriors, we will love what He loves and hate what He hates.[2] We will fight in formation with Him. We will be always under His control. There is no place for passivity, laziness, fear, arrogance, insolence, or spite.

The world wants us to be disqualified from the fight, either by our loitering on the sidelines as observers or by our going off on our own personal battles. The world does not want us to count in the battle against evil. The choice is ours.

INTO THE BATTLE

Jesus told us that the kingdom of heaven has erupted all around us with a new relentlessness and forcefulness. He said that the men who see this happening are seizing it with a holy and uncompromising fierceness. We are called to be these zealous men who violently grasp hold and press into its fullness. We are called to love God and hate evil with unshakable ardor and perseverance. We are called into the vortex of the struggle between good and evil, between right and wrong, between Jesus and Satan. We are not to remain apathetic or uncommitted. We are to take the fullness of our calling to the kingdom by force.[3]

As a disciple of Jesus, we are called to His war. This is

244

part of what it means to follow Him. He has an assignment for each warrior who joins Him, an assignment to be carried out in this lifetime of many battles. Successfully completing this assignment leads us to triumphantly achieve our destiny. This is for all who dare to pay the price and follow their Commander where He leads.

If we will answer the call, Jesus will show us our sword— the testimony of our life.[4] He will examine it in detail with us and demonstrate that it is of great value to Him. He will polish it to a brilliant luster. He will help us sharpen it. He will give it balance. He will show us how to handle it to do great damage to the forces of hell.[5]

Once we pick up the sword, we cannot lay it down. There is no scabbard hanging from the belt of our battle dress. We have no provision to put it away for a while. When we are at rest, it is stuck point down in the ground an arm's length away, always ready to be used. When we walk between battles with our Commander, we are learning from Him how to handle it better. All along, we are allowing Him to sharpen it by whatever means He prescribes. He is sharpening it for the next battle. And the next battle will come. And we will swing our sword for Him. And it will be of great consequence.

There are two extremely important things for us as warriors to remember when we go into battle.

Jesus has already won the war. He has defeated Satan and His demons and has paraded them through the streets. He has made provisions for us to share in this victory. But there are many battles yet to fight. Satan knows his time is short.[6] Although defeated, our foe has not given up. Each man has individual battles to fight. Each man has corporate battles to fight, joining with others who are called to those same battles.

Also, we do not carry a shield. Jesus is our shield.[7] We

are to follow Him and stay behind Him. If we get out in front of Him in a battle, or begin to fight the battle on our terms by our methods, or we head off to find and fight our own battles, we do so at our own peril, and we will suffer the consequences. The forces of hell will have full access to our families and us. We are no match for them by ourselves. We need a shield and we lack our own. Jesus, and He alone, is our shield. He is our protection. We must stay behind Him at all times by following as He leads us into battle.

The shofar call to battle has been sounded. Let us rally under the battle flag of our Warrior Commander and enter into the war with Him!

It all begins with us. It all depends on Him.

❖❖❖ CHAPTER NOTES ❖❖❖

The Scriptures are a chronicle of war. Throughout their pages, the imagery of armies and battles, of campaigns and weapons is vibrant. Much of the Old Testament deals with the conquest of the Promised Land by the Tribes of Israel, as well as the subsequent invasions by the conquering nations around them. An underlying theme of the New Testament is our war against all that is in the world—the lust of the flesh, the lust of the eyes, and the pride of life. Jesus is the center of this age, and Satan and his demons play major roles as His foes.

How many of us give lip service to Jesus as the Conquering Ruler? How many of us live under the overriding image of Him as the Good Shepherd and Prince of Peace? He is all three, but He is ultimately the Victorious Warrior and Vanquishing Ruler.

1. Our Commander

Jesus describes Himself as a Man of War.

(Exodus 15:3) The LORD is a man of war; The LORD is His name.

He describes Himself as the Commander of the army of the LORD.

(Joshua 5:13-14a) When Joshua was by Jericho, he lifted up his eyes and looked, and behold, a Man [Jesus] was standing before him with His drawn sword in His hand. And Joshua went to Him and said to Him, "Are You for us, or for our adversaries?" And He said, "No; but I am the Commander of the army of the LORD. Now I have come."

He parades His defeated foes—Satan and his demons—through the streets as a conquering hero.

(Colossians 2:15) He disarmed the rulers and authorities and put them to open shame, by triumphing over them in Him.

He is described as He battles. He is awesome and mighty. He is fierce.

(Revelation 19:11-15) Then I saw heaven opened, and behold, a white horse! The One sitting on it is called Faithful and True, and in righteousness He judges and makes war. His eyes are like a flame of fire, and on His head are many diadems [crowns], and He has a name written that no one knows but Himself. He is clothed in a robe dipped in blood, and the name by which He is called is The Word of God. And the armies of heaven, arrayed in fine linen, white and pure, were following Him on white horses. From His mouth comes a sharp sword with which to strike down the nations, and He will rule them with a rod of iron. He will tread the winepress of the fury of the wrath of God the Almighty.

2. Love What Jesus Loves and Hate What Jesus Hates

(Psalm 97:10a) O you who love the LORD, hate evil!

3. Kingdom Of Heaven Is Seized By Fierce Men

Since John the Baptist began teaching about the reality of the kingdom of heaven here in the present age, it has been made manifest all around us. Its march through mankind and history has been relentless. For us to walk into all of its fullness, we must aggressively pursue it and grasp hold of it forcefully.

(Matthew 11:12) "From the days of John the Baptist until now the kingdom of heaven has suffered violence, and the violent take it by force."

4. Our Testimony Is Our Weapon

The testimony of our life is our weapon as men. The more obedient the life, the stronger the sword. The purer the life, the sharper the edge.

(Revelation 12:11) And they have conquered him by the blood of the Lamb and by the word of their testimony, for they loved not their lives even unto death.

5. Jesus Trains Us For The Battle

For a soldier to be worth anything in battle, he must be properly trained. He must understand the grand strategy. He must know how to execute tactics. As soldiers in Jesus' army, we must be trained to fight His way on the battlefields of His choosing. Jesus is our drill instructor.

(Psalm 144:1) Blessed be the LORD my Rock, who trains my hands for war, and my fingers for battle.

6. Satan's Time Is Short

Satan has lost the war. But his pride and arrogance will not allow him to surrender. His hatred for God and his contempt for God's followers will not allow him to quit. Instead, he is ramping up his aggressiveness against the armies of the Lord. The evidence of this is all around us. His plan is to take as much ground in the Church as possible before the end comes. His strategy is to infiltrate and to make it ineffective. His tactic is to exploit the lust of the eyes, the lust of the flesh, and the pride of life in the lives of each believer.

(Revelation 12:12b) 'But woe to you, O earth and sea, for the devil has come down to you in great wrath, because he knows that his time short!'

7. Jesus Is Our Shield

Our only true defense in battle is Jesus. If we stay behind Him and in step with Him, we are safe.

(Psalm 28:7a) The LORD is my strength and my shield; in Him my heart trusts, and I am helped.

◆◆◆ STUDY GUIDE ◆◆◆

There is a war being fought around us today. Though primarily spiritual in nature, it is manifested in the physical world through men and by men. It is a war between Jesus and Satan. It is a war between the children of God and the children of Satan. Every child of God is involved in this war, whether he wants to accept this fact or not. All believers are called to stand in the ranks of the army of God. At the head of this great army stands Jesus—our Commander and Warrior King.

1) Look at the definition of *warrior*. What words do you see that jump out at you?

2) Look at the definition again. Have you ever considered Jesus as a warrior? Why or why not?

3) Have you ever considered the fact that you are a warrior in His army? When you do so now, describe your feelings.

4) Why do you think that any man who is called by Jesus would refuse to join Him in the battle? Make a list of possible reasons for not joining Him.

5) A commander commands. Look at the definition of *command*. What does the word mean?

6) If you decide to answer Jesus' call to battle and choose to join His ranks of warriors, what is your responsibility to your Commander?

† PRAYER THOUGHTS †

Ask Jesus to give you a heart for the battle—a warrior's heart. Ask Him to purge any passivity or laziness or fear or arrogance or insolence or spite or pride from your heart. And then ask Him to teach you when, where, and how to fight the battles He has chosen for you.

Jesus the Deliverer

We understand the reality of the unseen world around us. We have explored the idea of demonic infestation. We understand the basics of how we are infested and why we are infested. Now it is up to each of us to respond.

Do we see the telltale evidence of demonic control within us and in our families? Can we see inherited traits and health problems that have come down our family lines to us? Can we see these same traits in our children? Or our grandchildren? Do we see areas in our lives that are out of control? Areas of sinful behaviors? Nagging problems with immorality, lust, anger, over-eating, alcohol, illegal or prescription drugs, anger, fears and phobias, or pornography? Are we struggling with homosexual thoughts or desires? Do we believe we are in the wrong body, that we should have been created as the opposite sex? Are we 'driven' to the point where we can't relax or enjoy life? Do we have a compulsive/obsessive personality? Are we having problems sleeping? Do we struggle with self-hate or entertain thoughts that it would be better for all if we were dead? Do we cut, mutilate, hurt ourselves, or tempt self-destruction with overtly dangerous activities? Do we look for ways to fail at things? Are we confused mentally and struggle with excessive doubts and indecision? Do we find ourselves reacting against anything that is Godly? Do we harbor deep feelings of hatred, unforgiveness, envy, jealousy, or bitterness toward specific persons, groups of people, or people in general?

Many things listed in the questions above are common to mankind. But did Jesus ever intend for us to live in such straits of continuous struggle and defeat as a follower of His? What would be the point? Where is His power in this?

No, Jesus did not. He intended us to live a life of victory over our flesh. Jesus didn't say that we wouldn't have struggles—we will. He didn't tell us that all would be smooth sailing—those are not the seas we traverse in this world. Jesus didn't say that we would live a life of peace with all men—He told us we would be persecuted and reviled for His name's sake. Jesus didn't tell us there would be an absence of sickness and disease—this is part of the fallen world in which we live. We may experience these things and more through the working out of His plan in our lives. But we are not to be struggling down in the pigpen with these things. We are to be flying high above them like eagles.

If we do see these patterns of problems traveling down our family lines to us, our children, and our grandchildren, and that we are gripped by struggles that we cannot overcome on our own, do we understand that demons are involved? Demons that have a mission to steal, kill, and destroy within our lives and the lives of those in our family line? Do we understand that we will not be able to successfully walk with Jesus as a disciple until these demons are gone?

So what do we do?

Look to Jesus. He came to free the oppressed.[1] He still 'goes around doing good and healing those oppressed by the devil'.

THE BASICS OF DELIVERANCE

Deliverance is a very serious decision in our walk with Jesus. Once we begin, we must see it through to the end. The demons will get stirred up. They do not want to be consigned to the abyss.[2] We do not have to fear this. Jesus reigns over all things. There are three basic steps to being delivered from demonic infestation.

We must first ask Jesus to show us truth in this matter, truth about demons present in our lives and in the lives of our family members. If we seek Him with a pure heart, He will reveal the truth to us. He will show us the telltale signs of demonic presence in our families, our family lines, and ourselves. We will see patterns of control, illnesses, and weaknesses that span generations.

Then, we must begin to war against the demons area by area. There is a listing of common *Demonic Groupings* and areas of oppression in the *Appendix*, along with their practical manifestations. There is also a *Prayer of Renunciation* to recite that will begin to loosen their grip by canceling their permissions to remain inside of us. As we work through the list, it is important that we take a good look at our lives and confess our sins and the sins of our ancestors, living or dead. We must allow Jesus to point out the areas of infestation and the doorways of entry. This is a heart-wrenching process. The ugly realities of our lives and the lives of our previous family generations will be laid bare. It may be tough for us to come to grips with the fact that certain activities of our parents, grandparents, or great-grandparents opened doorways to generational curses that are being borne out in us and in our children. But truth is truth. It must be accepted and repented of for us to move ahead with this. Jesus wants a willing heart that is eager for the truth, no matter how distasteful. He does not want us to be defensive or evasive. All of this is preparation for freedom.

Finally, we must submit to the deliverance process. We must prayerfully select a deliverance ministry and make an appointment. Jesus must lead in this selection process, because the approaches taken by ministries vary. Jesus will lead us to the right person. And even though the approaches may be different, the end result is the same—it is Jesus who commands the demons into the abyss. During our deliverance, we must be open and honest. We may see or be made aware of things that are shocking. It is not the time for wavering or self-denial. It is a time of honesty and humility. Jesus will send the demons out—all of them—if we do our part. If we hold back, some of them will be held back. That is His justice. God's Justice

Jesus does the delivering. The anointed deliverance ministers are His instruments. He sets up court with His Father. Once their rights have been cancelled, the demons are then commanded to repair any damage they have done to our bodies, pull up any seeds of wrong thinking that have been planted within us, and are then cast into the abyss. There, the demons will remain until the end times.

Jesus oversees the process. He passes judgment on the demons. In His name, they are cast out. This is all very Biblical.[3] It is just not very prevalent in the church today. As a result, people remain in oppressive bondage their entire lives. Most live in ignorance that they are infested and that they could be set free from their tormentors.

WALK THE WALK

After deliverance, we will be able to deal with the rest of our issues with Jesus.

We will have two new challenges to face, though. Without the demons, the *real us* will finally surface. We may not like what we see. Years of infestation tend to put deep grooves in our souls in the form of wrong thought processes, poor character traits, reacting to circumstances, relating poorly to others, and self-focus. But they are just grooves of the flesh, and we can overcome them if we allow Jesus to finish His work of redemption in us.

Next, we must keep new demons from moving in.

Because all of the generational permissions have been cancelled, we will have a say in this. We must be vigilant. If we open the doors, new permissions may be granted, and we could become infested again. These new areas of demonic oppression can ultimately be passed down to our children, so the stakes are high. We need to understand clearly why Jesus told the paralytic He healed by the pool to 'stop sinning or something worse will happen to you'.[4]

We will now be able to walk successfully with Jesus as His disciple.

Free in Him.

When sin entered the world through Adam, four products of sin were set in motion—more sin, sickness, disease, and death. Additionally, rules of engagement were established by God for the battle between Himself and Satan. Clear legal rules were laid out. Clear legal consequences (judgments) were prescribed.

Satan has usurped jurisdiction over the earth from Jesus. As the squatting despot, he has set up his false kingdom on earth by assigning territories to his demons and setting up a reporting hierarchy and authority structure. Jesus and His angels in heaven war against them. This is clear from the book of Daniel.

(Daniel 10:4-6, 12-13, 20b, 21b) On the twenty-fourth day of the first month, as I was standing on the bank of the great river (that is, the Tigris) I lifted up my eyes and looked, and behold, a man [Jesus] clothed in linen, with a belt of fine gold from Uphaz around his waist. His body was like beryl, his face like the appearance of lightning, his eyes like flaming torches, his arms and legs like the gleam of burnished bronze, and the sound of his words like the sound of a multitude...Then he said to me, "Do not fear, Daniel, from the first day that you set your heart to understand and to humbled yourself before your God, your words have been heard, and I have come because of your words. The prince of the kingdom of Persia withstood me twenty-one days, but Michael, one of the chief princes, came to help me, for I was left there with the kings of Persia...But I will return to fight against the prince of Persia; and when I go out, behold, the prince of Greece will come...There is none who contends by my side against these, except Michael your prince."

We need a deliverer rom all of this spiritual warfare. Man is not capable of saving himself from such fiends. On his own, man is subject to the power of angels and demons.

Jesus came to deliver us from sin, sickness, disease, and death. He came to deliver us from demonic oppression. He came to legally enforce the canceling of their permissions in our lives. He came to cast them out of man.

1. Freedom In Jesus

(1 John 3:8) Whoever makes a practice of sinning is of the devil, for the devil has been sinning from the beginning. The reason the Son of God appeared was to destroy the works of the devil.

2. The Abyss

The Abyss is a deep bottomless pit. It is a place of imprisonment for demons. Demons do not want to go there because they will be confined until the end times. Then, they will be released to torment man upon the earth. Even Satan will be imprisoned there after the Battle of Armageddon for 1,000 years as Jesus reigns on the earth. Afterward, he will be released to deceive the nations, leading up to a final battle against God where fire comes down from heaven and devours the rebellion. After this final defeat, Satan will be cast into the Lake of Fire along with Death, hell, his demons, and all who did not call upon Jesus for salvation.

(Luke 8:30-31) Jesus then asked him, "What is your name?" And he said, "Legion," for many demons had entered him. And they begged Him not to command them to depart into the abyss.

(Revelation 9:1-4, 11) And the fifth angel blew his trumpet, and I saw a star fallen from heaven to the earth, and he was given the key to the shaft of the bottomless pit. He opened the shaft of the bottomless pit, and from the shaft rose smoke like the smoke of a great furnace, and the sun and the air were darkened with smoke of the shaft. Then from the smoke came locusts [demons] on the earth, and they were given power like the power of scorpions of the earth. They were told not to harm the grass of the earth or any green plant or any tree, but only those people who do not have the seal of God on their foreheads...They have as king over them the angel of the bottomless pit. His name in Hebrew is Abaddon, and in Greek he is called Apollyon.

(Revelation 20:1-3) Then I saw an angel coming down from heaven, holding in his hand the key to the bottomless pit and

a great chain. And he laid seized the dragon, that ancient serpent, who is the devil and Satan, and bound him for a thousand years, and threw him into the pit, and shut it, and sealed it over him, so that he might not deceive the nations any longer, until the thousand years were ended. After that he must be released for a little while.

(Revelation 20:10, 14-15) And the devil who had deceived them was thrown into the lake of fire and sulfur where the beast and the false prophet were, and they will be tormented day and night forever and ever...Then Death and Hades were thrown into the lake of fire. This is the second death, the lake of fire. And if anyone's name was not found written in the Book of Life, he was thrown into the lake of fire.

3. Biblical Basis Of Deliverance

Freeing people from the oppression of the demonic was not a side bar in Jesus' equipping of His disciples. It was a major focus of their training and activities.

(Mark 16:17a) "And these signs will accompany those who believe: In My name they will cast out demons."

(Luke 10:17) The seventy-two returned with joy, saying, "Lord, even the demons are subject to us in Your name!"

Jesus still oversees deliverance today, all in His perfect authority and judgment.

4. Something Worse

After the demons are gone, we want to keep them out. If we persist in our sinning, new demons can be given permission to enter. These demons will be worse than the ones who have left us. Persistent sin causes us to give over greater rights to our freedom by exposing us to powerful demonic forces. That is why we must walk consistently in our freedom and not go back to our evil ways.

(John 5:12-14) They asked him, "Who is the Man who said to you, 'Take up your bed and walk'?" Now the man who had been healed did not know who it was, for Jesus had withdrawn, as there was a crowd in the place. Afterward Jesus found him in the temple and said to him, "See, you are well! Sin no more, that nothing worse may happen to you."

For most of us, our modern culture has minimized the true reality of Satan's kingdom and its power at work in the world around us. When we do catch glimpses of this kingdom, often times we see it rebranded as harmless or irrelevant to our lives. It is anything but harmless or irrelevant. It is at work around and in us. We are no match against such power. Jesus is. He is our deliverer.

1) Take a look at the definition of the word *deliver*. While there are many applications for this word, you will likely see *save, rescue*, or *come through for*. When you see these words, what comes to mind?

2) According to the Chapter Notes, what five things did Jesus come to deliver us from?

3) When you look at all that is going on in your life, do you believe you need a deliverer from the things listed above?

4) Do you believe that Satan and his demons have invaded your life?

5) In what ways do you see their power at work within you?

6) If you have not already done so using the resources in the book, *WATM?*, use the listing of common demonic spirits in the *Appendix* and ask Jesus to reveal to you any areas of demonic control in your life. Make a list of the areas that you see.

7) Take a look at your list. Can you see these same areas of control at work in previous generations in your family? If so, list the areas and the family members involved.

8) Do you want Jesus to deliver you from these and to break their power in your life?

† Prayer Thoughts †

Use the prayer in the *Appendix* of this book. Insert the *main* demonic group names—one at a time—in the blanks of the prayer as you pray through each demonic group that Jesus has shown you is at work in your life.

Truly repent before your Creator for each area of control given over.

Once you have completed this, Jesus, your Deliverer, will hold these demons down until you go to the deliverance minister He has chosen for you—He will hold them down *as long as you do not once again grant them permission though sinful choices.*

Ask Jesus to lead you to the deliverance ministry He wants for you. Do not delay! Freedom is waiting for you!

JESUS THE HEALER

We live in a world filled with hurting people. This is a fact that can be verified by standing on a street corner in any major city in the world, by traveling to any third-world country, by visiting a nursing home or a prison, or by looking in the mirror. Some are hurting as a result of a physical problem. Sickness and disease are rampant upon the face of the earth. Many more are hurting as a result of emotional problems. Emotional issues do not discriminate based on genetics, location, or even social status. And then there are the broken relationships. Most of these are caused by a lack of forgiveness, manifested as either the withholding of forgiveness or the lack of receiving it from others. Spiritual infestations are more common than people want to believe. Most people are unknowingly victimized by spiritual consequences related to the actions of preceding generations in their family lines.

With all of this hurt comes the associated pain. Pain is universal. It is common to man. It is not just physical in nature. It can also be emotional, spiritual, mental, and relational. Each type of pain can be intense and resistant to our most concerted efforts to alleviate it. Each type has its own affect on a person. Left untreated, these pains can become debilitating.

With all of this pain and associated suffering comes the attempt to control and manage it. So man grasps for things to treat the pain and make it go away. This self-medication takes many forms—actual narcotic or anti-depressant drugs, alcohol, food, activities, relationships, or material things, to name just a few. But, man's attempt to lessen the pain via self-medication never cures the root problem. Instead, the pain is only masked, allowing the user to tolerate it to some degree. These self-medications provide short periods of relief, but the pain always returns, and with it the need to re-medicate. Over time, it takes more and more of the same 'medication' to achieve the same result. Over time, addictions occur.

On and on goes the cycle. The big cover-up. Nothing gets solved. The hurts are still there. Why? Because only the symptoms are being treated—the pain, the stress, the unpleasantness, the disappointment. The root causes remain buried deep and untouched. They are not reached. They are not probed. They are not resolved.

PAIN HURTS

We collect wounds throughout our lives. Some of these came to us before we were born. Some were acquired when we were young and susceptible to them. Some occurred through our familial relationships or our friendships. Some came as a result of physical sicknesses, infirmities, or deformities, others through abuse. Unhealed, these wounds fester deep within us.

And with these untreated wounds, comes the pain—pain that we don't want, need, or understand. Some of the pains are small, and we think we can manage them in the margins of our lives. Some are huge and defy our best management efforts. Large or small, we can't get away from any of them. The pain pesters us day and night. Certain things trigger more of it in our lives. We just want it to go away. But we want it to go away on our terms. We don't want to go down to the foundational issues that are causing the pain. We would have to deal with too much for that. We would need to have the wounds healed, wounds that we believe are better left alone. We just want the symptoms to go away—the pain, the stress, and the peripheral problems.

And what do we do? We medicate them. Drugs. Alcohol. Sex. Food. Spending. Religion. Status. Jobs. Children. Pets. Houses. Entertainment. Cars. Toys. Sports. Friends. Activities. TV. Novels. Busy-ness. Social media. The Internet. The list goes on. Because we are only medicating the symptoms, the pain keeps coming back. Over time, whatever we are using for medication can become serious addictions. We become altered by them. We become controlled by them. They affect every aspect of our lives.

All of this happens because we do not want to deal with the wounds of our lives, nor do we know how. So we cover them. We bury them so deep that no one can smell the stench of their unhealed rottenness. Only we know what wounds are there. Only we feel the deep emotional pain. We try to ignore the pain, but it is always there. We try willing it away, but it persists.

Over time, several things may occur as a direct result of our not dealing with the wounds. We suffer physical maladies that cannot be explained. We experience severe pains that drugs will barely touch and for which no doctor can find the cause. Insomnia persists. Emotional issues drain us. We become increasingly angry, increasingly bitter, increasingly contemptuous, or increasingly cynical. We have relational issues. We push away the very people who love us, wanting no one to get too close and see the real us and the wounds we are shielding. We find ourselves holding grudges. We have difficulty forgiving people. We develop sinful habits based on our attitudes of entitlement. We grant increasing control to the demonic as we give ourselves over to these actions and the attitudes behind them.

What we need is a healing. A complete healing.

THE GREAT PHYSICIAN

Jesus came to heal. A good portion of His ministry here on earth was consumed by His healing of others—physical problems, emotional wounds, spiritual issues, and relational rifts—the complete healing of the body, soul, and spirit of men. Jesus dealt with them all. Jesus healed them all.

Jesus healed physical problems.[1] Blindness, deafness, dumbness, leprosy, paralysis, birth defects, fevers, bleeding disorders, dropsy, epilepsy, severed ears, and other infirmities are specifically named or inferred from the Gospel accounts. We know He healed more than these specific ailments because He went about 'healing every sickness and every disease among the people'. He encountered and healed every malady that was common to man in that day. Given the squalor of their existence and the lack of modern medicine, one can only imagine. He also demonstrated complete power over life and death by raising people from the dead, the most memorable being Lazarus.

Jesus dealt with emotional wounds.[2] He moved freely among the outcasts and sinners of His day. He spent time with those who were hated among their own people. He fed them with spiritual truth. He listened to the stories of their lives. He spoke love to them. He understood them. They responded. They healed.

Jesus certainly dealt with spiritual issues.[3] Foremost, He brought salvation to mankind, to all who would believe. Beyond this, He cast many demons out of people. The Gospels are full of these accounts of spiritual deliverance from the demonic.

Jesus dealt with relational riffs, beginning with His molding of the disciples into a tight-knit group (Just think of how the hot head Peter or Simon the Zealot managed to get along with Matthew the tax collector, the one who collaborated with the despised Romans to extort money from the Jewish people!). As Jesus spent time with the social outcasts, He surely did much work healing their

264

relationships as well. To do this, He had to deal with their attitudes of unforgiveness toward others. He had to show them their personal need for forgiveness—from others and from themselves.[4]

The physical ailments were of the body. Salvation was of the spirit. The emotional, relational, and spiritual deliverance problems were of the soul. Jesus healed the whole man.

A study of Jesus' healing ministry reveals the key to His healing for us. Unless the person was totally incapacitated, there was an action required of each who was healed. Some had to touch Him. Some had to call out to Him. Some had to ask to be healed. Some had to verify that they wanted to be healed. Some had to beg Him. Some had to go and wash. Some had to believe. All had to pursue His healing.

And so it is for us. We must come to the place where we are so desperate to be healed that we are willing to do whatever He asks us to do. For our physical infirmities, we may have to change our eating habits, start exercising, or re-evaluate our use of medications. For our emotional wounds, we must confess their reality and allow Him to open each one and clean out the festering rottenness. We have to forgive others, and we must forgive ourselves. For our spiritual issues, we have to submit to the process of deliverance and face our demons. For our relational issues, we must become real and true and vulnerable. We have to drop our guard and stop protecting our hearts from potential hurts.

Jesus is the Great Physician. We can trust Him with our wounds and infirmities. We must bring them to Him. He has healed countless others—body, soul, and spirit. He can heal us so we can walk effectively with Him.

Jesus wants to heal us completely. He will heal us.

♦♦♦ CHAPTER NOTES ♦♦♦

Jesus is known as the Great Physician for a reason. He heals the whole man—body, soul (mind, will, emotions), and spirit. Some healings were physical only. Others were physical, emotional, and spiritual.

(Luke 7:21) In that hour He healed many people of diseases and plagues and evil spirits, and on many who were blind he bestowed sight.

1. Healings Of Jesus

There are many accounts of Jesus' healings in Scripture. In fact, He healed every affliction common to the people of that day. He still heals today.

(Matthew 9:27-30a) And as Jesus passed on from there, two blind men followed Him, crying aloud, "Have mercy on us, Son of David." When He entered the house, the blind men came to Him, and Jesus said to them, "Do you believe that I am able to do this?" They said to Him, "Yes, Lord." Then He touched their eyes, saying, "According to your faith be it done to you." And their eyes were opened.

(Mark 7:32-35) And they brought to Him a man who was deaf and had a speech impediment, and they begged Him to lay His hand on him. And He taking him aside from the crowd privately, He put His fingers in his ears, and after spitting touched his tongue. And looking up to heaven, He sighed and said to him, "Ephphatha", that is, "Be opened." And his ears were opened, his tongue was released, and he spoke plainly.

(Luke 17:12-14) And as He entered a village, He was met by ten lepers, who stood at a distance and lifted up their voices, saying, "Jesus, Master, have mercy on us." When He saw them He said to them, "Go and show yourselves to the priests." And as they went they were cleansed.

(Matthew 9:2, 6b-7) And behold, some people brought to Him a paralytic, lying on a bed. And when Jesus saw their faith, He said to the paralytic, "Take heart, my son; your sins are forgiven."...He then said to the paralytic—"Rise, pick up your bed and go home." And he rose and went home.

(Mark 3:1, 5b) Again He entered the synagogue, and a man was there with a withered hand...[Jesus] said to the man, "Stretch out your hand." He stretched it out, and his hand was restored.

(Luke 4:38-39) And He arose and left the synagogue and entered Simon's house. Now Simon's mother-in-law was ill with a high fever, and they appealed to Him on her behalf. And He stood over her and rebuked the fever, and it left her, and immediately she rose and began to serve them.

(Matthew 9:20-22) And behold, a woman who had suffered from a discharge of blood for twelve years came up behind Him and touched the fringe of His garment, for she said to herself, "If I only touch His garment, I will be made well." Jesus turned, and seeing her He said, "Take heart, daughter; your faith has made you well." And instantly the woman was made well.

(Luke 14:2, 4b) And behold, there was a man before Him who had dropsy...Then He took him and healed him, and sent him away.

(Luke 22:50-51) And one of them struck the servant of the high priest and cut off his right ear. But Jesus said, "No more of this!" And He touched his ear and healed him.

(Mark 3:10) For He had healed many, so that all who had diseases pressed about Him to touch Him.

(John 11:43-44a) When He had said these things, He cried with a loud voice, "Lazarus, come out." The man who had died came out, his hands and feet bound with linen strips, and his face wrapped with a cloth.

2. Jesus Mingled With The Outcasts

(Matthew 9:10) As Jesus reclined at table in the house, behold, many tax collectors and sinners came and were reclining with Jesus and His disciples.

3. Jesus Cast Out Demons

(Mark 1:27) And they were all amazed, so that they questioned among themselves, saying, "What is this? A new teaching with authority! He commands even the unclean spirits, and they obey Him."

(Mark 9:17b-18, 20, 26a) "Teacher, I brought my son to You, for he has a spirit that makes him mute. And whenever it seizes him, it throws him down, and he foams and grinds his teeth and becomes rigid. So I asked Your disciples to cast it out, but they were not able."...And they brought the boy to Him. And when the spirit saw Him, immediately it convulsed the boy, and he fell on the ground and rolled about, foaming at the mouth...And after crying out and convulsing him terribly, it came out.

4. Forgiveness Is Key

It is difficult to forgive those who have wronged us. It is difficult for others to forgive us for what we have done. It is even more difficult for us to forgive ourselves. Forgiveness is a requirement for healing.

(Matthew 18:21) Then Peter came up and said to Him, "Lord, how often will my brother sin against me, and I forgive him? As many as seven times?" Jesus said to him, "I do not say to you seven times, but seventy-seven times."

(Colossians 3:13b) As the Lord has forgiven you, so you also must forgive.

One of the most familiar aspects of Jesus' ministry on earth was His role as a healer. Scripture leaves no doubt about this. It was a major part of His ministry as *God with us*. People of that day needed His healing touch. We still do today. Jesus has not changed. He will always be *God with us*.

1) List one physical condition you would like Jesus to heal.

2) List one emotional hurt or problem you would like Him to heal.

3) What single relationship needs His healing touch?

4) Describe the pain that each one of these causes you. Be detailed.

5) List what substance, behavior, activity, person, or material thing you have learned to use for medication against each of these pains.

6) Have you ever considered that Jesus is just as interested in healing you today as he was the people we read about in the Gospels? If not, why not?

† PRAYER THOUGHTS †

Jesus is alive today! He is here with us. Jesus came to heal the whole man. Cry out to Him. Ask Him to heal the causes of your specific pain. And then wait for His answer—patiently. Do exactly what He says to do. It is required for your healing.

Jesus the Master

As Christians, we innately know that we are to be subject to the will of God. We know that He is supposed to be in charge and that we are not. However loosely we hold to these givens of our faith, they are nevertheless true. Some of us understand that we are to become followers of Jesus, His disciples. We understand that we are to follow as He leads and we are to do His bidding in our lives according to His will. We call upon Him as our Lord, but do we comprehend what this means?

The Greek word for *Lord* in the New Testament is *kyrios*. It denotes one who is the master or owner. This is the word used when Jesus was called 'Lord'.[1] Jesus is Kyrios. We are told that all things were put under His authority in heaven and on earth, and that at His name every knee shall bow.[2] That includes His disciples.

Even so, do we equate Jesus being our Lord to His being our Master? And if He is our Master, what does that make us?

Modern Day Slavery

Slave. Most of us do not like the word. We associate it with great injustice. It brings to mind a lack of choice. It is counter-cultural to our unalienable rights to life, liberty, and the pursuit of happiness. It is altogether too demeaning and too confining for our modern-day sensibilities. It presupposes that a master of sorts exists, one who is the owner of the slave. It goes against our natural aversion to being controlled. It strikes at the very heart of our concept of freedom.

Most of us believe we are far removed from the reality of slavery. We only know it from what we have read in books or have seen in movies or the occasional news report. It is something that has little to do with us today. It was not a tangible reality in our lives.

But is this really true?

The Bible has much to say about the reality of slavery. The primary message found in the New Testament is that God in His mercy sent Jesus to die for our sin. But the concept of slavery to sin is the symbiotic twin to this theme. The reason that Jesus had to come is that every man is born a slave to sin without any possibility of a true relationship with God. From the moment of conception, sin rules over us with a power that only the blood of Jesus can break. Sin is our master and we are its slaves. Jesus came to free us from this master. He came to set us free.

Jesus buys slaves out of the slave market of death from their owner, sin. When this occurs, that slave is not set free to follow the whims and desires of his own will. He becomes the property of Jesus. Jesus replaces sin as the Master over that slave. The slave is then led away from his old master by his new Master, Jesus. That is a crucial paradox of Christianity. One is set free to become a slave—a slave of Jesus, the purchaser by His blood.

When we read the New Testament in most modern translations, we are not likely to see the word *slave*. Instead, we encounter the word *servant*. We like that better. We are servants of Jesus. We are merely servants of sin. That does not sound so bad. That is manageable. But this is a mistranslation. The word translated as 'servant' (*doulos* in the Greek) actually means 'slave'. It occurs over one hundred times, so it is not the exception or a misprint.

The implications of this are significant—if Jesus is our Lord, we are not merely His servants. We are His slaves!

Jesus owns us. A servant is someone hired by another and paid a wage. A slave is owned, the possession of another. Jesus didn't hire us, He bought us with His blood.[3] He bought us from our former master—sin.[4] And since He bought us, Jesus owns us. He is our new Master.

Masters have rights over their slaves. The slave has none. The master controls the life of the slave. The slave does not. The master can treat the slave as he wishes. The slave has no recourse. The master commands the slave to do his bidding. The slave has no input into what he will be doing, or when, or for how long. The master is to be honored in all things. The slave has no honor but that which the master confers upon him personally or relationally by that master's status or standing. The master takes care of the slave, providing the necessities for life. The slave is dependent upon this care. The master is preeminent. The slave is not greater than his master in anything.

A slave has only one concern. This is to carry out the instructions of his master in such a way that the master is pleased with the effort and is honored by it. A slave has no say in things. A slave has no control of things. A slave has no personal rights.

This brings great clarity to the reality that each of us faces. Before Jesus saves us, sin is our master. And as our master, sin has all of the rights of a master, as stated above. Sin is in control. The slave of sin must do the bidding of his master in all things. As a slave of sin, the drive for more freedom from all personal constraints put in place by moral law and society does not lead to freedom from this master. Because this desire for freedom is self-focused, it leads to an ever-deepening state of slavery to sin, the master. Larger and stronger shackles replace the former as the captive is led deeper into captivity.

We are all slaves to something. We must each choose a master.

RUNAWAY SLAVES

As Christians we say that we 'belong to Jesus'. We say it, but do we live it?

After Jesus bought us from our former master, sin, and started leading us away from the slave market of sure death, did we turn to look back? Were we willing to go obediently along with our new owner to our new life? Or were we like many who, after being purchased from the cruel master of sin, turned around and ran away from their new master, Jesus?

For most, our running away didn't happen all at once. Perhaps we started by casting a few furtive glances in the direction of our old master. Then, maybe we started sneaking back for short visits. Before long, we were being fitted for the shackles once again. But we thought we were smart. We were sure that we could slip out of the fetters and head back to Jesus without anyone noticing. So we kept returning. Suddenly, we found out we were wrong. We found ourselves being carried off into deep captivity once again—not the captivity of eternal damnation, but a captivity of temporal destruction. And we found that we could not return on our own accord.

Why would we do such a thing? Why would we run from our Savior?

Rebellion. That is our surface problem. Underneath our rebellion, our *knowing* that we should be the masters of our own lives, lays a deep-seated arrogance and a puffed-up pridefulness. We are sure that we know better than God. We are sure that we can play both sides and win. And our pride overtakes us.

All of us have a tendency to get prideful and forget where

we came from. We quickly forget what we once were. How we thought. How we acted. And the more ugly our former life and our former deeds, the quicker we want to forget, move on, and act like nothing of the sort had ever happened. In all of our forgetting, we fail to remember to whom we once belonged—that destructive master, sin.

And so we run away from Jesus. We go back. We revisit our sinful ways.

Yes, we each must choose a master.

SLAVES OF PRIVILEGE

Throughout the history of slavery, it mattered to the slave who his master was. If he had a just master, the slave could expect to be treated fairly. If his master was good-hearted, the slave could expect to be treated well with ample kindness. If he had a prosperous master, the slave could expect to never be in want, with all of his needs met and taken care of. If the master was of high rank and standing, the slave even enjoyed privileges that came with his master's status in terms of recognition, treatment, and deference.

Our Master is the King of all kings and the Lord of all lords. He is faithful and true. He is tender hearted toward us and understands our frailties. He has brought us into His family. We sit at His table and break His bread. We share in His resources. We share in His life.

Let us understand this fully—that we are blessed to have Jesus as our Master. Let us accept this willingly—no longer desiring to go 'back to Egypt' and its sure slavery, even for a short visit. Let us rest in the ownership of Jesus completely—without further struggle against Him. Let us give ourselves to Him fully. Let us serve Him with great vigor. Let us be identified with Him unashamedly. Let us love Him completely. Let us follow Him unquestioningly, learning His ways as His disciple.

We are all slaves to something. We must choose a master. We can't follow Jesus if we are following our old master.

We are both owned as slaves by Jesus and welcomed as His brothers. It is a concept that we struggle with. We like the 'brothers' part of this. We like to think of ourselves as joint heirs with Jesus. We like to consider the privileges that come with this. In doing so, we somehow do not fathom the other more pressing reality that we are slaves to Jesus— that He bought us, that He owns us, that He has things He requires of us.

God is a jealous God. So is our former master, sin. So is Satan, our former slave driver. Satan is jealous of our position and privilege. He is jealous of our destiny as a believer. He wants to negate that. He wants us to be enslaved once again by sin so that we will be of little effect for the Kingdom of God on earth. So he works us to that end, trying to get us to run away from Jesus, back to our old master.

1. Jesus Our Lord

(John 13:13) "You call Me Teacher and Lord, and you are right, for so I am."

(John 20:28) Thomas answered Him, "My Lord and my God!"

(Romans 14:7-9) For none of us lives to himself, and none of us dies to himself. For if we live, we live to the Lord, and if we die, we die to the Lord. So then, whether we live or whether we die, we are the Lord's. For to this end Christ died and lived again, that He might be Lord both of the dead and of the living.

(Revelation 17:14) They will make war on the Lamb, and the Lamb will conquer them, for He is Lord of lords and King of kings, and those with Him are called and chosen and faithful.

(Revelation 19:16) On His robe and on His thigh He has a name written, King of kings and Lord of lords.

2. Everything Is In Subjection To Him

(Hebrews 2:7b-8a) You have crowned Him with glory and

honor, putting everything in subjection under his feet.

(Philippians 2:10-11) So that at the name of Jesus every knee should bow, in heaven and on earth and under the earth, and every tongue confess that Jesus Christ is Lord, to the glory of God the Father.

3. Bought For A Price

The purchaser owns what has been purchased.

(1 Peter 1:18-19) Knowing that you were ransomed from the futile ways inherited from your forefathers, not with perishable things such as silver or gold, but with the precious blood of Christ, like that of a lamb without blemish or spot.

4. From Slaves Of Sin To Slaves Of Righteousness

From the moment of our salvation, we are no longer slaves to sin. We have been set free. We now must make a conscious decision if we want to run back to our old master, sin, and serve him once more.

(Romans 6:17-18) But thanks be to God, that you who were once slaves of sin have become obedient from the heart to the standard of teaching to which you were committed, and, having been set free from sin, have become slaves of righteousness.

♦♦♦ STUDY GUIDE ♦♦♦

Most of us live daily lives far removed from the control of any one person—be it a king or some other form of supreme human authority. The idea of one man being owned by another ranges from the unimaginable to the repugnant. Yet, the concept and the reality of slavery are prominent in the Scriptures. The same is true for the concept and reality of a supreme ruler. We acknowledge this fact mentally through our ideas about God or Jesus, but few of our minds and even fewer of our hearts accept this at face value with all of its ramifications for our lives.

1) Look at the definition of *slave*. Write its basic definition when it is used as a noun.

2) What does it mean to be *legally owned*?

3) Write down the definition of *lord*. How does this word relate to *slave*?

4) Read **Revelation 19:16**. Jesus is called the *King of kings* and the *Lord of lords*. What do you think this means?

(Revelation 19:16) On his robe and on his thigh he has a name written, King of kings and Lord of lords.

5) What rights to the life of a man would the King of kings and the Lord of lords have?

6) Can you truly call Jesus your King and your Lord if you have denied Him His right to direct your life as He sees fit? Why or why not?

7) On a scale of 1 to 10, how much of your life do you really allow Jesus to direct?

I Control my Life   1 <<—>> 10   Jesus Controls my Life

8) How many times a day do you pause before you do something or make a decision and ask Him what He wants said, done, or decided? Why is this the case?

9) In what ways have you turned Jesus into your *copilot* where He only assists you in what you are doing or is allowed to direct only when you get tired of directing?

† PRAYER THOUGHTS †

Repent from these ways before Him. Seek His forgiveness. Give Him the right to use your life to accomplish His Father's plan. Begin to ask what He wants, and then obey Him.

Jesus is the Lord of all. He bought us with His blood and owns us. He has all the rights of ownership over our lives. In His great love and mercy, He will direct us along the way as His disciple.

JESUS THE LOVER

Love has become a cheap commodity in the world's marketplace today. As a word, we throw it around as a matter of habit. We love our wife. We love our children. We love our pet. We love the warm weather. We love to play or watch our favorite sport. We love our favorite sports team. We love cheeseburgers and fries, especially with a milkshake. We love our friends. We love our hobby. We love our boat. We love Christmas. We love the new gift we received. We love our job. We love our house. We love to go to on vacation.

We love God.

We are confused. We call our affections 'love'. We call sex 'love'. We call our likes 'love'. We call our preferences 'love'.

Yes, love has lost its meaning to us. In doing so, its value has been lost as well.

It has become cheap.

TRUE LOVE

What does *love* mean? Let's go back to the basics.

In the Greek language, there are four distinct words that form the concept of love. *Phileo* is known as brotherly love. It is used to describe affection for friends or the feelings of companionship that we have. It is most akin to the word 'like'. *Storge* describes the love between a parent and a child or the love between siblings. It is supportive and caring and natural. *Eros* is sensual or sexual love. It is concerned with pleasure, mostly our own. *Agape* is unconditional love. It is love that transcends feelings and emotions, and exists despite all things, even to those who are unlovable. It is mostly associated with God Himself for 'God is love (agape)'. Agape has been called the 'love of the will', but isn't it more than that? It has to be if it is truly God's love. It is a seeking love. It is a passionate love. It is a love based on principle. It is a love that desires only the good of its recipient.

Jesus is the manifestation of God's love for us. We can see what He did for us on the cross. He emptied Himself of the glory of heaven and gave us His life as a sacrifice for our sin. We know what we were when He did this for us. We know what we still are. We can also see how He loves others. We can read how He interacted with the people of His day when He walked the earth—His compassion and pursuit of their elusive hearts. We can experience Him this same way daily in our lives—this same passion and pursuit.

We can learn to love Him deeply as well.

THE BRIDE

For us who are married, we have at least once seen a bride on her wedding day. As we think back, we recall her beauty, her perfection, the slight blush on her cheeks, the sparkle of life in her eyes, and the excitement in her voice. Yes, she was the vision of loveliness. She was about to give herself to a man. She was desired greatly by her husband.

But the wedding day was the consummation of weeks, if not months, of preparation for the bride.

Foremost, the bride prepared herself for her husband. She made sure that she would be pleasing to him. She prepared her heart. She made it pure. She forsook all other things as less important and put him in that place. She made it a priority to know her husband more deeply—what he thought about things, what he liked or disliked, and his dreams for them together. She spent time with him to make this knowing a reality. She acknowledged his love for her and assured him that it was a mutual love.

The church is Jesus' bride.[1] He has set it aside for Himself. When He returns, He will take His bride to Himself. As part of the church, we are Jesus' brides. Each of us.

What have we been doing to prepare ourselves for Him?

THE BRIDEGROOM

We know from scripture that Jesus is the bridegroom who is coming for His church in the future.[2] As His betrothed, He is preparing us to sit at His wedding feast table with Him.[3] His desire is to present us to Himself without blemish or spot. He does this by spending time with us personally, helping us prepare, and teaching us to love Him by example.

Jesus' love for us is patient and kind. It is not boastful or rude. His love is not self-serving. It is not easily irritated by what we do or don't do. It does not keep score. It is not based on anything but what is best for us. His love never gives up on us. It never loses faith in us. It is always hopeful. It endures through every circumstance. It lasts forever.[4]

This is the love He has for us, His bride. It is to be our love for Him. It is to be our love for each other.

JESUS MY LOVER

Thinking of Jesus as our lover is not perverted or blasphemous. This is the true picture of His love for us. It is the love of a bridegroom for his bride. It is deep and abiding. It is fresh and pure. It is passionate and pursuing. It is a love without reservation. It is a love without shame. It is a love where all is seen. It is a love of affirmation. It is a love full of desire. It is a love full of hope. It is a love that seeks the best. It is a love of mutual satisfaction. It is a love of mutual enjoyment. It is a rejoicing love. It is an intimate love.

When we leave all sexual connotations out of our mental processing of the word pictures above, what remains is pure agape love. God's love. It is the perfect love of a perfect lover.

Ultimately, this love is the one thing that sets a disciple apart from all others who have some acquaintance with Jesus. *While we might begin our relationship with Him based on fear, it is our recognizing and responding to His love that distinguishes us as a disciple.* It is our following Him out of our love for Him, and this alone.

Not fear.

Not desire for gain.

Not thoughts of fame or of glory.

Love. Agape love.

It is Jesus' love for us.

♦♦♦ CHAPTER NOTES ♦♦♦

The concept of Jesus' love for us is a fact stated in the
Bible. We accept this fact. It sinks into our brains and
settles there. But does it sink into our hearts? How does
Jesus love us? Is it a sterile love? Is it from the will only? Or
is it more than this?

Agape love is often misunderstood. Yes, it is a love from
the will. But we understand this to mean it is somehow a
dry, sterile, heartless love. How fervently will we follow one
who loves us only from the will? How will this heal us and
make us whole?

Jesus loves us within the full spectrum of agape love. It
is alive. It is active. It is vibrant. It is full of heart because it
comes from the heart of God.

1. Every True Believer Is His Bride

Each of us is the bride of Jesus. We are to present
ourselves as a chaste (clean, spotless, and pure in thought
and deed) virgin to Him. One that has remained true to
Him. One that was kept for Him and not ourselves. One
that was not given over to the world.

*(2 Corinthians 11:2) For I feel a divine jealousy for you, since
I betrothed you to one husband, to present you as a pure
virgin to Christ.*

2. Jesus Is The Bridegroom

Jesus chose us for a deep relationship with Him. He sees us
as His bride. He desires to know us and celebrate our
relationship forever.

*(Ephesians 5:25b-27a) As Christ loved the church and gave
Himself up for her, that He might sanctify her, having
cleansed her by the washing of water with the word, so that
He might present the church to Himself in splendor.*

*(Isaiah 54:5a) For your Maker is your husband, the LORD of
hosts is His name.*

3. Wedding Feast

The wedding feast will last throughout eternity. It will be a celebration like no other. Forever.

(Revelation 19:7-9a) Let us rejoice and exult and give Him the glory, for the marriage of the Lamb has come, and His Bride has made herself ready; it was granted her to clothe herself with fine linen, bright and pure—for the fine linen is the righteous deeds of the saints. Then the angel said to me, "Write this: Blessed are those who are invited to the marriage supper of the Lamb."

4. Jesus' Love For Us

The love Jesus has for us is pure. It is the fullness of God's love personified. It is everything that love is supposed to be.

(1 Corinthians 13:4-8a) Love is patient and kind; love does not envy or boast; it is not arrogant or rude. It does not insist on its own way; is not irritable or resentful; it does not rejoice at wrongdoing, but rejoices with the truth. Love bears all things, believes all things, hopes all things, endures all things. Love never ends.

♦♦♦ STUDY GUIDE ♦♦♦

Deep in the heart of every man is the longing to be loved. This longing is so strong that we will abandon almost everything to gain it and risk almost anything to experience it. Because of sin in the world, man's love is not entirely pure. It is many times laced with selfishness, motives, and expectations. Yet, we long for it.

1) Look at the definition of *love*. Excluding anything with a sexual connotation, what are some of the meanings?

2) When a person is in love, what kind of feelings does this create?

3) When a person is in love, how is this expressed to the other person?

4) When a person is in love, what are they willing to do for the other person?

Jesus created us to be loved by Him, and, in turn, for us to *learn* to return this love in all of its intensity. This is the great eternal romance of God and man.

5) When you think about Jesus, what feelings come to mind?

6) When you think about your love for Jesus, how do you express this to Him?

7) When you think about your love for Jesus, what are you willing to do for Him?

† PRAYER THOUGHTS †

Eternity is a long time. There will be none of the distractions caused by sin in a fallen world. It will be Jesus and us. How are you preparing yourself for your Bridegroom?

Jesus created us for a great romance with Himself. If you

have not been doing your part in this love relationship, confess this to Him and repent. Ask Him to show you how to love—Him first and then others. He will show you. He is the expression of God's love.

JESUS ESTEEM

Self-esteem. 'The feeling one has for their value as a person.'

There is much discussion surrounding the subject of self-esteem. We hear about it on a regular basis, usually within the context of someone's failure or inability to deal with their life's realities. It is taught as a foundational given in schools and universities across the globe. Much is made of it, whether in having a healthy amount of it or being devoid of enough of it. It has become the touchstone of modern society and a major tenet of faith in the religion of self.

The lack of self-esteem is a subject for our time. It is blamed as the causal element of most societal ills of the day—the lack of motivation, the lack of achievement, the rise of evil. The presupposition of self-esteem is that we are supposed to feel great about ourselves and our value as a person. And therein lies the problem. How can anyone who takes an honest look at themselves, with all of their failures and weaknesses, feel good about what they see? Even if a person's mind is clouded as to the concepts of personal responsibility and sin, how can anyone feel good when their life is littered with the byproducts of the sin around them and within them?

The same is even truer for us. How can any of us not feel some sadness before our Savior? Really? After what He went through to pay the price of our sin?[1]

Jesus was beaten. He was mocked. He had His beard plucked out. He was slapped. Men spit in His face. They beat a crown of thorns deep into His scalp. They whipped

Him until the flesh was torn off, exposing arteries and tendons. He was paraded through the streets. Large spikes were driven through his wrists at the junctures where the major nerves passed to inflict maximum pain. Other spikes were likewise driven through the cluster of anklebones to fix Him to the cross. He was raised naked against the sky for the entire world to see. He had to pull against the nails in His wrists and push against the nails in His ankles to take a quick breath or He would suffocate. He suffered extreme thirst. And worst of all, He bore the horrible penalty of our sin before the purity of His Father. He died of heart failure. For us.

In spite of this, we have sinned willfully, and we continue sinning willfully. Yes, if we understood, truly understood, how could any of us feel good about ourselves? How could we even raise our eyes to look into His?

But is this how Jesus intended for us to live? In a perpetual state of guilt and shame? Paralyzed on the sidelines of discipleship because of what we have done in the past? Disqualified from following Him due to our association with evil? After all, each of us has sinned. Each has fallen short. It may be a matter of degrees, but none of us are without the blemish of sin upon us. Jesus had to die for each of us. No exceptions.

This is an important step in understanding who Jesus is for us—understanding and coming to grips with what our concept of self should be as sinners before Him and His holiness.

UNHOLY MEN BEFORE A HOLY GOD

We have been confronted by the reality of Jesus. We have seen Him in a fresh way. We have seen His sufficiency, His adequacy for our lives. He *is* the answer to our deepest problems and our most haunting questions. He has something for *every* facet of our being. Jesus has provided a way out of our darkness and apathy. He has invited us to join Him in a great adventure.

We know all of this. The truth has sunk down deep into our hearts and souls. We know we should act on this information. We want to act on it. But something is holding us back. There is a barrier between Jesus and us. A barrier between the feelings of gratitude, excitement, and hope that want to propel us forward and our actually moving forward. A barrier of guilt and shame. Somehow, in spite of all that has been discussed, we still do not feel worthy of further service to Jesus.

We must allow Jesus to guide us beyond this place of self-inflicted uselessness to make peace with a great truth. We do not deserve anything from Jesus and neither does anyone else. We don't deserve to be valued in His eyes. We don't deserve a place of honor. We don't deserve to be adopted into His family. We don't deserve to be called His brother. This may not be what we want to hear. But it is truth. We do not deserve these things.

But yet, Jesus places value on us. While we were still sinners, He died for us.[2] Jesus left the glory of heaven and came to earth for this purpose. He did not have to do this. He wanted to do this. What we deserved has nothing to do with what we received. That makes our salvation all the more wondrous and ponderous.

GUILT AND SHAME

Guilt and shame are the result of our failing to live as God intended. There are two aspects to each—*feelings* and *position*. 'Feelings' are how we see ourselves. They are a product of our soul—our mind, will, and emotions. They are internal to us and reflect our perception on a particular subject at a specific time. 'Position' is how God sees us. Our position is our standing before Him. It is legal and it is binding.

From a positional point of view, guilt is the opposite of innocence. Emotionally, it is what we feel when we have failed morally—when we have sinned. Positionally, shame is the opposite of honor. Emotionally, it is usually caused by a consciousness that we are guilty of something and deserve to make restitution.

While guilt can be a feeling we experience, it is more accurately a legal term. When we sin, we are guilty. Justice demands this to be so. Only forgiveness—the declaration that the debt is paid—can erase guilt. If we have not been forgiven, we are both guilty before the law and can feel guilt because of the offense. Once we have been forgiven, we can feel guilty, but positionally before the law there is no longer any guilt related to the offense. Instead, it has been replaced with the pronouncement of innocence. What this means is that our past lives of sin, once confessed and repented of, are pronounced 'forgiven', and the debt for that sin is pronounced 'paid in full'. All guilt is removed by Jesus' payment for our offenses. *We are no longer guilty!* If we still *feel* guilty, it is our believing the lies of our flesh or of demons. We need to reject the thoughts and move on.

Likewise, shame can be a feeling we experience, but it also speaks of our position before Jesus. Jesus died to ransom us from sin and death. His death took us from a position of shame to a position of honor. When we understand that Jesus is not ashamed to call us brothers in spite of what we have done, why do we think we should live in shame?[3] We have been adopted into God's family.[4] Where is the shame in that? Our lives before were shameful. Our behaviors before were shameful. Our positions before were shameful. They lacked honor. But our lives are no longer shameful if we have repented, accepted Jesus' forgiveness, and moved away from our sin. It is proper and right to feel a sense of humility when we consider our past lives and sins. But it is wrong to be held captive by shame. Our life's story is not about shame, but rather about honor in the love God has for us and the position He has bestowed upon us. Jesus scorned the shame of His experience on the cross.[5] We should do likewise and come to Him only with a humble, grateful heart. Paralyzing shame is another lie from our flesh or from demons. We must reject this and move on.

Even in our guilt and shame, we can see that Jesus is the answer. Only He can take away both.

OUR WORTH

We are a valuable person in the eyes of Jesus. Let us put all of our guilt and shame aside, and take on the esteem of Jesus. It is not self-esteem. It has nothing to do with self (us) or anything we could be admired or respected for. No. It is about Jesus—who He is and what He is respected for. It is about what He did and what He says about us. It is about how He sees us.

Put Jesus esteem in place of self-esteem. Let the value He places on us define our lives. In doing so, we will feel a surge of His life in ours. In doing so, we will come to a peace with our past. In doing so, we will be able to move beyond our former ways and enter into His ways. In doing so, our testimony will be one of power and might—His power and might.

We are highly valued in the eyes of Jesus. We have great worth.

There is nothing good in us apart from Jesus. Our life is a proof of this for all to see. All that is good in our life is because He is good. Any worth it has is because He has said it has worth. It is only useful because of His plan for us and His desire to use us in that plan. All that we are is Jesus. There is nothing else.

1. Jesus Suffered

We don't like to dwell on the death of Jesus or His sufferings on our behalf. But it is only through His sufferings and death that the price of our sin was paid and a cure for our suffering purchased. It is only through His resurrection that we are made alive.

(Isaiah 53:5) But He was pierced for our transgressions; He was crushed for our iniquities; upon Him was the chastisement that brought us peace, and with His wounds we are healed.

(John 19:3b) And [they] struck Him with their hands.

(Mark 15:29-32) And those who passed by derided Him, wagging their heads and saying, "Aha! You who would destroy the temple and rebuild it in three days, save Yourself, and come down from the cross!" So also the chief priests with the scribes mocked Him to one another, saying, "He saved others; He cannot save Himself. Let the Christ, the King of Israel, come down now from the cross that we may see and believe." Those who were crucified with Him also reviled Him.

(Isaiah 50:6) I gave My back to those who strike, and My cheeks to those who pull out the beard; I did not hide My face from disgrace and spitting.

(Matthew 27:28-30) And they stripped Him and put a scarlet robe on Him, and twisting together a crown of thorns, they put it on His head and put a reed in His right hand. And kneeling before Him, they mocked Him, saying, "Hail King of the Jews!" And they spit on Him and took the reed and struck Him on the head.

(John 19:1) Then Pilate took Jesus and flogged Him.

(John 19:17a) And He went out, bearing His own cross, to the place called the Place of a Skull.

(John 19:28) After this, Jesus, knowing that all was now finished, said (to fulfill the Scripture), "I thirst!"

2. He Loved Us While We Were In Our Sin

God knew every sin of ours before He sent his Son to die for those sins. Yet, He loved us.

(Romans 5:8) But God shows His love for us in that while we were still sinners, Christ died for us.

3. Jesus Is Not Ashamed Of Us

Jesus is not ashamed of us. Even when Satan stands before Him to accuse and deride us because of our sin. Jesus knows that if we cooperate, His work of sanctification will draw us to sin less and to obey more. He knows that His power will be unleashed in us as we are obedient—the power that crushes all that Satan is doing.

(Hebrews 2:11) For He who sanctifies and those who are sanctified all have one source. That is why He is not ashamed to call them brothers.

4. We Have Been Adopted

Adoption speaks of love, blessings, security, relationship, and inheritance. Adoption takes us out of a place of need into a place of provision. Adoption takes us from a position of guilt and shame to one of innocence and honor.

(Ephesians 1:5a) He predestined us for adoption as sons through Jesus Christ.

5. Jesus Scorned His Shame

Jesus scorned the shame of the cross because He understood His position before His Father. He put it behind Him and walked into His present glory.

(Hebrews 12:2) Looking to Jesus, the founder and perfecter of our faith, who for the joy that was set before Him endured the cross, despising the shame, and is seated at the right hand of the throne of God.

An important aspect of our being human is our emotional ability. We were created to feel things deeply. When we stuff our emotions down deep inside and deny their very existence, we become less than the man we are to be. But our feelings can be deceptive. They are a product of our thought process—our understanding and our perceptions. With wise understanding and correct perception, our feelings will line up with truth. For this reason, we must examine them *and* correct them if needed.

1) Briefly look back on your life. Consider all you have and have not done. Write down your feelings about this.

2) Are there any feelings of guilt? Why? What are the sources of these feelings?

3) Are there any feelings of shame? Why? What are the sources of these feelings?

4) Look at what you have written. Are these sources of your feelings things you have confessed to Jesus and received forgiveness for?

5) If not, confess them and receive His forgiveness right now. If you already have received His forgiveness, why do these feelings linger?

6) Write down the definition of *innocent*.

7) Write down the definition of *honor*.

8) How can innocence co-exist with guilt?

9) How can honor co-exist with shame?

10) Thinking in terms of being *paralyzed*, look at the definition of *paralyze*. In what ways have your guilt and shame made you powerless and ineffective for Jesus?

† PRAYER THOUGHTS †

Forgiven men are innocent. Forgiven men are honored. Jesus has done both for us. We are to accept these gifts, not on our merit, but because Jesus has given them to us. We are to live in the reality of these gifts every day. Ask Jesus to show you how He sees you. You have great value in His eyes.

JESUS POWER

The task seems overwhelming. Even though we have come to see an all-sufficient Jesus with His many facets in our lives, we still tremble at what is before us.

Why?

Could it be that we now see ourselves with clarity that has escaped us until now? That our efforts up to this point have not produced much Godly fruit? That with all of our false pretense stripped away, we are left naked before the piercing gaze of our Lord? That we finally realize the folly of attempting a life lived apart from our Creator and His power?

And in this moment, do we feel our inadequacy start to crush out the excitement of our new walk with Jesus?

This is the final step in successfully following Jesus as His disciple—understanding how to walk each day in His power. Step by step. Minute-by-minute.

INSECURITY

After all that we have gone through to get to this place with Jesus, it is normal for our confidence to be shattered, for feelings of inadequacy to overtake us, and for insecurities to surface in our souls. Should we not expect this? After all, we have examined ourselves in the mirror of truth, coming face to face with our failures. We have been weighed in His scale and found to be wanting in our holiness and purity.[1] We have been ground in His righteous mortar by His holy pestle—broken and humbled. We have been sifted and had our falseness winnowed. We now stand as we truly are before Him.

We know we are not up to the task before us. Even though we see the path to our destiny clearly. Even though we want to pursue Jesus with everything within us. Even though we are ready to lay our lives down for the sake of His call.

Yet, questions swirl in our heads.

How can we walk with Jesus? How can we keep ourselves on His path? How do we keep moving and not get stuck at a place where we are half way, with one foot on the path and one foot off it? How can we follow Him with abandon, living dangerously in His hand?

We must walk in His power.

MAN'S POWER

As man has taken the rightful place of God in his own life and went his own way, he has sought to control his environment. A man's power comes from three major sources. We have seen these at work in our own lives. We have used them to get what we wanted and to maintain some aspect of control over the world around us.

Position. We spend much effort and time maneuvering to better our lot in life. We want the job title where we work. We work to get a position of leadership, any position. We demand to be recognized as the head of our household. Why? Because there is much power found in a position. The more important the position, the greater the power. The greater the power, the more we can control. And it is about control because the more we can control, the higher our sense of security.

Persona. Our persona includes our physical appearance and our projected personality. Our cultures are based on these things, and by them every man is judged. Our appearance is the physical image we project. Our size, shape, and adornment all say something about us to the

300

world around us. We adopt and project a personality that reinforces the image we want and the goals we have. With our appearance and force of personality, we have power—power over people and circumstances. In this, we find our security.

Possessions. We chase after wealth. We amass possessions. But they are not just any possessions. They must be the right possessions. Those that speak of status in our own eyes and in the eyes of those we seek to impress. Because with having money or possessing those symbols of status comes power. Power by perception. It matters to us what others think. If they think highly of us because of what we have, own, or can afford to do, we have power. In our minds, we equate this perception of status to security.

Have we not been guilty of these behaviors in our lives? Do we not gain a healthy dose of affirmation from them? Do we not find some security in them? Do we not feel an aspect of control through them?

But now, as we look at them under the bright light of truth, can we see that we have been bankrupt in our thinking? That the sources of our power only work for us as we walk on our own path?

That they will not work for us as we walk on Jesus' path?

Isn't this the thought that causes us to tremble as we contemplate following Jesus? Realizing that what we have known of power is really not power after all? That the kind of power we have wielded in the past cannot propel us down Jesus' path in our walk as His disciple? That this type of power is inadequate for us to fulfill His great calling on our lives?

TRUE POWER

Jesus is awesome. His power has been on display for millennia.[2] From His creation of all that is known and unknown, to His re-creation of heaven and earth at the end of time. From His miracles before Pharaoh, to His miracle at work in each of us. From His own birth in mere human form, to His resurrection as the all-powerful God. From His lightening and thundering and earthquakes, to His speaking in a still, small voice.

He caused bread to rain down from heaven. He brought forth water from a rock. He caused the sun to stand still. He gave victory to His warriors. He turned water into the finest wine. He broke open the prison and loosed the chains of Paul and Silas. He transforms lives today.

Jesus has power. Power that never fails. Power that works in us. Power that fulfills His plans. It is power that transcends the meager power of man with all his positions, personas, and possessions. It is power that is everlasting and not temporary. It is power above circumstances. It is power that He makes available to each of His disciples.

POWER FOR OUR WALK

Confidence for our walk with Jesus must come from His power alone. It is adequate for the task ahead. It affirms us each step of the way. It makes us secure in Him.

What must we do to take possession of this power? We must walk into it. But we cannot merely walk into it. We must walk humbly before our God, knowing what we are without Him in our lives.[3] And we must leave behind all that will void His power—our wills, our sin, and the cares of this world.[4]

Our wills negate Jesus' power. They make us double-minded, which is a condition of the heart. There is no power in being half-hearted. There is only instability. That is why Jesus calls us to love Him with all of our heart, soul, strength, and mind. With our everything.

Sin separates us from Jesus' power. It does not separate us from His love, for nothing can. But sin is a breaking of our fellowship with Him. It is darkness instead of His light. It must be confessed and forsaken.

The cares of this world choke out Jesus' power. What we will eat. What we will wear. How we will make money. The upkeep of our possessions. All that we worry about. For in our worrying, we display our unbelief that He will take care of us even more than He does the birds of the air. Jesus said that the way is narrow. For us to fully squeeze through that narrow place to walk as His disciple, we must abandon the cares of this world. If we do not, we will get stuck with one leg on His path and one leg on ours. This is where many fall away.

How will we know if we are walking in Jesus' power?

We will see evidence of it in our lives. We will see consistency in our walk. We will see new strength in our relationships. We will see a fresh boldness in our actions. We will see a passion in our purpose and in our steps.

We will see fruit in our lives.[5] The fruits of the Spirit— love, joy, peace, patience, kindness, goodness, faithfulness, gentleness, and self-control.

We will see the Beatitudes at work.[6] We will become poor in spirit, not thinking highly of ourselves. We will mourn over our present failings as they occur. We will be meek, having our strength under His control. We will hunger and thirst for Jesus' righteousness and not our own. We will have a bent toward mercy as Jesus leads us to be merciful. We will purify our hearts, making room only for what Jesus puts there. We will seek peace in our dealings with others—

not compromise, but the quiet confidence of Jesus as He deals through us. And we will not shy away from persecution because of our walk with Jesus, but will see it as His affirmation of our actions.

Jesus' power. Let us each claim it for our own. Let us each possess it. Let us each allow it to flow through us as we walk with Him.

♦♦♦ CHAPTER NOTES ♦♦♦

We are powerless without Jesus. We cannot overcome our flesh. We cannot overcome the world. We cannot overcome Satan and his demons. We cannot overcome our fears, doubts, and inadequacies. We cannot even walk consistently. We will fail and fail miserably.

His power is essential for our lives.

1. Apart From Jesus, We Have Been Found Wanting

We know what we are like apart from Jesus. Let us never forget this.

(Daniel 5:27) You have been weighed in the balances and found wanting.

(Luke 3:17) "His winnowing fork is in His hand, to clear His threshing floor and to gather the wheat into His barn, but the chaff He will burn with unquenchable fire."

2. The Awesome Power Of Jesus Manifested

How easy it is to forget the power that Jesus possesses while we are in the midst of our pursuits and our struggles. We are limited. Jesus is unlimited. We are bound by our humanness. Jesus is boundless in power.

(John 1:3) All things were made through Him, and without Him was not any thing made that was made.

(Revelation 21:1) Then I saw a new heaven and a new earth, for the first heaven and the first earth had passed away, and the sea was no more.

(Exodus 7:3-4) "But I will harden Pharaoh's heart, and though I multiply My signs and My wonders in the land of Egypt, Pharaoh will not listen to you. Then I will lay my hand on Egypt and bring my hosts, my people the children of Israel, out of the land of Egypt by great acts of judgment."

(Acts 2:1-4) When the Day of Pentecost arrived, they were all together in one place. And suddenly there came from heaven a sound like a mighty rushing wind, and it filled the entire house where they were sitting. And divided tongues as of fire appeared to them and rested on each one of them. And they

were all filled with the Holy Spirit and began to speak in other tongues as the Spirit gave them utterance.

(Matthew 28:5-6) But the angel said to the women, "Do not be afraid, for I know that you seek Jesus who was crucified. He is not here, for He has risen, as He said. Come, see the place where He lay."

(Exodus 19:16-18) On the morning of the third day there were thunders and lightnings and a thick cloud on the mountain and a very loud trumpet blast, so that all the people in the camp trembled. Then Moses brought the people out of the camp to meet God, and they took their stand at the foot of the mountain. Now Mount Sinai was wrapped in smoke because the LORD had descended on it in fire. The smoke of it went up like the smoke of a kiln, and the whole mountain trembled greatly.

(1 Kings 19:12b) And after the fire the sound of a low whisper.

(Exodus 16:14-15) And when the dew had gone up, there was on the face of the wilderness a fine, flake-like thing, as fine as frost on the ground. When the people of Israel saw it, they said to one another, "What is it?" For they did not know what it was. And Moses said to them, "It is the bread which the LORD has given you to eat."

(Exodus 17:6) "Behold, I will stand before you there on the rock at Horeb, and you shall strike the rock, and water shall come out of it, and the people will drink."

(Joshua 10:13) And the sun stood still, and the moon stopped, until the nation took vengeance on their enemies.

(John 2:7-9a) Jesus said to the servants, "Fill the jars with water." And they filled them up to the brim. And He said to them, "Now draw some out and take it to the master of the feast." So they took it. When the master of the feast tasted the water now become wine...

(Acts 16:25-26) About midnight Paul and Silas were praying and singing hymns to God, and the prisoners were listening to them, and suddenly there was a great earthquake, so that the foundations of the prison were shaken. And immediately all the doors were opened, and everyone's bonds were unfastened.

3. Walking Humbly With Jesus

Even though we have access to all of Jesus' power in our lives, even though we are called into battle by His side, even though through the proper use of the power of His name we can command demons to flee, yet, we must walk humbly with Him. All that we have access to comes by way of Jesus.

(Micah 6:8) He has told you, O man, what is good; and what does the LORD require of you but to do justice, and to love kindness, and to walk humbly with your God?

4. Cares Of This World

Besides sin, which separates us from Jesus until it is forgiven, nothing can negate His power in our lives like the cares of this world. We all have physical and emotional needs—food, clothes, shelter, money, jobs, love, affection, affirmation, and nurturing. When we fail to recognize that He knows more about what we need than we do, we forget His power in our unbelief. We spend time worrying about what He already knows about and has a plan set in place for. This worrying can choke out everything else that is good in our lives, and can drown out Jesus' voice.

(Matthew 6:26) "Look at the birds of the air: they neither sow nor reap nor gather into barns, yet your heavenly Father feeds them. Are you not of more value than they?"

(Luke 8:14) "And as for what [the seed] fell among thorns, they are those who hear, but as they go on their way they are choked by the cares and riches and pleasures of life, and their fruit does not mature."

5. Our Fruit

We should see fruit in our lives. The fruit confirms the type of 'branch' our lives have become. It confirms that we are firmly grafted into Jesus and sustained by His power.

(Galatians 5:22-23a) But the fruit of the Spirit is love, joy, peace, patience, kindness, goodness, faithfulness, gentleness, self-control.

6. The Beatitudes

We should see a change in our character as we walk in Jesus' power.

(Matthew 5:3-12) "Blessed are the poor in spirit, for theirs is the kingdom of heaven. Blessed are those who mourn, for they shall be comforted. Blessed are the meek, for they shall inherit the earth. Blessed are those who hunger and thirst for righteousness, for they shall be satisfied. Blessed are the merciful, for they shall receive mercy. Blessed are the pure in heart, for they shall see God. Blessed are the peacemakers, for they shall be called sons of God. Blessed are those who are persecuted for righteousness' sake, for theirs is the kingdom of heaven. Blessed are you when others revile and persecute you and utter all kinds of evil against you falsely on My account. Rejoice and be glad, for your reward is great in heaven, for so they persecuted the prophets who were before you."

It is a basic scientific law of thermodynamics that left to themselves, things do wind down and go from order to disorder. It takes the application of an external power source to make anything operate and progress. It is the same with our walk with Jesus. Left to ourselves, our walk with Him *will* wind down. Left to us, the things He has called us to do *will* remain undone.

1) According to the book, *WATM?*, what are the three sources of man's power?

2) Look at each of these and write down how you have used that source of power to find security for yourself.

3) Look at each of them again. Why will these sources of power *not* work for you as you walk down Jesus' path of discipleship to your destiny?

4) When you consider this fact, how do you feel? Be specific.

5) Make a list of ten ways Jesus' power has been displayed throughout history for all to see.

6) Look at the list. If Jesus can do these, do you think His power is sufficient for your walk with Him? And for all that He has called you to do?

7) According to the book, *WATM?*, what three things will keep us from having this power in our lives?

8) According to the book, *WATM?*, how will we know when we have Jesus' power in our lives?

† **PRAYER THOUGHTS** †

We need Jesus to work through us in order for us to be all that He wants us to be and in order to accomplish all that He wants us to accomplish. Ask Jesus to fill you with His power and to help you use it with humility.

❧ PART 4 ☙
THE POSSIBILITIES

Where does this all lead? What happens after we fight our way through our past life of failings or complacency and get into line behind Jesus?

A redeemed life.

We will have the opportunity to live out our remaining years for Jesus—whether one year or forty—to participate in the great adventures Jesus has planned for us, to learn His ways, and to know His heart.

Jesus did not save us so we could waste our lives here on earth. He saved us so we could live life more abundantly. More fully. More generously. Once we have taken the necessary steps to become His disciples, we will be able for the first time in our lives to walk into this abundant life.

We have a life before us, full of potential.

Potential speaks of all that is possible but has not yet become actual. All of our possibilities as a disciple of Jesus exist. They are stored away. They are being kept for that day when they can be released in all of their fullness. And what is the triggering mechanism to release this power of our future? Our destiny?

Only one thing. We must now walk into it.

It requires our committed action. We must take the first step. With everything that is within us, we must walk. And then, we must keep on walking.

Where will Jesus lead us? What adventures await us? Only He knows. One thing is certain—our lives will never be the same. Jesus will begin revealing pieces of His plan for us. He will start showing us specific opportunities for a significant life in Him. He will show us how to be a blessing to men and a threat to Satan. He will gradually define our destiny for us.

After a lifetime of insignificance and struggle, after years of going our own way, after shamefully discounting Jesus' purchase price for our lives, it may be difficult for us to grasp the significance of this life ahead. It may seem nebulous or ethereal, something that we cannot quite come to grips with. It may even seem impossible. This section will help us catch a vision for the possibilities that lie within our grasp. These possibilities must be taken forcefully. By each of us.

The demons tremble. Jesus awaits. Our Father watches.

LATTER RAIN

Time keeps ticking away. Once it is gone, it cannot be retrieved. It does not matter our social status, gender, age, location on earth, amount of wealth or its lack, or level of diligence. Each day passes away the same for one man as it surely passes for another. 24 hours. 1,440 minutes. 86,400 seconds.

If we hit the 'snooze' button on the alarm clock and roll over for another ten minutes of sleep, we seem to be behind those ten minutes all day long. At the time we decided to hit that button and burn those minutes, we did not hold that short amount of time to have much value. How many times have we then later on in the day reckoned those same minutes as precious and wished that we had them back?

As we look back over our lives, how many times have we hit the 'snooze' button on our Christian experience? On our relationship with Jesus? How much time have we burned in self-absorbed pursuits? In self-focused activities? In going our own way? How much time have we counted as unimportant in our lives since we met Jesus and pledged to follow Him?

For most of us, there are certain days of the year when we stop and realize that another year has passed by and we take stock of our lives. For some, it may be a wedding anniversary. For others, it could be Fathers Day. Or perhaps it is New Years Day, some other holiday, or our birthday. Whatever the day, a retrospective pause is taken, and our progress from the last pause pondered. We look back on all of the long years of our lives. We contemplate the relative speed in which they passed, slowly at first and then seemingly more rapidly. We also peer forward into the misty future to the years to come, those we have yet to experience.

How do they look?

Perhaps, not so good looking backwards. For many, they are mostly wasted years. Years of spiritual leanness. Years holding vast periods of time that we treated as unimportant. Years that we can never get back.

Jesus has good news for us, though. As we have started to follow Him as His disciples in earnest, we share in the promise of a future. And in that future, we can look forward to another event. The latter rains in our lives.[1]

This is not the religious movement that goes by the same name here. It is the work that Jesus will do through us as we surrender more and more to Him, align ourselves with His will, and walk closely to Him as disciples. It is a period of productivity for the Kingdom that stretches from the present on into the future. From where we are to where we will be.

ANOTHER OPPORTUNITY

In ancient times, the Israelites experienced two seasons of rain. Being farmers and herders, rain was a topic of great interest to them. Their entire economy revolved around crops and animals. The season of the *former rain* was an annual period of rain in the late fall. The harvest was in and the earth was at rest. The season of *latter rain* came in the spring. With it came all of the hopes for another year of bountiful crops and good pasture land. The latter rains brought with them the promise of life. *Potential.* Without these rains, crops would be stunted, and consequently, the people faced the prospect of a year of famine. Without these rains, the grazing fields did not produce the lush growth needed to support the herds, raising the specter of leaner animals and higher mortality rates.

And so it is with us. The times of the former rains are past. Any harvest we had from the past is now history. Whatever our lives produced is over and done with. It is what it is. It might have been a harvest of abundance along with fields of plenty. Or, perhaps not. Whatever the case, we cannot go back to the past. We cannot fill our barns or fatten our herds retroactively. That time is over.

Many of us have wasted precious time. We know this. We feel it deeply. But do we want this to be the legacy we leave upon the earth when we die? Or, do we want to finish well and accomplish something that is significant? Do we want our lives to matter? For Jesus? For our families? For our future generations?

These times of the latter rains will become our legacies in life. What we accomplish for Jesus as He leads us through the many battles will become how we are ultimately remembered. They will be blessings to the people of God and arrows in the hearts of the enemies of our King. They will produce an abundance spiritually in the lives that we touch. They will be passed down our bloodlines, defining the trajectories of our children, our grandchildren, and all who come after us for a thousand generations![2] For Satan and his demons, they will mark another toll in the long sounding of their death knell.

This should be of great encouragement to all of us. That we could mess up our lives so badly or waste years of valuable time and then get another chance is truly a blessing of grace and mercy from Jesus.

What will be our end when our shadows on earth pass away? Do we want Jesus to be pleased with the time He has redeemed in our lives, this time of the latter rain? Do we want to stand tall on that last day and see heaven opened to reveal Jesus standing at the right hand of God our

Father? Do we want Him to reach out His hand to ours and say, 'The work here is done and it is time to go'? Do we want to bow before Him and His Father and receive our crown? Do we desire for our family to see us enter into His presence in peace? Do we want it to be a celebration of a life well lived, and not a dirge for a life of regrets?

We have this opportunity. That is one of the benefits of fighting our way out of our present darkness and slumber and into the mighty army called Jesus' disciples. Into a life of abundance. Into a season of the latter rain.

We can end our lives well. Jesus will be honored. Our Father will be glorified.

✦✦✦ CHAPTER NOTES ✦✦✦

We have a chance to start over. This is a great gift from Jesus. Starting over is starting over. It is leaving the past behind. It is setting off in a new direction on a new leg of the journey with Jesus. It is moving toward our destiny.

As we begin anew, we do get a jump-start from one perspective. Our life's experiences up until now are real. Even if they are bad experiences, they add value to our new walk. They give us a sense of perspective. They help ground us. They keep us humble. They make up our life's story.

And then we move forward to a remaining life lived with honor and purpose to glorify Jesus and our Father.

1. The Rains

It is appropriate that the rains are named as they are. They fit perfectly with our life stories. The former rains come in the late fall or early winter. They come after the work is done. They cannot be used for that year's harvest. The latter rains come in the spring. They signify provision for new growth. New potential.

We cannot go back. We can only go forward to a better harvest.

2. A Thousand Generations

A thousand generations is a long time. This term is used in the Bible to signify something that will last *forever*. Incredible as it seems, Jesus stands ready to honor our efforts as His disciples for a thousand generations—forever!

(Psalm 105:8) He remembers His covenant forever, the word that He commanded, for a thousand generations.

(Deuteronomy 7:9) Know therefore that the LORD your God is God, the faithful God who keeps covenant and steadfast love with those who love Him and keep His commandments, to a thousand generations.

♦♦♦ STUDY GUIDE ♦♦♦

Just as the spring rains bring the promise of new life in the northern hemisphere, so does our new walk with Jesus. The rains do not discriminate where they fall, be it ground that has never been tilled, or ground that has produced abundant fruit. The starting point for all the ground is the same—life-giving water from heaven. Water that can transform even the most parched soil into a lush field.

1) What emotions do you feel when you anticipate a fresh walk with Jesus?

2) Make a list of the things you want to walk away from (attitudes, actions, people, habits, etc.).

3) Make a list of the things you want to walk toward.

4) Look up the definition of *potential*. How does this word fill you with hope for the future?

5) Find the definition for *legacy*. If you continue your walk with Jesus, in what ways will your life be a gift to those you leave behind when you die?

6) Why is it important to you to leave such a gift?

† PRAYER THOUGHTS †

Jesus is merciful to us. He knows He made us from the dust of the earth. He gives us an opportunity to begin where we are and to walk victoriously with Him to our destiny. Ask Jesus for a fresh vision for your life and then follow close after Him to its fulfillment.

LIFE SWORD

Swords are weapons used in hand-to-hand combat. They are designed to do damage to the enemy. While used to some extent defensively, a sword is primarily an offensive weapon. They contain one or two edges made for cutting and a point made for thrusting. These edges can be honed to razor sharpness using the proper tools. The sharper the sword, the deadlier to the enemy.

Swords come in various lengths, shapes, sizes, and weights. Their intended usage determines these characteristics. Much skill and sophisticated knowledge is needed to make a proper sword. Care must be taken in the design of the sword so it is manageable by him who wields it. It must not be too heavy or too light. It must not be too thick or too thin. It must not be too long or too short. It must not be too wide or too narrow. It must not be too rigid or too flexible. The grip area must take into account the need for either one or two hands for swinging the weapon. Above all else, the sword must be well balanced with an adequate pommel below the handle or it will be difficult to swing and sluggish to maneuver in battle.

The earliest swords were constructed out of wood with stone or bone sections for the cutting surface. Later swords were produced from bronze, iron, and steel. Each material had different characteristics related to the manufacturing technology of the day. Metal swords were made by hammering red-hot material into the desired shape. Dipping the hot blade into a liquid quenched the metal. This process gave the sword the hardness needed to withstand the rigors of contacting other hard objects in battle, but increased its brittleness. To counteract this, the blade was tempered by elevating its temperature for long periods of time. Tempering techniques made the metal flexible, so that it would not lose its shape or shatter in battle.

Much skill is needed to wield a sword properly. Hours of practice are required to move from a rudimentary ability to mastering the weapon in preparation for battle. Without this exercising, the user is doomed to sure defeat.

OUR TESTIMONY

The most powerful weapons we possess are the name of Jesus and our testimony. We have been granted limited use of Jesus' name (See the *Chapter Notes* for more detail). We own the testimony of our lives.

The name of Jesus is the most powerful weapon of all. At the end of time, His name will cause every knee to bow whether in heaven, on earth, or under the earth. As our King, Lord, and Brother, when Jesus authorizes us to use His name, things get done. His name carries the same authority as His person, so when it is properly invoked, all of creation must react. This is not optional.[1]

Our testimony is our second most powerful weapon. A testimony is a declaration of fact from our personal knowledge or experience. Its usual context is in a legal setting where the one making the claim is under an oath to tell only the truth. Our life's story regarding the transforming power of Jesus is our testimony. It can be expressed in what we say or demonstrated by how we live. The common denominator is Jesus—His saving, supernatural power of love at work. Therein lies the power. Our testimony may be disputed by men, but what we know as fact cannot be refuted by them.

Our testimony is the sword of our life.[2] Our *life sword*.

Jesus designed the type of sword our lives would be before the foundations of the earth were laid, according to His calling for each of us. Our sword was then hammered and shaped by the realities of our life, both good and bad. Bad choices, mistakes, and complacency make our swords useless by degrees in battle. Good choices, time spent with Jesus, and obedience to Him make them more lethal.

Jesus is the one who takes our old, rusty, dull sword, and re-shapes it. He uses times of patiently waiting upon Him to quench it. He uses the hot trials in our lives to temper it. He uses his personal teaching time with us to sharpen it to a razor's edge. And He uses our times of rest between the battles to shine it to a brilliant luster. He is our pommel—the One who gives our sword balance. He is the One who teaches us how to use our sword to inflict maximum damage on the enemy in battle. He is the One who trains us to be dangerous men. He puts the fierceness for the battle in our hearts. He does all of this so we can fulfill the destiny that He planned for us before we were born.

The demons know these things as well. They are subject to the name of Jesus and must obey commands given in His name, when given with the proper jurisdiction (in other words, when given specific commands, for specific things, in specific situations where we have the authority to do so under the direction of Jesus. See the *Chapter Notes* for more detail). This is the power of Jesus' name. Likewise, the demons know that the truths about Jesus in our life's story have a powerful effect on those around us. Even more so, they know that they cannot successfully assail a pure life that has no hidden sin. This is the power of our testimony.

INTO THE BATTLE

When a man comes to that place of authenticity where sin has no hold on him and he has nothing to lose, he becomes a dangerous man in any fight. That is why Satan and his demons want to keep us on the sidelines. That is why they want to keep us wounded and bound up. That is why they want to silently infest us. That is why they want to keep us emasculated. That is why they want to defeat our ability to follow Jesus. *They want to keep us out of the fight.*

So, we must go through the steps necessary to become dangerous men. We must allow Jesus to make our swords ready for the battles that lie ahead. We must submit to His training. Once underway, we must continue to walk with Jesus as His disciple. Ever obedient. Ever learning. Ever pure. Ever free.

Then, when the shofar is sounded and we are called to battle, we will be ready.[3] We will fearlessly follow our Commander into combat. We will fight in concert with Him and execute His orders. We will make Jesus proud with our bearing in the battle, and bring glory to His name in our perseverance.

In doing so, we will glorify His Father, our Father.

The testimony of our life is our sword in battle. Some of us may be cringing at this thought because we think that all we have is a two-inch, single-blade, fold-up pocketknife based on our lives so far. But, it is all about the transformation. Our 'BC' might have been evil. Some of our 'AD' might have been only marginally better. But the testimony of how our life is *now* is the key—how far we have come, what we had to overcome, where Jesus has led and how. These are the things our swords are made from. Our remaining days can be significant upon the earth. Our swords can be used mightily in battle. Much can be accomplished for our Commander.

1. Using The Power Of Jesus' Name

There is much misunderstanding about the use of Jesus' name. Well-meaning but misinformed people throw it around carelessly. It gets invoked for purposes that do not line up with His plan. Because of this, there is no power attached to the words—no matter how intently or how intensely they are spoken—and much damage occurs.

Jesus' name is like a nuclear weapon in a knife fight. It is powerful and effective. It carries the authority of Jesus Himself if used properly. And it must be used properly. Otherwise, it will bring demonic forces down upon us with a fury.

In the strictest sense, all things in heaven, on earth, and below the earth are subject to obey the name of Jesus.

(Philippians 2:9-11) Therefore God has highly exalted Him and bestowed on Him the name that is above every name, so that at the name of Jesus every knee should bow, in heaven and on earth and under the earth, and every tongue confess that Jesus Christ is Lord, to the glory of God the Father.

So the issue of using His name properly does not lie in the name itself. It lies in our authority to use it. We must obey Jesus on this. If He tells us to use His name to accomplish something that we are doing with Him, we are to use it. It will have great effect against evil. If He does not tell us to use it, we should not. The battle is His, not ours. If we get out from behind His shield, we will run into trouble quickly.

Demons have an organized hierarchy. Authority is distributed according to territory and rank within that territory. If we attempt to use Jesus' name to rebuke a demon that we have nothing to do with (in other words, one that is not involved in what we are working on for Jesus), all it will do is aggravate that demon and grant him access to us and our families. We have no jurisdiction over him or his territory because Jesus did not give it to us. It is nothing more than our getting out in front of Jesus, our shield. We are exposed to the full firepower of the enemy.

An example of this would be if we were driving around in our vehicle and saw something we didn't like that was not our concern, and we rebuked the demons involved with that place or situation in Jesus' name. Because we had nothing to do with it (Jesus did not have us directly involved with that battle), we would just be taking on the wrath of that demon and all others under his authority. Nothing good would happen in our life as a result, and much bad could.

So, we are to use Jesus' name as a tactical nuclear weapon that is very specifically targeted to what we are involved in, and do so only when we have our Commander's permission to do so. In this way, we will have the jurisdiction to use it to great effect in the battle.

The passage in the Book of Daniel is telling about the power of demons.

(Daniel 10:12-13, 20b, 21b) Then he (Jesus) said to me, "Do not fear, Daniel, from the first day that you set your heart to understand and to humbled yourself before your God, your words have been heard, and I have come because of your

words. The prince of the kingdom of Persia withstood me twenty-one days, but Michael, one of the chief princes, came to help me, for I was left there with the kings of Persia...But I will return to fight against the prince of Persia; and when I go out, behold, the prince of Greece will come...There is none who contends by my side against these, except Michael your prince."

We need to stay behind our shield, Jesus.

2. The Sword Of Our Testimony

(Revelation 12:11) And they have conquered him by the blood of the Lamb and by the word of their testimony, for they loved not their lives even unto death.

This is a rich verse that speaks directly to our life sword. The 'him' in this verse is Satan. We corporately will overcome Satan as we individually fight the battles that Jesus has for us to fight and accomplish what He has for us to accomplish. How is it done? We overcome the enemy by the blood of the Lamb, Jesus, in conjunction with our testimony—our life's story. The relationship between the blood and our testimony is the key here. The power of Jesus' blood is found in its atoning payment for our sin. So, with respect to our testimony, it is speaking of our pure life where we are no longer bound by the sins of the past that have been forgiven. It is a life that Satan and his demons cannot successfully assail because of our commitment to purity through obedience to Jesus. This is the key to having a strong, dangerous, and effective life sword.

But there is one other thing. The last part of this verse is also important. These who overcame Satan and his demons had nothing left to lose. They had come to peace with their past lives. They had acknowledged their past sinfulness. They had scorned their past shame in humbleness. They had accepted themselves positionally before Jesus. They had picked up their swords and turned toward their destiny. There was nothing else to do but live fully for Jesus until He called them home. They were willing to lay down their lives for their Commander. Minute by minute. Hour by hour. Day by day. Year by year.

Taken together, this is how we will finish well and leave our legacy.

3. Shofar

The shofar is a ram's horn used by ancient Hebrews as a call to assembly or battle. Based on the effects of this trumpet when they were blown by Gideon's three hundred or at Jericho, it must call forth the very angels of God to the battle.

✦✦✦ STUDY GUIDE ✦✦✦

Jesus has called us into battle alongside Him. Our enemy is more powerful than us as mere men, so hand-to-hand combat is out of the question. We need a weapon—an effective weapon.

1) According to the book, *WATM?*, what two weapons do we possess for the battle?

2) Look at these two weapons. For these to be effective, we must know how to use them. According to the book, *WATM?*, what is the primary rule on using Jesus' name in battle?

3) Look up the definition of *tactical* in the dictionary. What does it mean?

4) According to the book, *WATM?*, who owns our testimony?

5) What does our testimony consist of?

6) Since the demonic world cannot prevail against the name of Jesus, where will they concentrate their attack?

7) Beyond working with Jesus, how do we keep our life sword ready for battle?

8) On a scale of 1 to 10, how ready is your life sword for battle?

Not Ready   1 <<——>> 10   Ready

† PRAYER THOUGHTS †

If your sword is rusty and dull, it is time to give it to Jesus and allow Him to polish and sharpen it. If it is brittle, it is time to allow Him to temper it. If it lacks balance, it is time to invite Jesus to give it His balance. We are heading for battle. Each of us needs a sword Jesus can rely on. Ask Him to prepare yours.

WE WILL NEVER DIE

Mankind has been looking for a means of slowing the approach of physical death or outright escaping it for millennia. From ancient times, this search focused on finding a mythical river or water source with restorative healing powers. Magical elixirs and all manner of snake oil remedies have been foisted upon a public eager to stop the march of time. There is something in man that yearns for an extension of his existence.

EVERLASTING BEINGS

Man was originally created to be an everlasting being, one who physically lived forever by eating fruit from the Tree of Life that grew in the Garden of Eden.[1] That is how Jesus created man for the Godhead—to walk with Them through an endless future in fellowship. It was not until sin entered into the world that physical death took root in creation and spiritual death in man.

Most of us will walk upon the earth for seventy or eighty years. Factoring out infant mortality, wars, plagues, curable diseases, and the affects of poor diet, this has not changed much over a couple of millennia. Yet, it is still much shorter than the life spans we read about in the Genesis account. Beyond Enoch and Elijah, and up to the Rapture, all men must die physically.[2]

But yet, through Jesus, we can be born again spiritually, passing from spiritual death to eternal life. While we have not existed since eternity past, and are therefore not eternal, we now will live on forever in Jesus, even after our physical death. Our understanding of this important fact has been lost in our 'live for today' materialistic culture where everything is focused upon our physical life here on earth in the present. In fact, we commonly refer to eternity as the 'afterlife' as if the 'here and now' were the main attraction and our life after death is some type of a letdown. But the spirit of a redeemed man lives on forever after the brief physical life has ended. Do we take pause at this in all that we do?

Forever is a long time. A very long time. It is so long that our minds, which are locked into a time and space continuum, cannot even comprehend what 'forever' means. 'Absolutely without end' can't be measured in terms of time, space, distance, mass, speed, or relativity. It does not have an ending point. It has only one duration, and that is *forever*. It does not fit into anything that man can use to frame it. One thing we do know, 'forever' is permanent instead of temporary.

REWARDS

So why is it important for us to ponder our existence in the eternal? Because it reinforces our temporary status as citizens in this life on planet earth.

We tend to put a lot of emphasis on our present life. In and of itself, this is not a bad thing. We are supposed to live our lives to the fullest degree possible as our acknowledgment of Jesus' sacrifice for us. We are supposed to worship our Creator every time we ponder His magnificent creation. We are supposed to marvel in gratitude at every breath and heartbeat.[3]

But man goes far beyond this in his efforts to live life. Man tends to worship himself instead of Jesus' creation. He tends to focus on the life instead of the Giver of Life. He tends to accumulate—things, money, lands, houses, vehicles, prestige, food, clothes, experiences—the list goes on and on. All of these are passing, just as man passes.[4]

Nothing physical can be taken from this life into the next, nor can anything temporal, such as educational degrees or power or position. But yet, we spend much time on the pursuit of these things instead of in the pursuit of God.

Eternity frames our purpose for being. If we were created for everlasting fellowship with Jesus, why would we not be spending time now, in this life, cultivating and developing this relationship? After all, we have only a short span of time to get things moving forward in this regard. Wouldn't it be a travesty if we only learned to recognize Jesus when we face Him after we die? To get to heaven and not really know who He is relationally? To wait until then to spend quality time with Him?

What are we thinking?

Yet, this is the attitude of many. Life in the here and now gets fenced off from life in eternity. Life here is for us. We will get around to God when we die, or so we think.

The eternal emphasizes the importance of our actions while we are here on earth. Jesus taught us there are varying levels of eternal rewards in heaven.[5] Sure, all believers will get into heaven, but all believers will not dwell in that kingdom equally so. Jesus taught us that the extent and content of our reward is based solely upon what we do for His kingdom with what we are given in our life on earth. If we are given much in terms of knowledge, revelation, opportunity, and means, then much is expected. If we are given less, something less is expected. It is the concept of return on investment. Jesus expects a return on the blessings and opportunities He provides to us in this life.

Additionally, we know that we will reign with Jesus when He rules the earth personally for 1,000 years.[6] That means we will be put in charge of things. Again, it is clear that he who was faithful in the little things while walking on earth will be given more responsibility in bigger things after his physical life is over. Our positions in the eternal will be determined by our temporal actions in this life.

This likely extends to our dwelling place as well, both during the thousand-year reign of Jesus on earth, and afterward in the New Jerusalem upon the new earth. Some dwelling places will be larger and more magnificent than others. Some will be located closer to the throne of God.[7]

And there is one more aspect to this idea of rewards. We know that we, as the Bride of Christ, will sit with Jesus the Bridegroom at the wedding feast table. Given that all believers from all ages will be present, it must be a very large table. As with any table, there are only two places or seats next to the head of the table where Jesus sits. The rest of us will be spread down both sides as far as the eye can see. The positions at that table will be based on our actions here on earth. Do we want to be seated as close as we can to Jesus or far away in the seats reserved for those who treated their salvation with little regard? Is it important to us to have intimate conversation with Him?

Our relationship with Jesus will be forever and ever. Our rewards will be forever and ever. Our ruling position will be forever and ever. Our position at the feast table will be forever and ever.

That is a long time based on our short time here.

MOTIVATION

Is it wrong to focus on our rewards and positions in the next life? If it were, would Jesus have emphasized the importance of our actions in this life in relation to these things in the next? This is not about earning one's salvation. That is something none of us could ever do. It is about earning our eternal rewards.

God the Father is perfectly just. His perfect justice demands that people not be treated the same, but that consequences be based on the actions of those people with respect to their opportunities. This same perfect justice requires that our rewards be different as well, based on our actions relative to His plans for our lives.

Our focus should be on the most important factor that overrides all of the reasons given above. That is our relationship with Jesus. If our relationship is pleasing to Jesus, God the Father is glorified. And that is why Jesus does what He does.

♦♦♦ CHAPTER NOTES ♦♦♦

Man spends a lot of time, effort, and money trying to extend his life on earth when eternity beckons all of us just around the next corner. Jesus had a lot to say about preparing for eternity, not just spiritually concerning one's salvation, but also in terms of rewards and positions. With all that takes place each day in our lives, it is difficult to keep the eternal perspective. We have places to go, things to do, people to see, and bills to pay. The *now* of life crowds in on us, pushing the *then* of eternity into the margins.

But, eternity is always out there. It is a trip we will all take. It is our final frontier. It is not the *afterlife*. It is *the* life! Perhaps we should be spending more time preparing for that trip than our vacation or holiday this year?

1. Tree Of Life

The Tree of Life that was in the Garden of Eden now awaits us in heaven.

(Genesis 3:22-24) Then the LORD God said, "Behold, the man has become like one of Us, in knowing good and evil. Now, lest he reach out his hand and take also of the tree of life and eat, and live forever"—therefore the LORD God sent him out of the garden of Eden to work the ground from which he was taken. He drove out the man, and at the east of the garden of Eden He placed the cherubim and a flaming sword that turned every way to guard the way to the tree of life.

(Revelation 22:1-2) Then the angel showed me the river of the water of life, bright as crystal, flowing from the throne of God and of the Lamb through the middle of the street of the city; also, on either side of the river, the tree of life with its twelve kinds of fruit, yielding its fruit each month. The leaves of the tree were for the healing of the nations.

2. Those Who Never Die

There are two marvelous stories in Scripture that tell of two men who did not die and were taken physically to heaven. Equally marvelous, those Christians who are alive when

Jesus returns will share in this same experience of being taken up bodily into His presence.

(Genesis 5:24) *Enoch walked with God, and he was not, for God took him.*

(2 Kings 2:11) *And as they still went on and talked, behold, chariots of fire and horses of fire separated the two of them. And Elijah went up by a whirlwind into heaven.*

(1 Thessalonians 4:16-17) *For the Lord Himself will descend from heaven with a cry of command, with the voice of an archangel, and with the sound of the trumpet of God. And the dead in Christ will rise first. Then we who are alive, who are left, will be caught up together with them in the clouds to meet the Lord in the air, and so we will always be with the Lord.*

3. Numbering Our Days

We don't like to think about how short our life on earth is. If we were truly willing to ponder this fact and grasp its significance, would we ever waste a day pursuing the meaningless things of this life?

(Psalm 144:4) *Man is like a breath; his days are like a passing shadow.*

(Psalm 90:12) *So teach us to number our days that we may get a heart of wisdom.*

4. We Can't Take It With Us

We came into the world with nothing and we will leave with exactly the same amount.

(Luke 12:16-20) *And He [Jesus] told them a parable, saying: "The land of a rich man produced plentifully, and he thought to himself, 'What shall I do, for I have nowhere to store my crops?' And he said, 'I will do this: I will tear down my barns and build larger ones, and there I will store all my grain and my goods. And I will say to my soul, 'Soul, you have ample goods laid up for many years; relax; eat, drink, be merry.' But God said to him, 'Fool! This night your soul is required of you, and the things you have prepared, whose will they be?'"*

(1 Timothy 6:7) *For we brought nothing into the world, and we*

cannot take anything out of the world.

(Ecclesiastes 5:15) As he came from his mother's womb he shall go again, naked as he came, and shall take nothing for his toil that he may carry away in his hand.

5. Everlasting Rewards

Scripture is clear about the reality of rewards based upon our actions on earth. Jesus, Himself shall give them to us.

(Mark 10:29-31) Jesus said, "Truly, I say to you, there is no one who has left house or brothers or sisters or mother or father or children or lands, for My sake and the gospel, who will not receive a hundredfold now in this time, houses and brothers and sisters and mothers and children and lands, with persecutions, and in the age to come eternal life. But many who are first will be last, and the last first."

(Matthew 5:11-12a) "Blessed are you when others revile and persecute you and utter all kinds of evil against you falsely on My account. Rejoice and be glad, for your reward is great in heaven."

(Revelation 2:23b) "And I will give to each of you according to your works."

(Revelation 22:12) "Behold, I am coming soon, bringing My recompense with Me, to repay each one for what he has done."

(1 Corinthians 3:8) He who plants and he who waters are one, and each will receive his wages according to his labor.

(1 Corinthians 3:13-14) Each one's work will become manifest, for the Day will disclose it, because it will be revealed by fire, and the fire will test what sort of work each one has done. If the work that anyone has built on the foundation survives, he will receive a reward.

6. One-Thousand Year Reign

(Revelation 20:4, 6b) Then I saw thrones, and seated on them were those to whom the authority to judge was committed...But they will be priests of God and of Christ, and they will reign with Him a thousand years.

(Rev 21:1-2) Then I saw a new heaven and a new earth, for the first heaven and the first earth had passed away, and the sea was no more. And I saw the holy city, New

Jerusalem, coming down out of heaven from God, prepared as a bride adorned for her husband.

7. Many Dwelling Places In Heaven

(John 14:2) "In My Father's house are many rooms. If it were not so, would I have told you that I go and prepare a place for you?"

♦♦♦ Study Guide ♦♦♦

The world speaks of existence after death as the *afterlife,* as if this brief time on earth is *the life.* The goal then becomes to concentrate on the things of this life at the expense of the things in the next. Jesus tells us in the Gospels that we have it all wrong. Our priorities are backwards. Eternity is a lot longer than 70 or 80 years here. We need to prepare.

1) Think about your week. You have 168 hours to spend. Write down in detail how many hours you spend on things of eternal consequence versus things that will pass away.

2) Make a list of what you can do to increase your focus on the eternal.

3) Look at **Matthew 6:19**. What does this say to you?

(Matthew 6:19) "Do not lay up for yourselves treasures on earth, where moth and rust destroy and where thieves break in and steal."

4) Write down the definition of *reward* when it is used as a noun.

5) Write down the definition of *eternal.*

6) What do you think about a man who would spend most of his effort accumulating things of no eternal value instead of concentrating on rewards that he can keep eternally?

† Prayer Thoughts †

It is easy to live for the immediate and disregard the future if you don't really know what that future will bring. As Christians, we have been told about our futures. The question then becomes, *'Will we prepare for it?'* If you have not been preparing, confess this to Jesus and ask Him to give you His eternal perspective.

IMPACT

An impact is made when two objects strike each other. A hammer and a nail. A ball and a bat. A car and a guardrail. In order for an impact to occur, the objects must be moving toward an intersecting point. The *instance* of the impact releases vast quantities of energy. The *result* of the impact is that motion is produced or impeded and trajectories are altered. The *legacy* of the impact is that the current state of all objects involved has been changed forever.

As a disciple of Jesus, we will have an impact. Our lives with Jesus will move according to His plan. They will intersect with other lives and events at critical junctures. Supernatural energy will be released at the point of contact with these other lives and events. The trajectories of all will be altered. Sometimes, courses will be changed from destruction to life. Sometimes they will be accelerated. Sometimes slowed. Whatever the nature of these impacts, things will be different for all involved. Lives changed. Ideas challenged. Evil confronted. Blessings bestowed.

Jesus called us to be both salt and light in this world.[1] Salt impacts the taste of foods and liquids, bringing out and enhancing their individual flavors. It acts as a preservative. It has cleansing properties. It can be used for healing. Light impacts the visibility of anything it engulfs, bringing forth the true image of the object. It exposes the unseen. It exerts pressure on any object in its path. It dispels the darkness. Both salt and light make big impacts.

Our lives are to matter. They are to have impact.

Normal People do not Change the World

Normal changes with the passing of time in any culture. It follows the general flow from morality to evilness, from truth to falsehood, from clarity to confusion.

Normal people do not stand steadfast against the flow of the world around them. They bend to the pressure of their cultures. Slowly, they change as the flow sweeps over and around them, propelling them steadily downstream. This is why it is not possible for normal people to change the world—the world is always changing them.

Jesus has a better way. He wants to walk us out of our 'normal' and into His supernatural 'abnormal'. He wants our lives to have a world-changing impact.

If we will follow Jesus' lead on this, we will no longer be content to go with the flow around us, be it the flow of the culture of the world or the flow of the culture within the church today. Instead, we will want to impact the state of both for Him. We will want to show these cultures and the people within them the Jesus we have come to know—the real Jesus. We will want to challenge them out of their two-dimensional creation of Him and into a multi-dimensional relationship with Him.

Likewise, we will seek to change our impact on our family. To teach them the importance of principle and purity, helping them to stand on the first and rest in the second. To teach them to pick up their swords for Jesus and to swing them mightily as warriors with Him in battle. To teach them the value of living life to the fullest as Jesus intended by losing their lives fully for His sake. To teach them to pass all of this down to future generations.

If we will surrender our wills, purify our souls, and begin our walk, Jesus will change us from normal to abnormal, supernaturally.

340

Will we join Jesus wholeheartedly in this walk? Will we run with Him to the call of battle? Will we lay down our lives with His for the sake of our families, our future generations, and for others He sends us to? Will we rest in the arms of our Savior?

We can accomplish much with Jesus. Our lives can have an impact. We can fulfill our destiny. In doing so, we will honor Jesus and glorify our Father who is in heaven.

I count everything as loss because of the surpassing worth of knowing Christ Jesus my Lord...

that I may gain Christ...that I may know Him and the power of His resurrection.[2]

♦♦♦ CHAPTER NOTES ♦♦♦

Many of us want to make a difference. We want to count. We want to have an impact. We don't just want to accumulate or consume. We want to give a vision to our families. We want them to see a purpose in this life. We want to help them chart a course to a fulfilled life. A substantial life. A significant life.

Jesus has given us the opportunity to do all of this and more. Under His direction, it will be done correctly. Under His control, it will be done mightily.

1. Disciples Are To Be Salt And Light

(Matthew 5:13-16) "You are the salt of the earth, but if salt has lost its taste, how shall its saltiness be restored? It is no longer good for anything except to be thrown out and trampled under people's feet. You are the light of the world. A city set on a hill cannot be hidden. Nor do people light a lamp and put it under a basket, but on a stand, and it gives light to all in the house. In the same way, let your light shine before others, so that they may see your good works and give glory to your Father who is in heaven."

2. All Things Are Loss Compared To Jesus

(Philippians 3:8-11) Indeed, I count everything as loss because of the surpassing worth of knowing Christ Jesus my Lord. For His sake I have suffered the loss of all things and count them as rubbish, in order that I may gain Christ and be found in Him, not having a righteousness of my own that comes from the law, but that which comes through faith in Christ, the righteousness from God that depends on faith— that I may know Him and the power of His resurrection, and may share His sufferings, becoming like Him in His death, that by any means possible I may attain the resurrection from the dead.

✦✦✦ STUDY GUIDE ✦✦✦

The world is a big place, a powerful place. It tends to make a big impact on us. It flows around us, threatening to uproot us and sweep us from our feet. As Christians, we are called to stand against this pull of the world around us.

1) In what ways do you see the world impacting your life and sweeping you away from where Jesus wants you to be?

2) In fast-moving water, it is important to have your feet firmly planted. Jesus is our rock, the place of sure footing. List the things you need to do to remain firmly planted on Him so you can resist the flow of the world.

† PRAYER THOUGHTS †

It is impossible to stand against the flow if you are holding on to some of what is floating by. Ask Jesus to show you the ways of the world you are grasping hold of. Make a list of whatever He shows you.

Just by standing firm, we impact the culture that is trying to sweep us away. We slow it and we divert it with our stance. If you are having trouble getting your footing, cry out to Jesus. It takes supernatural force to stand against the flow of the world.

344

EPILOGUE

From the first pages of this book to the last, we have encountered a living Jesus. We have come to understand that He is real and that He is engaged. We have seen that He is ever present. We have felt His great love and concern for us. We now know that He is sufficient for our journey.

Chapter by chapter, Jesus has traced a path for each of us to follow. It is a path specifically chosen just for us. It is a path that must be walked individually. It is a path that begins at the wide place of our being a Jesus follower in name only. It winds its way through our struggles to become His disciple. It ends at the narrow place reserved for His dedicated few.

We have heard Jesus challenging all that is conventional in our lives. Our concept of who He is. Our concept of who we are. Our concept of our relationship with Him. Our concept of the Christian life. He has challenged us to take up the mantle of authentic manhood as a single man, husband, father, or grandfather. He has challenged us to expand the horizon of our vision beyond the immediate, the familiar, and the comfortable. He has challenged us to pick up our sword and never lay it down. He has challenged us to become dangerous for Him.

Taken as a whole, these challenges represent a call to stand in a place where few men stand today. It is a place where nothing stands between Jesus and us—not our past, not old wounds, not sin habits, not our fears, not man-made religion, not even the demonic. It is the place of freedom in the uncharted territory of a vibrant love affair with our Creator.

The journey is set before us. It is epic in its proportions. Jesus says, "Come, follow Me."

❧ APPENDIX ❧

JESUS THE REDEEMER

Jesus is the redeemer of sinners. Every man starts life as a slave of sin. Jesus buys us back from our master, sin. He pays a ransom for our release—His blood. It was a debt that we could not pay ourselves. Only through Jesus can salvation come to us because only He can pay the price of our sin.

Those who have never asked Jesus to save them from their sins can do so now.

Follow each of the steps below from the heart.

HEAR THE GOOD NEWS

Christians are those who have understood their sinfulness and asked Jesus to save them from their sins. Salvation does not come through infant baptism, church membership, personal goodness, our parents, by doing good works, giving money, any other of our efforts, or even by just saying a prayer. It comes only by the graciousness of God to us.

(Ephesians 2:8-9) *For by grace you have been saved through faith. And this is not your own doing; it is the gift of God, not a result of works, so that no one may boast.*

The Bible tells us that God is holy and perfect in every way. Jesus told us we had to be perfect as our Father in heaven is.

(Matthew 5:48) *"You therefore must be perfect, as your heavenly Father is perfect."*

This perfect God cannot be around sinful man.

(Isaiah 59:2) *But your iniquities have made a separation between you and your God, and your sins have hidden His face from you so that He does not hear.*

All men are sinners.

(Romans 3:23) For all have sinned and fall short of the glory of God.

The punishment for our sin is eternal death in the lake of fire.

(Romans 6:23a) For the wages of sin is death.

This is a problem for us. How can we ever get to God, for all of us have sinned? The Bible has good news for us.

(John 3:16) For God so loved the world, that He gave His only Son, that whoever believes in Him should not perish but have eternal life.

God Himself provided a way for us to be with Him in heaven for all of eternity. He gave us salvation through His Son, Jesus. He gave it to us as a free gift.

(Romans 6:23b) But the free gift of God is eternal life in Christ Jesus our Lord.

Jesus died to make us righteous.

(1 Peter 2:24) He Himself bore our sins in His own body on the tree [cross], that we might die to sin and live to righteousness. By His wounds you have been healed.

This is the good news of the Gospel of Jesus, the Messiah.

UNDERSTAND THAT WE ARE ALL SINNERS

We have seen above that all men are sinners, deserving of death. *All* includes everyone and excludes no one. We are sinners before a holy God. Nothing that any of us has done or will do in this world can compensate for that or make it go away, even a little.

(Isaiah 64:6) We have all become like one who is unclean, and all our righteous deeds are like a polluted garment.

We must acknowledge this and take ownership of it. We

350

cannot blame anyone or anything for our failings. They are ours and ours alone. We stand naked before a holy God in our sin.

BELIEVE THAT JESUS IS THE SON OF GOD

Jesus is the Son of God. He was fully God when He walked as a man upon the earth. He is eternally God—He always was and always will be. There was never a time when He was not God. Jesus claimed to be God when He used God's name, 'I AM'.

(John 8:58) Jesus said to them, "Truly, truly I say to you, before Abraham was, I AM."

He asked His disciples who they thought that He was. Peter answered and was blessed by Jesus.

(Matthew 16:16) Simon Peter replied, 'You are the Christ, the Son of the Living God.'

Jesus told us that if we did not believe this, we would die in our sins.

(John 8:24) "I told you that you would die in your sins, for unless you believe that I am He you will die in your sins."

Believing is not just mental agreement or an intellectual understanding of the facts. It is an intimate knowing with all of our heart. It is a matter of having faith based on the evidence. Salvation is a heart issue, not a mental acknowledgement like: 'The sun is shining today'. Many have made this mistake in their lives. We must not make it in ours or we will not be saved.

TURN AWAY FROM ALL OF OUR SINS

We must turn away from our sins. All of them. To do this, we must confess them as best we can remember them—including the secret sins that we have harbored. Jesus already knows our sins. He will not be shocked.

Repentance is a turning away from our sins. It is not confessing them and then going back. It is not being sorry that we were 'caught' by Jesus doing something wrong. That is worldly sorrow. Godly sorrow is being grieved that our sin caused Him to go to the cross.

(2 Corinthians 7:10) For godly grief produces a repentance that leads to salvation without regret, whereas worldly grief produces death.

We cannot hold back. We must confess our sins to Jesus. Grieve over them.

ASK JESUS TO SAVE US

We must consciously ask Jesus to save us from our sins and become the Lord of our lives.

(Romans 10:13) For 'everyone who calls on the name of the Lord will be saved'.

Making Jesus *Lord* is putting Him in charge of our lives. Many make the mistake of seeking an easy salvation of words spoken in an emotional moment without counting the cost of following Jesus as their Lord. But Jesus tells us that we are to count the cost of belonging to Him.

(Luke 14:27-28, 33) "Whoever does not bear his cross and come after me cannot be my disciple. For which of you, desiring to build a tower, does not first sit down and count the cost, whether he has enough to complete it?...So therefore, any one of you who does not renounce all that he has cannot be my disciple."

(Luke 9:62) Jesus said to him, "No one who puts his hand to the plow and looks back is fit for the kingdom of God."

If Jesus is Lord over our lives, a significant change will take place. We will consciously exchange our life for His eternal life.

(Matthew 10:39) "Whoever finds his life [keeps his current life for himself and his own purposes] will lose

it, and whoever loses his life for my sake will find it."

Paul the apostle makes it clear how this works in our life.

(Galatians 2:20) I have been crucified with Christ. It is no longer I who live, but Christ who lives in me. And the life I now live in the flesh I live by faith in the Son of God, who loved me and gave himself for me.

(1 Corinthians 6:19b-20a) You are not your own, for you were bought with a price.

If we ask Jesus to save us and to become Lord over our lives with a sincerity of heart, He will save us and give us eternal life.

FOLLOW-UP

After we have done this, we should ask Jesus what we should do next. It is important that we find other believers to help us learn to walk with Jesus. There are many men's groups that were formed for this purpose. Local churches have classes for new believers as well. We will also want to be baptized by immersion (going under the water), just like Jesus was baptized. Baptism does nothing to enhance our salvation, but it is an important a step in obedience—one that identifies us with Jesus.

Then we must start our walk. Remember, we are to allow Jesus to lead us.

DELIVERANCE RESOURCES

There are several deliverance ministries and resources available. Two items have been included below to assist in your pre-deliverance work with Jesus. The first is a listing of the major demonic groupings. The second item is a prayer.

The listing of demonic groupings will be helpful in two ways. First, you can use the list to detect generational demons or curses that have been passed down your bloodlines. Secondly, it will help you see which areas of demonic control seem to exist in your life. Under each main heading is a listing of the possible manifestations of demons in that group (the ways that individual demons in that group show up in or through your life). These manifestations can indicate the presence of demons with specific assignments against you. You must allow Jesus to show you truth in these areas and point out what you are dealing with. Once you have noted the major areas of demonic influence or control, you can go to the prayer provided at the end of the list.

The prayer is used to begin tearing down the demonic kingdoms within you by canceling their permissions and rights to be there. The prayer can be used by inserting the name of the major demon grouping in the blanks and then praying through the prayer. Pray through the prayer one time for each major demonic group that you believe is present, inserting the name of that group in the blanks.

This will get you started down the road to freedom, but you will need to see an anointed deliverance minister for deliverance from the demon kingdoms within your flesh. Ask Jesus to choose one. He will lead each of you to the right one. Remember, their approaches vary but their end result is the same. Jesus commands the demons into the abyss.

DEMONIC GROUPINGS

LYING SPIRIT *(1 KINGS 22:21-22A)*

Charming, cheating, crafty, cunning, deceptive, deluded, dishonest, double-minded, exaggeration, excessive talking, falseness, flattery, gossiping, hypocrisy, insinuations, lies, manipulating, misleading, pretentious, seductive, tricky.

DEAF/DUMB SPIRIT *(MARK 9:25)*

Accident prone, anti-social behavior, apathetic, bi-polar, complacent, convulsions, confused, chronic fatigue, deafness, delusions, disorganization, dumbness, epilepsy, escaping into fantasy, feeling abandoned, foaming at the mouth, forgetful, hallucinations, hardness of heart, inability to focus, inactivity, inattention, incoherence, inertness, insanity, irresponsibility, isolation, laziness, lethargy, mental dullness or stupor, memory lapses, passivity, poor retention, repression, restlessness, schizophrenic, seizures, shyness, silence, sleepiness, sloth, slowness, stoicism, sullenness, trance-like actions, unreality, withdrawal.

HAUGHTY SPIRIT *(PROVERBS 16:18)*

Anger, argumentative, arrogant, blame shifting, boastful, bragging, brash, chronic dissatisfaction, conceit, contentiousness, controlling actions, critical, cursing, cynical, derision, dictatorial, disputing, disrespectful, domineering, egocentric, egotism, extravagant, false anointing, false spiritual gifts, feelings of superiority, hateful, headstrong, impatient, insolent, intellectual, intimidating, intolerant, irritability, loudness, manipulative, mean, mocking, obstinate, overbearing, perfectionistic, philosophical, prejudiced, pretentious, prideful, refusing correction, rude, scornful, seeking validation, self-centeredness, self-deception, self-importance, self-righteous, self-sufficient, smug, stubborn, unrepentant, vain.

PERVERSE SPIRIT *(JUDE 1:4)*

Abortion, adultery, bestiality, brazenness, carnality, child molestation, coarse joking, cursing, defiant, degradation, deviant, dishonoring, enticement, exhibitionism, fantasies, fetishes, filthy-minded, flirtatious, fornication, frigidity, harlotry, hateful, homosexuality, immodesty, immorality, impotence, incest, incubus (male demons having sex with humans), lesbianism, lust, masochism, masturbation, nymphomania, obscenity, pedophilia, perversion, pornography, sadism, sensuality, seduction, sex change, sodomy, succubus (female demons having sex with humans), transgender, transvestites, unfaithfulness, voyeurism, vulgarity.

BONDAGE SPIRIT *(2 PETER 2:19)*

Addictions to and/or cravings for alcohol / caffeine / drugs (including prescription) / food / nicotine / sex / sports / sugar / work, anorexia, bingeing, bitterness, boredom, bulimia, co-dependency, condemnation, control, covetousness, criticism, denial, dominance, drivenness, excesses, false guilt, false burdens or responsibilities, faultfinding, gluttony, greed, hyperactivity, hypochondria, insomnia, judging others' motives, materialism, moodiness, nervousness, obsessive/compulsive behavior, possessiveness, pressure, resentment, restlessness, self-analysis, self-destruction, self-hatred, self-mutilation, shame, soul ties.

FAMILIAR SPIRIT (OCCULT / WITCHCRAFT)
(DEUTERONOMY 18:10-12; ACTS 16:16)

Astral projection, astrology, automatic handwriting, black magic, channeling, charms, clairvoyance, conjuring, consulting the dead, crystals, divination, enchantments, false prophesies, fortune telling, hallucinations, handwriting analysis, hexes, horoscopes, hypnosis, incantations, levitation, jinxes, mediums, mind reading, new age spirits, occult, Ouija board, palm reading, psychic powers, ritual abuse, Santeria, Satanism, secret societies, sorcery, spirit guides, spiritism, tarot cards, voodoo, warlock, white magic, witchcraft.

ANTICHRIST SPIRIT *(1 JOHN 4:3)*

Acting steadfastly against God / Jesus / Holy Spirit / the Bible, agitation of others, believing false teachings, blasphemous, denying the deity of Jesus, denying the working of the Holy Spirit, hatred of the one true God and His followers, hindering others' spiritual growth, holding to false beliefs or doctrines, humanism, lawlessness, persecution of the Church, profanity, promoting divisions within the Church, rebellion, religiosity, skepticism, spiritual blindness, spiritual doubting, unbelief, unteachableness, worldliness.

WHOREDOM SPIRIT (IDOLATRY) *(HOSEA 4:12-13)*

Bible version worship, chasing after positions of power or authority, chasing after social standing or fame, creation worship (all forms of mother earth worship), counterfeit Gifts of the Spirit, cults, denominational superiority, doctrinal obsession or enslavement, esteeming anything or anyone above God (people, possessions, sports, activities, hobbies, etc.), false religions, false anointing, false gods, false worship (worshipping anything or anyone but God through Jesus), fraternities or sororities and their vows, humanism, legalism, love of money, materialism, mind over matter beliefs, religious ritualism, religious commercialization, traditions of men, romanticism, secret orders or societies, spiritism, worldliness.

SPIRIT OF JEALOUSY (NUMBERS 5:14)

Accusing, aggression, anger, arguing, backstabbing, belittling, bickering, bitterness, competition, contempt, contention, control/domination, covetousness, criticism, cruelty, discontentment, discord, disputing, dissatisfaction, distrust, envy, fault-finding, fighting, frustration, fury/rage, greed, hardness of heart, hatred, hostility, impatience, insecurity, intimidation, intolerance, irritation, judging, malice, manipulation, materialism, mocking, murder, negativity, possessiveness, quarreling, resentment, retaliation, revenge, sadism, sarcasm, selfishness, slander, spite, strife, suspicion, temper, treachery, unforgiveness, violence.

SPIRIT OF HEAVINESS (ISAIAH 61:3)

Aimlessness, anguish, bleakness, broken-heartedness, chronic weariness, crying, dark foreboding, death wishes, deep hurt, defeatism, dejection, depression, despair, desperation, despondency, discouragement, disappointment, disillusionment, fatigue, gloom, grief, guilt, helplessness, hopelessness, inability to cope, lethargy, listlessness, loneliness, melancholy, morbidity, mourning, negativity, oppression, pessimism, powerlessness, regret, self-condemnation, self-defeat, self-pity, self-rejection, shame, sorrow, suicide, undependability, unreliability, unworthiness, uselessness, weariness, wounded spirit.

SPIRIT OF INFIRMITY (LUKE 13:11)

All types of chronic lingering infirmities / diseases / sicknesses / infections (especially those that are prevalent in our family lines), abnormal physical attacks of any nature, allergies, arthritis, asthma, barrenness or miscarriages, bleeding, cancer, congestion, convulsions, diabetes, fungus infections, heart attacks, heart disease, high blood pressure, impotence, insomnia, migraine headaches, pains (unexplained or those that travel around the body), paralysis, seizures, warts and moles, weakness.

SPIRIT OF FEAR *(2 TIMOTHY 1:7)*

Abnormal, excessive, or irrational fears and phobias of all types (accusation, authority, condemnation, closed-in spaces, confrontation, correction, darkness, death, disapproval, embarrassment, failure, God, heights, humiliation, intimacy, man, persecution, poverty, rejection, sickness, water), agitation, anxiety, apprehension, compromise, cowardice, distress, distrust, dread, faithlessness, fear of losing salvation, feelings of inadequacy or inferiority, fretting, hoarding, hysteria, indecision, indifference, insecurity, lack of trust, mental torment, nervousness, nightmares, paranoia, passivity, procrastination, reclusiveness, self-awareness, self-rejection, skepticism, sleeplessness, stinginess, stress, suspicion, tension, terror, timidity, wavering, worry.

PRAYER OF RENUNCIATION

In the name of the Lord Jesus Christ, I come against the **{NAME OF SPIRIT}**, and every associated demon that is within me. I declare that I am covered by the blood of Jesus. I want nothing to do with you.

{NAME OF SPIRIT}, I renounce you.

I renounce every demon associated with you.

I do not belong to you.

I do not belong to myself.

I belong to the Lord Jesus Christ.

I am His divine property.

Jesus, I ask You to reclaim the ground that I or my ancestors gave over to these demons.

Jesus, I ask that You send whichever of these demons You will into the Abyss.

Jesus, I ask that You bind those that remain until the day of my deliverance.

Jesus, protect me from their lies and deception so I can hear Your voice clearly.

Jesus, sanctify me, my family, my home and property, and my future generations for use according to Your perfect plan for us.

Study Guide Word Definitions

activity: something that is done for pleasure and that usually involves a group of people

authentic: real or genuine
: true and accurate
: not copied or false

command: to tell (someone) to do something in a forceful and often official way
: to have authority and control over (a group of people, such as soldiers)

deliver: to set free
: to produce the promised, wanted, or expected results

disciple: someone who accepts and helps to spread the teachings of a famous person

diversion: something that people do because it is enjoyable, entertaining, or pleasant
: something that takes attention away from what is happening

eternal: lasting forever

fraud: a person who pretends to be what he or she is not in order to trick people

hobby: a pursuit outside one's regular occupation engaged in especially for relaxation

honor: a good name or public esteem
: respect that is given to someone who is admired

identity: who someone is
: the qualities, beliefs, etc., that make a particular person or group different from others

By permission. From *Merriam-Webster's Collegiate® Dictionary, 11th Edition* ©2015 by Merriam-Webster, Inc. (www.Merriam-Webster.com).

innocent: not guilty of a crime or other wrong act
: free from legal guilt or fault

legacy: something transmitted by or received from an ancestor or predecessor or from the past

lord: one having power and authority over others.
: a ruler by heredity right or preeminence to whom service and obedience are due.

love: strong affection for another arising out of kinship or personal ties
: affection based on admiration, benevolence, or common interests
: an assurance of affection
: warm attachment, enthusiasm, or devotion
: the object of attachment, devotion, or admiration

nature: the way a person or animal behaves
: the inherent character or basic constitution of a person or thing
: an inner force or the sum of such forces in an individual

obsession: an activity that someone is very interested in or spends a lot of time doing

paralyze: to make powerless or ineffective
: to make (someone or something) unable to function, act, or move

performance: an activity (such as singing or acting in a play) that a person or group does to entertain an audience

potential: existing in possibility
: capable of development into actuality
: something that can develop or become actual

pride: a feeling that you are more important or better than other people
: inordinate self-esteem
: conceit

program: a plan of things that are done in order to achieve a specific result

rebellion: opposition to one in authority or dominance
: open, armed, and usually unsuccessful defiance of or resistance to an established government

religion: an organized system of beliefs, ceremonies, and rules used to worship a god or a group of gods
: a personal set or institutionalized system of religious attitudes, beliefs, and practices
: a cause, principle, or system of beliefs held to with ardor and faith

religious: believing in a god or a group of gods and following the rules of a religion
: of, relating to, or devoted to religious beliefs or observances

respect: a feeling of admiring someone or something that is good, valuable, important, etc.
: high or special regard

reward: something that is given in return for good or evil done or received or that is offered or given for some service or attainment

selfish: having or showing concern only for yourself and not for the needs or feelings of other people
: seeking or concentrating on one's own advantage, pleasure, or well-being without regard for others

shallow: not caring about or involving serious or important
things
: having little depth
: lacking in depth of knowledge, thought, or feeling

significance: the quality of having notable worth or
influence
: the quality of being important

slave: one that is completely subservient to a dominating
influence

stubborn: refusing to change your ideas or to stop doing
something
: difficult to deal with, remove, etc.

tactical: of, relating to, or used for a specific plan that is
created to achieve a particular goal in war,
politics, etc.

trust: belief that someone or something is reliable, good,
honest, effective, etc.
: assured reliance on the character, ability, strength,
or truth of someone or something

warrior: a person who fights in battles and is known for
having courage and skill

ADDITIONAL PUBLICATIONS

Jesus In Disguise

Red Letters
A Jesus Devotional

History Hunters Series
Historical mysteries for middle schoolers
and young adults

Made in the USA
Monee, IL
16 August 2021